HER
SUTCLIFFE

HERBERT SUTCLIFFE

CRICKET MAESTRO

ALAN HILL

FOREWORD BY
FRED TRUEMAN

To Betty, for keeping an eye on play in another Yorkshire innings.

First published 2012
This paperback edition published 2022

The History Press
97 St George's Place, Cheltenham,
Gloucestershire, GL50 3QB
www.thehistorypress.co.uk

British Library Cataloguing in Publication Data.
A catalogue record for this book is available from the British Library.

ISBN 978 18039 9004 0

Typesetting and origination by The History Press
Printed and bound in Great Britain by TJ Books Limited, Padstow, Cornwall.

MIX
Paper from
responsible sources
FSC® C013056

Trees for LYfe

Contents

About the Author   7
Foreword   9
Introduction   13

1   An Orphan at Pudsey   19
2   A Glorious Dynasty   35
3   A Yorkshire Welcome   50
4   Holmes and Sutcliffe   65
5   Alliance with the Master   81
6   Triumphant in Australia   94
7   The Aura of Authority   112
8   Conquerors on a Gluepot   131
9   The Captaincy Furore   157
10 Peerless at the Summit   178
11 555 at Leyton   193
12 The Imperturbable Maestro   214

13	The Snare of Bodyline	232
14	Sutcliffe and Hutton	253
15	Fanfares in Retirement	275
	Statistical Appendix	299
	Bibliography	327
	Index	329

About the Author

John Arlott, when reviewing Alan Hill's biography of Herbert Sutcliffe, voiced his praise of an acclaimed cricket biographer, whose balanced style, he said, 'constantly leads the reader to think, thus heightening both his concentration and interest.' Alan Hill has twice won The Cricket Society's prestigious Literary Award for his biographies of Sutcliffe and Hedley Verity. His other books include studies of Les Ames, Peter May, Jim Laker and the Bedser twins.

About the Author

Foreword

by Fred Trueman OBE

It is wonderful news that a good and loyal friend of Yorkshire cricket, Alan Hill, has produced another book on our great men of the past. Herbert Sutcliffe's career presents a story of amazing achievement by a player who was a model example for any young cricketer.

Herbert was a proud man and he had every right to be so. The determined orphan lad had made good and become the revered champion of Yorkshire and England. Anyone who could earn the respect and friendship of people like Bill Bowes and Hedley Verity was entitled to claim that he had given of his best in life as well as cricket. Herbert was always spick and span in appearance and as courageous in his crippled old age as he was as the master batsman against the world's fastest bowlers. He once told me that there were some players who could play fast bowling and others who couldn't. 'But, you know, if everybody told the truth, no one really likes it,' he said.

Herbert still holds the highest average for an English Test batsman. They say he was a terrible man to get out. He was at his best in a crisis. In his day, batting technique was really put to the test on uncovered wickets. Herbert and his Yorkshire and England opening partners, Percy Holmes and Jack Hobbs, had few, if any, equals on the real 'stickies'. Alan Hill writes about the heroics of Sutcliffe and Hobbs in those epic struggles against Australia at the Oval and Melbourne in the 1920s. Only two magnificent players could have survived in such conditions. They did and England won.

Herbert was also acknowledged as one of the most unselfish batsmen of his time. He didn't hog the limelight unless it was necessary for him to shield a lesser player. I doubt whether there were many more loyal cricketers. Brian Sellers owed much to Herbert, as Yorkshire's senior professional, during our great days in the 1930s. Douglas Jardine also had the good fortune to have Herbert at his side on the bodyline tour. Herbert did not see anything wrong in our tactics, and was unswerving in his support of his captain in a controversial series.

In his retirement, when I got to know him, Herbert was a great encourager of young Yorkshire players, particularly those who had the good sense to listen. I did listen to him. He watched me as an eighteen-year-old and said I would play for England. In a way, rather like Herbert's prophecy about Len Hutton when he was a young boy, his praise raised expectations about my ability in Yorkshire. It was a bit of a millstone. But Herbert didn't scatter compliments like confetti. He knew his cricket and cricketers. Herbert also thought I had potential as a batsman. I did score nearly 10,000 runs, including three centuries. But when you are bowling around 1,000 overs a season, as I did, it isn't easy to put more spadework in as a batsman. I could graft when necessary, but I didn't always play as straight as Herbert would have liked.

Herbert became a close friend and my wife and I entertained him at our North Yorkshire home. I think he found it a peaceful retreat after the harsh atmosphere of at least one of his nursing homes. He did surprise us one morning. It was about 10.30 and Veronica brought out the coffee. 'Good Lord, haven't you got anything stronger?' he asked. His old eyes twinkled when Veronica suggested that he might like a gin and french. 'Yes, that would be better,' he said. It was his favourite tipple. And he needed it. Herbert was a strong man but he was in constant pain with his arthritis. I reckon he deserved his gin.

Many people, as Alan Hill relates, have said that Herbert was a severely practical performer. He had to cut out the frills as an opening batsman. He had to lay the foundations for the dashers. Herbert had the ideal temperament for this job. He was a magnificent judge of line and length. But it would be wrong to suppose that he was a slowcoach. He could hit sixes with the best of them. Herbert once hit Ken Fames and the rest of the Essex bowlers all over Scarborough. He went from 100 to 194 in forty minutes.

Maurice Leyland could wield the long handle pretty well himself. He was batting with Herbert at Scarborough. I once asked Maurice how many he scored during the onslaught. Maurice said: 'Sixteen. I only had four balls – that's all Herbert left me – and I hit each one of them for four.' Maurice wasn't often left standing as a batsman. Anyone who could do that must have been one hell of a player.

Introduction

Pride can so often be confused with pomposity. In his thrusting ambition, Herbert Sutcliffe could not escape the darts of envy, even among his own folk at Pudsey. The orphan boy, in his sporting odyssey, was blessed with a vision and resolution to rise above his humble origins. He was equipped by nature to live above the average. From his earliest years he displayed a dignity and earnestness which drew him into the embrace of influential benefactors.

Countless cricket chronicles have misleadingly fostered the haughty image, which was, in reality, a reflection of his unabashed self-confidence. It did induce a reverential awe, and for some, including his Yorkshire and England successor, Leonard Hutton, led to a view of Sutcliffe as a slightly forbidding figure. Yet his actions, fully expressed for the first time in my book, belie this portrayal. Sutcliffe was, as many people have pointed out, the reverse of the egotist. He was unselfish and loyal as a cricketer and unfailingly courteous as a man. Along with his great England batting partner, Jack Hobbs, Sutcliffe was committed to advancing the cause of the professional cricketer. 'Our profession as a respected one started with Jack and Herbert. They gave us a new status,' said Stuart Surridge, the former Surrey captain and a close business associate and friend of the Sutcliffe family.

In the 1930s Sutcliffe, as the senior professional, became a father figure to a host of aspiring young Yorkshire professionals. He was given the title of the 'maestro' in the Yorkshire dressing room. Bill Bowes and Hedley Verity, two illustrious colleagues in a glorious decade, were devoted to Sutcliffe. They regarded him as a kindly mentor and respected his insistence on a strict code of cricket conduct and meticulous appearance. Ellis Robinson, the Yorkshire off-spinner and one of the new guard before the war, remembered his senior's calmness in the most difficult of circumstances, both on and off the field. 'He set a perfect example to we who got into the Yorkshire team,' said Robinson. 'One of his great attributes, which many failed to appreciate, was, for want of a better word, his guts. Many times I have seen him black and blue, taking the brunt of the bowling on his body, rather than play the ball and thus resisting the chances of getting out.'

Exploring the riches of Herbert Sutcliffe's career has been a challenging and rewarding task. He was a cricketer who deserved to be admired almost without reservation. His indomitable spirit as the mainstay of Yorkshire and England shone brightly in the memories of those who stood alongside him. He is remembered for his imperturbable temperament. The late Les Ames said that Sutcliffe would go first into his side mainly because of the Yorkshireman's unruffled approach and tremendous belief in himself. In Australia, the scene of many of Sutcliffe's greatest triumphs, Sir Donald Bradman and Bill O'Reilly both paid tribute to the qualities of an unyielding and combative cricketer. 'He was virtually unshakeable,' said O'Reilly. 'You could leave him for dead with a ball and he'd almost leer at you.'

A legion of collaborators have enabled me to retrace the steps in a fascinating trail winding over eighty years. In placing on record the caring father and magisterial family man I am greatly indebted to the support of Bill and John Sutcliffe and their sister, Mrs Barbara Wilcock. They have provided many character insights and much valuable illustration material. For my impressions of Sutcliffe's early years in the Nidderdale village of Summerbridge and the sketch of his father, Willie, I am pleased to acknowledge the assistance of Barry Gill, the secretary of the Dacre Banks Cricket Club. At Pudsey, where Sutcliffe moved while still a young boy, I have found diligent supporters. Ralph Middlebrook was my friendly guide on an important research visit to the town. Mr Middlebrook enlisted the much appreciated aid of Roland Parker, Richard Smith, Ruth Strong and Mrs M. Tordoff, of the Pudsey Civic Society, to immeasurably strengthen my portrait. They, along with Mr J.W. Varley and Dr Sidney Hainsworth, both lifelong friends of Sutcliffe, have provided intriguing recollections of a hitherto largely uncharted period leading up to, and including, his service with the Yorkshire Regiment in the First World War. There have been many expressions of Sutcliffe's humanity and tributes to his gracious character. A telling example was his enduring friendship with John Witherington, one of his most devoted admirers. I am extremely grateful to Herbert Witherington, of Whitburn, Sunderland, for allowing me to quote from the long-running correspondence with his brother.

My thanks are also due to Tempus and their enterprising sports publishers for reissuing my award-winning biography. They have ended a long wait for those who missed the original edition published sixteen years ago. I am pleased that others will now have the opportunity to rejoice in a cricket gladiator who matched the Australians on their own ruthless terms and came out best.

I must also acknowledge the courtesy and help of Mr Stephen Green, the MCC curator at Lord's; Mr Ross Peacock, assistant librarian of the Melbourne Cricket Club; and the British Newspaper Library staff at Colindale, London. I have delved happily and profitably into the writings of A.W. Pullin ('Old Ebor') and J.M. Kilburn in the *Yorkshire Post*. Other allies on the Yorkshire scene have included Ron Burnet, Raymond Clegg, Michael Crawford, Capt. J.D.W. Bailey, Robin Feather, J.R. Stanley Raper, Ted Lester, Tony Woodhouse, John Featherstone, F.G. Jeavans, Mick Pope and Tom Naylor. My good friend, the late Don Rowan, was a constant rallying force during the course of a marathon project. Testimonies to Sutcliffe's greatness as a cricketer and a man have come from people in many walks of life. A small army of collaborators have provided a rich brew of anecdotes to be stirred by this biographer. They include Lord Home of Hirsel, Tom Pearce, Freddie Brown, Tommy Mitchell, Arthur Jepson, John Langridge, Len Creed, David Frith, Cyril Walters, Max Jaffa, Philip Snow, Rex Alston, H.M. Garland-Wells and Stuart Surridge. Doug Insole, Wilf Wooller and Peter May have also offered their observations on Sutcliffe as a Test selector in the late 1950s.

In my assessment of the epic achievements of Sutcliffe's career, I drew hugely on the wisdom of Bob Wyatt, a shrewd, perceptive and kindly collaborator. As always on my visits to his home in Cornwall, I found pleasure in his hospitality and the buoyancy of a remarkable man. I was also privileged, in the last years of their lives, to gain a rapport with Les Ames and Sir Leonard Hutton. With their passing, cricket lost two notable elder statesmen and my conversations with them illuminated my understanding and added to my appreciation of an illustrious cricketer.

Finally, it is opportune to refer to the obituary tribute of Ellis Robinson, who cherished his association with Herbert

Sutcliffe. 'To those of you who never saw Herbert play, you missed some unforgettable and majestic hook shots off the world's fastest bowlers. I treasure the fact that I had the good fortune to have played alongside Herbert and been his colleague and friend.'

Alan Hill
Lindfield, Sussex
June 2007

1

An Orphan at Pudsey

'Herbert was involved with fine people and because he was
good at cricket they wanted to help him.'

> Roland Parker, the former Pudsey
> St Lawrence club captain

The brass band boomed vigorously, discharging its volleys of
sound among the excited, swaying people. Behind the march-
ing musicians followed a torchlight procession of Yorkshire
villagers, each one caught up in the delirium of a momentous September day. Held aloft by the rejoicing cricketers,
above the forest of torches, was a gleaming goblet-shaped cup,
donated by the gentry of the Nidderdale district.

Willie Sutcliffe, his life soon to be cruelly terminated, was
one of the celebrants on this day in 1894. The last train had
steamed into the valley and he alighted to be borne, along
with the rest of his victorious teammates, on a joyful promenade. Dacre Banks had defeated local rivals Glasshouses by
122 runs at nearby Birstwith to win the Nidderdale League
Challenge trophy. Throughout the night, the elegant cup was

filled to the brim, time and time again, for all wanted to toast the champions.

Presiding at the presentation ceremony at Birstwith in the afternoon was the Revd Alexander Scott, the vicar of Pateley Bridge. He had missed the opening stages of the title decider in order to fulfil a long-standing engagement to officiate at the marriage of two young friends at Wakefield. As he told the cricketers afterwards, he was so keen to attend the match that he was actually out of the church and into a cab, and on his way to the railway station, before the bridal party left. He arrived at the Birstwith ground to join a capacity crowd of 900 spectators. A quick glance at the scoreboard told him why the Glasshouses contingent were in a jubilant mood.

Dacre Banks, after winning the toss, were toiling against a confident attack. Willie Sutcliffe was bowled in the first over. His captain and fellow opener, George Brooks, soon followed him to the pavilion. The Holmes brothers, Jack and Richard, 'trundled so well,' reported the *Nidderdale Observer*, that four wickets went down for 27 runs. The decline was halted by Robinson and Gill, who 'obtained a complete mastery of the bowling and took the score to 92 before another wicket fell'. Gill reached his half-century as the bowlers wavered. The report considered that 'the excitement must have been too much for them, as not one of them could find a good pitch and came in for punishment'. The Dacre Banks' tail wagged merrily and Ellis, coming in tenth man, 'commenced to hit out brilliantly, landing a ball from Richard Holmes clean out of the field for six.' Ellis moved briskly to an undefeated 33, scored in under half an hour.

The opening alarms were forgotten in the late flurry of runs. Dacre Banks totalled 179. Sutcliffe, eager to restore his pride after the batting lapse, took four wickets in a spell of sustained aggression. Only two of the Glasshouses batsmen reached double figures. Their gloom was matched by the lowering clouds. The match was abandoned in the failing light. At 57 for eight wickets, Glasshouses were probably beyond recovery, but their decision to surrender their claims to the cup and try again another day provided an unsatisfactory climax to the game.

The celebrations in Nidderdale were but a prelude to an event of greater significance for Yorkshire and England. Two months later, on 24 November, at their cottage home in Gabblegate, Summerbridge, Willie Sutcliffe and his wife, Jane Elizabeth, announced the birth of their second son, Herbert. Herbert's later allegiance to Pudsey, where he moved while still a baby, along with his elder brother, Arthur, is not in dispute, but the good people of Nidderdale cherish their association with a great cricketer. The Sutcliffe family home still stands in a cluster of cottages in the renamed East View facing on to the Pateley Bridge–Harrogate road.

Herbert's father, Willie, had fine credentials as a cricketer and a man. 'A more kindly disposed gentleman never went into a cricket field and it was wished that Dacre had more like him,' was the verdict of one contemporary. In Nidderdale he was referred to as 'above average in local cricket'. As a medium-pace bowler, he was noted for his accuracy, and it was said of him that he could hit unguarded stumps four times out of six. He obviously possessed considerable potential because he attended trials at the Yorkshire nets at the same time as George Hirst. Willie Sutcliffe, in one unconfirmed account, worked at a local sawmill at Dacre Banks. His employer was a Peter Wilkinson, who, as president of the local club, offered Sutcliffe the appealing proposition of a job to persuade him to play cricket at Dacre Banks. In those days of modest fixture lists, Sutcliffe was able to share his cricket services between Dacre Banks and Pudsey St Lawrence, after the move across the moors to the West Riding township. At Pudsey he assisted his father, the publican at the King's Arms. His brothers, Arthur and Tom, also played for the St Lawrence club.

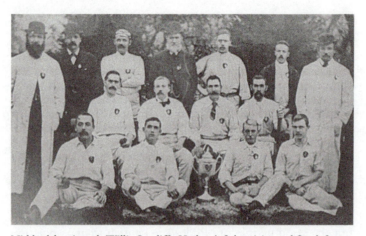

Nidderdale triumph: Willie Sutcliffe, Herbert's father (pictured first left in front row) was a member of the Dacre Banks XI which won the Nidderdale League Cup in 1894. (J.B. Gill)

The Sutcliffe boys, Herbert and Arthur – and their new baby brother, Bob – were plunged into grief when their father died in the summer of 1898. Willie Sutcliffe was a rugby centre three-quarter as well as a cricketer. He had suffered a severe internal injury while playing rugby in the previous winter. The injury, diagnosed as a twisted bowel, was aggravated in a cricket match. He died within a few days. He was aged thirty-four.

Willie's widow, Jane, and her bereaved family returned to Nidderdale. The elder boys, later to be joined by Bob, were enrolled at Darley School, about three miles from their former home at Summerbridge. Herbert's iron temperament, and his ambition to rise above his origins, was probably forged during this unhappy time. He and his brothers had to watch their mother in the throes of consumption as she battled bravely to fend for her young sons. By the time she remarried Tom Waller, a clogger master in the boot trade at Darley, the illness had taken a distressing hold on her life. She was allowed only a short term of happiness. Jane is also believed by the Sutcliffe family to have become pregnant with another child. It was this burden, on top of her already poor health, which led to her death, at the age of thirty-seven, in January 1904.

Whether, as has been said, Tom Waller was illiterate and considered unsuitable to raise his stepsons is a matter for conjecture. The fortunes of Herbert Sutcliffe might have taken a different course had Waller been entrusted with his upbringing. Entries in the Darley School register reveal that Herbert and his younger brother, Bob, left the school to resume their formal education at Pudsey some time before their mother's death. The elder Arthur was reunited with his brothers afterwards. A decision had clearly been taken, probably at the instigation of 'three remarkable ladies' back in Pudsey, as to the future custody of the children.

Rallying to the rescue of the orphaned boys were Willie Sutcliffe's sisters, Sarah, Carrie and Harriet, who ran a bakery and confectioners in Robin Lane, Pudsey. Carrie, as the middle aunt in age, became Herbert's guardian, and Arthur and Bob found equally caring foster mothers in Sarah and Harriet. From the aunts, all devoted Congregational churchgoers, the boys learned the disciplines of religion. Herbert, in fact, was unswerving in his devotions throughout his life; he was a Sunday school teacher as a young man; and his cricketing star first flickered in church teams at the turn of the century. 'Herbert was involved with fine people and because he was good at cricket they wanted to help him,' commented one Pudsey townsman.

The Sutcliffe boys were ushered into a kindly but strict household in Robin Lane. In addition to the aunts, Arthur Sutcliffe ('Uncle Arthur'), a cricket stalwart of the Pudsey St Lawrence club, was there to keep a fatherly eye on them. The boys slept in a loft above the bakehouse, and they had to make a nightly ascent by ladder to go to bed. Barbara Wilcock, Herbert's daughter, wincingly provided a memory of a Sunday ritual of her childhood. 'Herbert used to take us [Barbara and

her brother, Bill] to a freezingly cold church to attend long
services. Afterwards, we went to see Aunt Harriet, who would
be cooking the Sunday joint on the kitchen range. She would
cut off titbits for Bill and myself.' They were then allowed to
enter the austere parlour, a dubious privilege because it was
reserved for Sundays; a fire had only just been lit and it was as
cold as the church.

Herbert Sutcliffe described how his real craze for cricket
began at the age of eight (this would be soon after his return
to Pudsey and can be counted a new dawn in his life in a
sporting as well as a domestic sense). From this time onwards,
his great ambition was to play for the St Lawrence club where
his uncles, Arthur and Tom, along with his father, Willie, had
played. He had first to blink back the tears when he was
rejected by the Congregational Church club. 'Nay, lad, you're
too small; come back when you're bigger,' he was told by the
club officials when he asked to be allowed to practise at the
Long Close ground. As he regularly attended the church, the
refusal was, to say the least, uncharitable; but the undaunted
Herbert was more hospitably treated by the neighbouring
Stanningley Wesleyans. When Stanningley heard about the
rebuff they lost no time in inviting him to join their team.
Herbert was overjoyed and always remembered their kindness to him in later years. In his boyhood, Herbert was looked
upon as more of a bowler than a batsman; and in one notable
display in the 1907 season he took all ten wickets in a match.

Herbert's enthusiasm and promise brought a coveted promotion in 1908 when he was called up to play for the Pudsey
St Lawrence second team. He had been spotted by Richard
Ingham, his first sporting benefactor and the St Lawrence captain, while playing in a Pudsey workshops competition on the
Britannia ground. Ingham, the exemplar of the self-made man,
was at this time a dignitary of considerable local standing and
head of a worsted spinning business at Pudsey. He was born in

the Sandy Lane district of Bradford, one of a family of twelve children. At the age of ten, he was a half-timer in a local mill. After his apprenticeship, he was the manager of a company in Malmo, Sweden before returning home to go into business on his own account at Crawshaw Mills, Pudsey.

Ingham was also a highly respected local cricketer. He had spent five seasons at Eccleshill in the Airedale League before moving to Otley. At Eccleshill, one of his colleagues was Albert Cordingley, a slow left-arm bowler, who at the turn of the century had vied for a place in the Yorkshire team with Wilfred Rhodes. Lord Hawke, in fact, had advocated Cordingley as the stronger candidate before Rhodes demonstrated his credentials. At Otley, Ingham was captain when the club beat Farsley by three runs at Yeadon to become the Airedale League champions in 1904. Business commitments brought Ingham to Pudsey in the following year. It was the start of an outstanding career with the St Lawrence club. He was captain from 1908 to 1919 and president of the club from 1920 until his death in 1935. Ingham, as a cricket all-rounder, demonstrated the astuteness which marked his success as a businessman. 'As a leader Dick is ideal,' was the verdict of a Pudsey contemporary, when Ingham came to live and work in the town. 'His natural Yorkshire shrewdness comes to his assistance in the captaincy of the St Lawrence team.'

Ingham served on the Pudsey town council for twenty-one years and was elected mayor in 1922/23. He was also a member of the Yorkshire County Cricket Club committee and chairman of the Bradford Park Avenue football club. During his long term in the council chamber he was amusingly described as having the 'practical man's distrust of oratorical thrills... he has a Yorkshire pungency which brings the dreamer back to earth with distressing acuteness.'

On his scouting mission in 1908, Richard Ingham had noted and marked the poise of the young Herbert Sutcliffe in

Herbert's cottage birthplace at Gabblegate (now renamed East View) which faces on to the Pateley Bridge-Harrogate road. (John Featherstone)

the workshops league match. He had watched, with growing attention, the efforts of the rapidly disillusioned bowlers. At first, as a gesture of kindness, they had sent down a sequence of encouraging lobs to the boy. Herbert was not impressed and treated the gentle deliveries with disdain. The bowlers soon realised that their generosity was unwarranted; but they had allowed Herbert his chance. They did not get him out until he had scored 70. Cricket was always a serious business for the aspiring Sutcliffe. He was diligent and zealous in the nets. The memories of the Pudsey seniors laid stress on Herbert's keenness. 'While the other team members, having completed their ten minutes in the nets, would gather in groups and chat,' said one man, 'Herbert bowled and fielded as if a match were in session and every run counted.' Herbert himself considered that his attitude at practice helped him to build up his concentration. A photograph from this time shows the young Herbert, immaculate and composed, in a St Lawrence team group. He faces the camera with a stare of pride. The older men appear almost like courtiers in his presence.

One of Herbert's early appearances for the St Lawrence Club was reported in the *Pudsey and Stanningley News*. The match was against the Stanningley and Farsley Britannia Second XI in September 1908. The newspaper commented:

> Pudsey St Lawrence's second string had to fight hard against Stanningley and Farsley in the latter part of the game, their last wicket partnership being a very stubborn one. Every praise is due to little Sutcliffe (the son of that well-known local cricketer, the late Willie Sutcliffe). He is really a wonderful good length bowler for his age. He was also top scorer with 27, and it was somewhat singular that the next best scorer, with 16, should be Will Armitage, a colleague of young Sutcliffe's father in his palmier days.

Herbert was still only fourteen when he made his first-team debut for St Lawrence midway through the following season. In the Saints' ranks before the First World War were Henry Hutton, father of Leonard Hutton, and Major Booth, the Yorkshire cricketer. Herbert thought that St Lawrence must have been a man short for the derby match against the seniors of Stanningley and Farsley. He was lucky enough to be given the vacant place:

> Anyway, I went, a terrified little figure [the phrase strikes an odd note for someone of his fortitude], wearing white shorts, into the field while our opponents rattled up a useful score. Then, when their innings was over, I waited about the pavilion watching the St Lawrence wickets fall regularly and, I am afraid, rather cheaply. I was not happy about it at all, but when my turn came – I batted at no. 6 – I was ready for the job. The feel of the bat gave me a comfort though I

cannot remember whose bat it was. I am certain it was not my own. For forty-five minutes that borrowed bat stayed in my hands, and though I scored no more than one run with it, I brought it out unbeaten when time came, and the match was saved.

In 1911, Herbert switched his allegiance to the rival Britannia club where, he said, 'my batting improved by leaps and bounds'. He finished the season with an average of 33.30. The decision to make the move was largely prompted by an offer of clerical employment by Ernest Walker, the Britannia captain and a textile mill owner at Pudsey. There was also the question of insufficient time for practice, a weighty matter for Herbert. He had left school at thirteen and was then serving an apprenticeship in the boot and shoe trade as a 'clicker' (fastening boot soles to uppers) with the firm of Salter and Salter in the Lowtown area of the town.

The apprenticeship ended abruptly during a busy time at the Pudsey factory. The priorities of cricket training meant that Herbert kept missing overtime work. Charles Salter, the owner, reprimanded his young employee, and told him that he must make up his mind whether he wanted to be a boot craftsman or a cricketer. Herbert was upset by the incident and worried about the reaction of his Aunt Carrie, of whom he was very fond. His anxiety was quickly allayed. 'Come and work for me,' said Ernest Walker, 'I'll double your wage and let you play cricket.' Roland Parker, a future St Lawrence captain, in relating this story, said: 'They all knew this boy [Herbert] because he was so obviously a star of the future.' In later years, Herbert referred to the immense debt he owed to Ernest Walker. 'There are leaders in every sphere of life who, by their example, personality, demeanour and character, make a big impression on young people. Ernest was the incarnation of the best in sportsmen – one of the best who ever lived.' Walker was an extremely good club cricketer and close to county standard. He and the young Sutcliffe would later share some fruitful opening partnerships for Britannia. Herbert's work at the Walker mill office also had other beneficial effects. It fostered an interest in book-keeping, which served him well in his later business career.

Herbert was doubly fortunate in winning the approval of two influential mentors. First, Richard Ingham, and then Ernest Walker had shrewdly recognised his potential. In 1911, Walker was more than pleased to bring Herbert into the Britannia fold. The mysterious element is that Ingham, with first call on Herbert's services, did not find a job for the youngster at his mill. Roland Parker recalled that Ingham and Walker were boon companions: 'By signing Herbert Ernest really stole a march on his friend.' In an interesting sequel, Herbert, perhaps a little rueful at his earlier defection to the rival cricket camp, did return to the St Lawrence club for one season in 1916.

Sutcliffe's rapidly blossoming talents as a batsman at Pudsey were brought to the notice of the Yorkshire cricket authorities at Headingley. In April 1912, he was invited to attend the county practices. Herbert remembered his apprehension and wildly fluctuating thoughts about his prospects. The indecision was soon quelled. The surety of purpose, which governed all his actions, prevailed. He was resolved to make a bid for county status.

'The fateful day of the Yorkshire practice arrived,' recalled Herbert. 'I must admit a certain amount of nervousness was inwardly felt on entering the ground.' He changed and wandered into the nets. George Hirst, the benevolent guide of this and later Yorkshire cricket generations, welcomed him with a beaming smile. 'I've heard a lot about you. Don't be nervous, just make yourself at home. You ought to be at home because we're all cricketers here. Play your own game and you'll be quite all right,' was his greeting as Herbert fumblingly buckled on his pads. 'All my nervousness vanished the moment I stepped into the net,' said Herbert. 'I was on my mettle from the start and set my teeth to fight hard.' The trial was a success and a few days later Herbert was invited to play for a Colts XVI against the county team. 'My luck in this match completely deserted me, for I was out in quick time in each innings for under double figures,' recalled Herbert. The failure provoked a discouraging response from one well-meaning friend. He compounded Herbert's disappointment with the words: 'All right in the nets, you know, Herbert, but short of temperament for the middle.' The adviser believed that frayed nerves would prove Herbert's undoing at county level. 'Stick to your job and enjoy club cricket,' he said. The criticism did not go unheeded, except that it had the opposite effect of bolstering Herbert's resolve.

At Headingley, where Herbert came under the exemplary control of George Hirst and Steve Doughty, the Yorkshire second-team coach, there was a strict emphasis on the importance of pad play. The adherence to this second line of defence was to prove an important discipline. Herbert said he never regretted the time he sacrificed while being taught to play with his legs. 'The swing and swerve ball had been developed so much that almost every team had experts who were able to do practically anything with the ball in the air and it was absolutely impossible for anybody to enter first-class cricket with the idea of playing with the bat alone.'

Herbert's early attempts to deploy the pad strategy did leave him worried and bemused. On his return to Pudsey club cricket, he was dismissed lbw on three successive Saturdays without scoring. Ernest Walker, as his club captain, was also puzzled by the lack of form. Walker registered a protest to Steve Doughty. 'What are you doing to young Sutcliffe?'

Boy with a future: Herbert (centre, front row) as a fourteen-year-old in the Pudsey St Lawrence team. On his right is Henry Hutton, father of Leonard Hutton. Richard Ingham, the club captain (fourth from right, back row) and Major Booth, the Yorkshire and England all-rounder (far right) are also feature in the photograph. (Richard Smith)

he asked. 'He can't get a run for us since he joined your lot at Headingley.'

Herbert did master this crucial phase in his cricket apprenticeship. It strengthened his defence to spread dismay among bowlers and it gave him extra confidence in attack. There were two learning seasons in 1912 and 1913 when his batting averages suffered as he digested the lessons of Hirst and Doughty. For a man who never surrendered his wicket gladly, it must have been galling to fail in executing new strokes.

By the summer of 1914, with war on the horizon, he had built up his armoury as a cricketer. At the age of nineteen, he unveiled his mastery in the Bradford League. The *Bradford Cricket Argus* described two innings of 54 and 76, in which he was undefeated, as 'first-rate expositions'. In June, Herbert was selected to represent the Bradford League against the Yorkshire Second XI at Park Avenue, Bradford. The county colts were pushed hard to gain victory by one wicket in an exciting match. Herbert hit 73, out of 179, in the League's second innings. 'As an exhibition of batting, the best performance was that of Sutcliffe,' reported the *Cricket Argus*. 'He batted with supreme confidence and good style against bowling of quite the best Second XI class. He went in at the fall of the third wicket, when only 33 runs had been scored, and was last man out after batting for two hours.' Sutcliffe's innings included two sixes and eight fours and was 'unmarred by a single chance'.

Sutcliffe was also associated with a future Yorkshire colleague, Emmott Robinson, in the county Second XI which twice beat their Surrey counterparts at Rotherham and the Oval in 1914. At Rotherham, the match was dominated by Robinson, who struck an unbeaten 172, and Barnsley bowler A.C. Williams, who took 12 wickets in the match. Yorkshire were the victors by an innings and 18 runs. Robinson augmented his run proceeds with two half-centuries for the county seconds in the seven wickets' success over a Huddersfield and District XI at Fartown. Sutcliffe's contributions were smaller but the *Yorkshire Post* noted the 'punishing power of his on-driving' and added: 'he is possessed of a good physique and should develop into a fine player.'

Sutcliffe moved up to open the Yorkshire colts' batting for the first time against an East Riding XI at Beverley in August. The selectors were rewarded with a second-innings half-century. 'He was confident and stylish in this two-hour innings, his best performance for the second eleven,' commented the *Cricket Argus*. 'In Sutcliffe Yorkshire have a capable right-hand batsman, with youth on his side. In his movements in the field he looks every inch a cricketer, and possessing as he does a variety of good strokes, it would seem to be a sound policy to persevere with him.' The report cannily balances praise and caution in its commendation.

Yorkshire players, not excluding the great Wilfred Rhodes, had to satisfy vigilant juries. The examinations were searching and there was no danger of swollen heads among even the most gifted of White Rose apprentices.

Back home in Pudsey, the enthusiasm for Sutcliffe was less restrained. Herbert's batting feats were relished as much as the Sunday dinner roast. His most ardent and loyal admirers were in the little Yorkshire township. One of them, Fred Ambler, a future mayor of Pudsey, lived opposite the Britannia ground. Ambler was a faithful valet in Herbert's early years. He carried his idol's long brown cricket bag and whitened Herbert's boots for a shilling a week.

Ernest Walker and Sutcliffe were Britannia's opening partners in the last cricket summer before the war. Their alliance obeyed the precepts of care, but a sense of purpose was always evident in their batting. It was demonstrated with a special fervour in one match against the old rivals, Stanningley and Farsley Britannia. The *Pudsey and Stanningley News* reported:

> Walker and Sutcliffe at once proceeded to give a pretty exhibition of batting. Sutcliffe gave a very hard chance off the first ball he received, but the two batsmen played steadily against good bowling. They were not parted until the score had reached 86 when Walker, who had just posted his half-century, was caught and bowled by Barnes. Sutcliffe also completed his 50; he was joined by Nettleton, and these two took their team to victory.

As proof of his increasing consistency, Herbert hit a stylish 82 for Britannia in the nine wickets' victory over Tong Park, and this was closely followed by half-centuries against Queensbury, Undercliffe and Baildon Green. It was his best season in club cricket. Herbert was fully entitled to say that he had a 'real royal time' in Bradford League and Yorkshire

Second XI cricket in 1914. His aggregate in all matches for the year was 1,278 runs; in nine innings for the Yorkshire Colts he scored 249 runs (average 35.57); and in 21 innings for Pudsey Britannia his tally was 727 at an average of 45.44. Ernest Walker, second in the club averages, totalled 365 runs, and only three other Britannia batsmen, Nettleton, Burton and Tordoff, exceeded 200 during the season. Herbert was unapproachable in the Bradford League as well. He overtook the previous record league aggregate of 693, established by Cecil Tyson at Tong Park.

Sutcliffe's association with Jack Hobbs was still an unregarded prospect. But it was fitting that his future England partner should join the galaxy of talents in wartime league cricket in Yorkshire, and surpass the record with Idle two years later. Hobbs's achievement was to be dwarfed by his shared conquests with Sutcliffe in other greater arenas. The record flourish in Yorkshire linked their names for the first time.

2

A Glorious Dynasty

'"How many has he got?" was a question which did not require an answer in Pudsey. In the old days it meant "John" later "Major", and then "Our 'Erbert".'

Yorkshire Post

The lofty greystone town which became Herbert Sutcliffe's adopted home, and to which he clung with affection for almost seventy years, stands on tiptoe in cricket renown. Pudsey glows with a sporting lustre, bright and strong enough to pierce the gloom of the smoking mill chimneys at the beginning of the century. This homely parish, now enveloped by its big city neighbours, Leeds and Bradford, glories in a tradition with few parallels.

It has fostered a remarkable dynasty of Yorkshire cricketers. The first was the steadfast John Tunnicliffe (Long John O' Pudsey), who shared a notable opening partnership with Jack Brown from Driffield. Tunnicliffe, a product of the Britannia club, was born on 26 August 1866. At sixteen, he was debarred from becoming a member of the club because of a rule which

limited the youthfulness of candidates to eighteen. A special
general meeting was called to amend the rule and open the door
to the tall, gangling boy, who, even at that age, was one of the
biggest hitters in the district. In 1891, playing for the Yorkshire
Colts at Sheffield, Tunnicliffe drove a ball over the pavilion and
into the back of a brewery yard on the other side of the road.

Such spectacular strikes did not always carry the field.
Tunnicliffe was judged a rash young cricketer. So persistently
did he commit batting suicide that he was deemed incorrigible. In 1892, his second season with Yorkshire, he was quietly
omitted from the team. It was thought that he had little
chance of regaining his place. He was, however, given another
opportunity to redeem his previous failures, when he was
included in the team which played Lancashire in the August
bank holiday match at Old Trafford. His turn to bat came on
the Tuesday afternoon. Lancashire had scored 471 on a good
wicket. Yorkshire, on a wicket freshened by heavy rain in the
early morning, were struggling against Briggs, Mold and Alec
Watson. There was a vast crowd, all very pleased at the discomfort of the Yorkshire batsmen, and the bowlers were in full cry.

It was not exactly the time in which a batsman would choose
to play for his existence as a county cricketer. Tunnicliffe had
learned his lesson. He was grimly resistant and the Lancashire
bowlers could not dislodge him. At the end of the innings he
was 32 not out. In the follow-on, Lord Hawke was sufficiently
impressed by Tunnicliffe's tenacity to send him in first. The
result was that the Pudsey man obtained a splendid half-century, by far the highest score, and secured his position in the
team, never to lose it again. Tunnicliffe had discreetly schooled
himself in defence, with the happiest of consequences. He
took on the mantle of a sheet anchor batsman, a role which
had never been adequately filled since the days of Louis Hall.

Tunnicliffe had, though, to wait until 1896 before he began
his association with Jack Brown. The story of their subsequent

record partnership against Derbyshire will be told later; but these two men were Yorkshire's pilots in 26 century first-wicket stands. Two of them, a telling feat at the time, were obtained in one match against Middlesex at Lord's in 1897. In the first innings they scored 139, and in the second, without being separated, they hit 146 to bring about a Yorkshire victory. Tunnicliffe and Brown, as is the case with all prominent opening alliances, could each prop up one end while the other attacked. Brown, in his later years of indifferent health, often preferred patient methods to his more characteristic brilliancy. Tunnicliffe would then show that the powers of his hitting had not declined. A writer in the *Cricket Magazine* commented:

> His great reach enables him to get well over the ball, which he watches closely, and he has a very strong defence. He perhaps hardly possesses a sufficient variety of strokes to be judged among the greatest of batsmen, but his driving power is tremendous, while, in consequence of his height, more half-volleys come his way than to a batsman of fewer inches.

It was often said of Tunnicliffe that he was worth his place in the Yorkshire team for his slip fielding alone. In Yorkshire, they said that catches hung on to him like hats on a hat-rack. He took 694 catches to earn comparison with Woolley, Hammond and John Langridge in this position. He was also a more than competent emergency wicketkeeper. Not all his catches were taken at slip. In the outfield he had a safe pair of hands when Jessop or other big hitters were on the rampage. Tunnicliffe only gradually established himself as a regular slip fieldsman. Once there, this Gulliver of a man, at 6ft 3ins, pulled off some astonishing catches. 'Whether from a smart cut off Hirst's expresses, or an incautious peck at Rhodes's "breakaways", how many a batsman has turned round to see the giant arm fully extended with the ball tightly held above the head, or maybe an inch or so from the grass,' commented W.A. Bettesworth in 1903.

Many tales were told about Tunnicliffe's spectacular catches. Two Yorkshiremen were overheard discussing his agility. One of them said:

> I tell you I once saw Jessop start to make a hit to long leg, but at the last moment he suddenly altered his mind, as he often does, and made a sharp late cut.
>
> Now Long John, as soon as he saw Jessop going to hit to leg, started for that side, because there was nobody at long leg. Just as he had moved he saw what Jessop was up to and tried to stop himself, with the result that he turned a complete somersault. But it is a fact that in falling over John remembered his duties and stretched out his long arm just in time to grasp the ball at slip.

His companion listened thoughtfully to this account. After a short pause he remarked casually:

> That's nowt. I remember that he and David Hunter [the Yorkshire wicketkeeper] once nearly had a scrap over a catch of his. It was in this way. He was fielding at short slip to Peel, very close in, and the last two men were battin', with three runs to make to win. 'Tunny' got a bit excited, and when one of the batters just touched the ball he copped it before it had time to reach Hunter.
>
> Of course, Hunter was in a rage. He said it was infringing on his prerogatives. Lord Hawke had to make peace between them.

In seventeen seasons with Yorkshire, Tunnicliffe scored over 20,000 runs, including 1,000 runs in a season twelve times.

After his retirement, he was the coach at Clifton College and later a member of the Gloucestershire county club committee.

Yorkshire's next recruit from Pudsey in 1908 was the ill-starred Major Booth, who received his grooming at the St Lawrence club in Tofts Road. Booth was the son of a prosperous local grocer and attended Fulneck School managed by the Moravian religious sect at the foot of the town. Booth and Alonzo Drake, who died of heart disease in 1919, were the rising stars before the First World War, and were confidently expected to spearhead the county's attack into the 1920s. Booth was one of Pudsey's favourite sporting sons during a sadly curtailed career. He was the first of the town's international cricketers, representing England in two Tests in South Africa in the 1913/14 series. His selection was acknowledged at a dinner attended by fellow Yorkshire cricketers George Hirst, David Denton, Roy Kilner and Wilfred Rhodes at the Queen's Hall, Pudsey at the end of the summer. He received the gift of a solid silver cup bearing the inscription: 'Presented to Major W. Booth by members of the Pudsey St Lawrence Cricket Club and friends in appreciation of the eminent position attained by him in the world of cricket.' George Hirst, as expansively friendly as ever, told the assembly: 'If your Major is successful in South Africa they should be pleased; if not, they should make excuses for him.' Booth was unable to live up to the expectations of his Yorkshire admirers in South Africa. But there were mitigating circumstances. On the Sunday before the first Test at Durban he was involved in a motor accident, thrown out of a car as it hit a bank approaching level crossing. He escaped with a minor back injury.

Booth, tall, good-looking and charming, was on the threshold of greatness at the outbreak of war. As a second lieutenant in the Yorkshire Regiment, he died leading his men into action on the battlefield of the Somme in July 1916. He was aged twenty-nine. There were many good judges who contended

Long John O' Pudsey: Tunnicliffe, predatory slip fieldsman, sheet anchor opening batsman and the first of a remarkable cricket dynasty. (MCC)

that his death deprived England of a fast bowler who might have restrained the havoc of Warwick Armstrong's Australians in 1921. In his brief career, Booth demonstrated that he could have become one of the great allrounders. He scored nearly 5,000 runs, twice achieving 1,000 in a season, and took 603 wickets at an average of 19.82. As a right-arm medium-pace bowler, who occasionally deployed a formidable offbreak, he was flatteringly compared to the great S.F. Barnes. *Wisden*, which named him as one of its Five Cricketers of the Year in 1914, commented upon his bewilderingly late outswingers. 'He makes the ball swerve away at the very last moment. There is, too, something puzzling about his flight, and if the wicket is doing anything he can make the ball pop up very nastily.'

Booth claimed two hat-tricks, bowling unchanged with Drake in two matches in 1914; he took over 100 wickets in three successive seasons – 1912-1914 – and three wickets in four balls three times. In 1912, against Middlesex, he had match figures of eight wickets for 136 and scored 107 not out. In 1913, his best season, he recorded a double of 1,228 runs and 181 wickets. Yorkshire had good reason to mourn the loss of

both Booth and Drake. Their rich promise can be gauged from
some of their last performances together. In 1914, they bowled
unchanged against Gloucestershire, Booth taking 12 wickets
and Drake eight, the first time this feat had been accomplished
since Hirst and Haigh in 1910. Drake then proceeded to make
cricket history in taking all 10 wickets against Somerset, finish-
ing with match figures of 15 for 51. In this triumphant finale
the all-rounders flourished mightily. Booth and Drake shared
313 wickets, and each scored more than 800 runs.

At Pudsey, Major Booth's memorial is a plaque in the
St Lawrence Church close by his old cricket ground. His sur-
name is also commemorated in a town side-street, Booth's
Yard. The Yorkshire players contributed to the plaque, which
was unveiled by Richard Ingham in 1920. The grief of his
sister is poignant and haunting. She was unable to accept that
Major had been killed and was reputed to have kept a light
burning in the window of their cottage in the hope that he
would return. His room remained undisturbed until she died
in 1950, when the cottage, near the Britannia ground, was sold.

John Tunnicliffe and Major Booth scattered the seeds of
their modest distinction in Pudsey's cricket fields. They were a
fertile setting for the emergence of a great cricketer. Herbert
Sutcliffe was to profit from this heritage in asserting his own
enduring command between the wars. In his turn, Leonard
Hutton fulfilled the high hopes of his townsmen. One of
the most remarkable aspects of the Pudsey tradition is that it
delivered to the world two magnificent sportsmen. Sutcliffe
and Hutton, one the acclaimed master, the other the gifted
apprentice in the mid-1930s, were close neighbours at Pudsey.
Sutcliffe's married home at Southroyd House was only the distance of a well-thrown cricket ball from that of his Yorkshire
and England successor. The Hutton family cottage still stands
snugly among its neighbours in a neat terrace overlooking the
glorious Fulneck valley at the foot of the town.

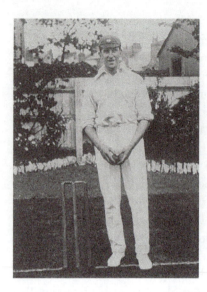

Major Booth, another of
Pudsey's favourite sporting sons,
whose career was curtailed by
his death in action in the First
World War. (Richard Smith)

The staggering successes of Sutcliffe and Hutton in their
great days were nowhere followed more attentively than in
Pudsey. The evening papers always sold well on summer afternoons. The cricket news was given out on a communal basis.
'How many has he got?' was a question which did not require
an answer. In the old days it meant 'John', later 'Major', and
later still 'our 'Erbert'. Afterwards, in a lingering wave of affection, it could only be 'Leonard'.

Ray Illingworth, the last in the illustrious line, if one allows
the short step into adjoining Farsley, did not pale by comparison with his predecessors. Illingworth, as one of the most
accomplished of England's post-war captains, did not betray
his origins. He brought renewed celebrations and ensured that
the eyes of the world remained fixed on his home town.

Going to watch all of these worthies was akin to a state
occasion for Pudsey and other Yorkshire followers at Park
Avenue, Headingley and Bramall Lane. They carried their par-
cels of sandwiches and perched expectantly on their seats as
the runs and centuries flowed with the regularity of a precisely

timed clock. The steel of the Pudsey cricketers, and indeed their independent characters, was forged in an industrial town where the spoils of grime had to be earned. Such labour had special dignity. 'Where there's muck there's brass,' was certainly relevant to Pudsey. Yet there were others who resented the curse of comedy which pursued their industry. A columnist in 'This World of Ours' in the *Yorkshire Post* wrote:

> I think it is about time that we allowed Pudsey a new repu-
> tation apart from the one given it by the mythical treacle
> mines and its sparrows which fly backwards to keep the
> dust out of their eyes. A native of the town will tell you that
> it is a place which never fails to produce a new cricket star.

This was penned in the late 1930s, when Leonard Hutton was emerging to enthral with his artistry. The image of a town bereft of sunshine beneath its sullen canopy was not easily dispelled. Before and long after Herbert Sutcliffe's boyhood, the phalanx of mill chimneys did release their plumes of black smoke to cast a dismal veil over the district. In the late eighteenth century, Pudsey was said to be the 'largest cloth-ing village in the West Riding'. One hundred years later, it still had over 100 independent cloth manufacturers, most of whom would be partners in the town's eight company mills. These mills were each owned by up to fifty small manufac-turers, who sold their pieces, or lengths, of broadcloth at the Coloured Cloth Hall in Leeds. They wove the cloth on han-dlooms in their own homes, but used the mill machinery for the early processes of spinning the yarn and fulling (cleans-ing and thickening) the cloth. In 1887, about 4,000 people in Pudsey were employed in the textile industry – almost a quarter of the population.

The introduction of steam-powered looms led to the demise of the small cloth manufacturers. By 1912, Pudsey had twenty-two textile mills and the owners announced their prosperity by building handsome villas in the town. Textiles was the dominant industry, but boot and shoe manufacturing was a close rival. Quarrying, too, had an important role, and most Pudsey houses were built of local stone. There were a host of other occupations. The town boasted three basketmakers, two tanneries, three watchmakers, a herbalist, ropemaker and monumental mason.

In the late Victorian era, Pudsey, despite its sooty drabness, still had a vast expanse of fields. So there were also four market gardeners, eight cowkeepers, with their small milk rounds, and thirty-one farmers. In addition, there were three surgeons, five solicitors (Pudsey folk were notorious for their excursions into litigation) and numerous clergy. To serve the pre-supermarket population of 15,000 people there were thirty-six grocers, twelve greengrocers, twenty-two butchers, eleven confectioners, four fishmongers and no fewer than fifty-one general shopkeepers.

The domestic scenario was one of Dickensian bleakness. The villagers were huddled together in their cottages in overcrowded yards. Some people, marginally better off, had gas or oil lamps, but in most of the humble dwellings the dancing firelight was supplemented only by tallow candles made from boiled mutton fat at an evil-smelling chandlery. Only a few households had bathrooms or indoor toilets. The rest had earth privies in their backyards. They were emptied periodically by local farmers, most of whom grew rhubarb which thrived on the massive applications of manure. Ruth Strong, the local historian, has wryly noted: 'As the population grew it is small wonder that the Pudsey district became nationally famous for its rhubarb.'

Away from the enclave of mills and dusty streets the villagers could roam abroad into a more pleasing terrain. They could walk in the country to Tong village and stride down the lovely winding lane to Fulneck and along the beck side to Troydale. One old resident remembered the summer days of her childhood in a cottage in one of the town fields. There she would sit under a nearby tree and enjoy a lavish helping of the renowned rhubarb and custard coupled with homemade brown bread and a slice of chocolate cake. A drowsy cow used to watch over the fence and nibble its own meal of sweet-peas. She recalled bluebells in the woods, stepping stones over a rippling stream and young lovers in their courtship trysts on Post Hill.

Two hundred years ago, the social life of Pudsey centred on local inns where sports such as cock and dog fighting, horse-racing and bull-baiting, a speciality of the Pudsey Feast (the local name for fair), drew the crowds. Quieter and less pro-voking pastimes prevailed in the advancing years of the next century. Then the church and chapel held sway, along with Sunday schools, brass bands, choirs and soirées. There was immense rivalry between the places of worship. In 1877, there were as many as nineteen in Pudsey, all expressed in the length and glitter of the Whitsuntide processions and later through the Sunday school cricket league, which was to prove a rigor-ous nursery for the young Herbert Sutcliffe.

The changing social pattern brought cricket out from under the umbrella of public houses and works and into the patronage of church organisations. Cricket became a magnifi-cent obsession with the formation of the Pudsey and District League in 1893. The St Lawrence and Britannia clubs were joined by the neighbouring villages of Bramley, Thackley, Calverley, Farsley and Rawdon. In the same year, the Sunday School League, with another twelve teams, soon to expand its ranks to twenty clubs, was formed. A sturdy resolution was displayed by the cricketers of Pudsey. It was a minimum requirement in the high, windswept town and on the rough, sporting wickets.

There was a fierce, even vicious, rivalry between the chief cricket protagonists, St Lawrence, representing the Top Enders, and Britannia, or to give it the modern designation, Pudsey Congs, in the bottom end of the town. The feud was as intense as that dividing Shakespeare's Montagues and Capulets. Love matches between the lads and lasses of the warring groups were not acceptable. They were strongly advised to find better halves. Before the turn of the century, on cricket derby days, there were rowdy, unpleasant scenes. Groups of rival supporters would hide behind the stone walls, tear up huge grass sods from the roadside, and pelt each other with the missiles. Even the ladies, in their high-brimmed hats, did not escape the barrage. In fact, the rivalry was not restricted to the boisterous youths. The girls were just as quarrelsome, 'fratching' noisily on the benches around the grounds.

The Pudsey Britannia club was formed in 1854 by the young men connected with 'the select class of the Lower Sunday School'. Three of the founders, Joseph Halliday, Joseph Musgrave and Joshua Lee, were later elected life presidents of the club. Britannia's first home was in Hammerton Fields, which was shortly succeeded by a move to the Junction Field, the site of the present playground and sports centre. This ground was opened on Whit Monday 1860 and was occupied by the club for twenty-one years. In 1863, an All-England XI visited the town to play twenty-two men from Pudsey and District. The England ranks included some of the greatest cricketers of the day. There was the Notts fast bowler, the swarthy John ('Foghorn') Jackson, his nickname deriving from his habit of blowing his nose loudly after taking a wicket. Edgar Willsher, a left-arm fast bowler from Kent, was also a member of the England attack. From Cambridgeshire came George Tarrant, another feared fast bowler, and his county teammates, Tom Hayward and Bob Carpenter, two of the best batsmen in the country. The Yorkshire representatives were George

Anderson, a rebellious character but a renowned batsman, and Joseph Rowbotham, a jovial eccentric from Sheffield, who later captained his county. Julius Caesar, from Surrey, lived up to his imposing name by registering the top score – 23 out of 79 – in the second innings of the Pudsey match.

The numerically stronger Pudsey proved formidable opponents. They had taken the precaution of selecting a quartet of Yorkshire players. These were Tom Emmett, John Thewliss, John Hall and Ikey Hodgson, the first of the county's famed line of slow left-arm bowlers. Hodgson took 11 wickets for Pudsey.

The All-England XI ultimately triumphed by the narrow margin of seven runs. It was a low scoring match in which overwhelming pace was the decisive factor. Willsher took 24 wickets, Jackson ten, and Tarrant six. Only two of the twenty-two Pudsey batsmen reached double figures in both innings. Their combined total amounted to 147 runs. Twelve months later, Pudsey gained their revenge on a pitch judged by its critics to be one of the worst in the county. They beat their All-England opponents by 105 runs in two days. It was the last of these fixtures. The England players, with the honours shared, decided not to put their reputations at risk on the ground again.

In August 1875, one of the great derby matches between Britannia and St Lawrence was played for £50 a side at Dudley Hill. It was watched, on the first day, by an estimated crowd of 3,000 spectators, and the receipts for the two days amounted to £68 18s. One Pudsey man remembered the excitement generated by the occasion, and the contingents of supporters travelling to the match in brakes and every mode of transport. Britannia won by seven wickets against a St Lawrence team which included Herbert Sutcliffe's two uncles, Arthur and Tom. Arthur was top scorer in both St Lawrence's innings. He hit 24 out of a total of 53 in the first innings and 44 out of 138 in the second innings.

A wintry scene at the Pudsey Britannia ground where Sutcliffe first won his spurs as a cricketer. (Pudsey Civic Society)

In 1881, Britannia moved to their present ground in Intake Road. An early history of the club reported that the 'officials and players had the satisfaction of being in possession of one of finest playing areas for miles around'. By 1890, the Yorkshire county authorities had taken note of Pudsey as a potential proving ground. With a view to fostering cricket in the area, they arranged a match against fifteen Britannia and District players. John Tunnicliffe, George Hirst and Willie Sutcliffe were selected for Pudsey. The Yorkshire team included such notables as Louis Hall, George Ulyett, David Hunter and Bobby Peel.

Over the next thirty years, Britannia were prominent members of the Pudsey and District, Leeds and Bradford Leagues. John Tunnicliffe, Ernest Walker and Herbert Sutcliffe were key figures who excited acclaim, and the club was endowed with the mellowing influence of good fellowship and team spirit. But history and tradition can be expelled by the whims of fortune. In the 1960s the famed Bottom End club tumbled into near oblivion. The lovely ground became a football field, and the old cricket pavilion, after being vandalised, was demolished. An historic club had to make a fresh start as a Sunday school team on a bleakly anonymous council ground.

Happily, for the club's future, there was a group of diehard enthusiasts who refused to accept that the decline could not be halted. The old Britannia ground was purchased in 1977 from the church commissioners. A voluntary task force, with exceptional devotion, relaid the square, and a new pavilion was erected. Cricket was resumed at Britannia on 20 April 1980. The official opening ceremony was attended by Bill Sutcliffe, the son of Herbert, and E.H. ('Tyke') Walker, the former president of the old Britannia club. The renaissance was sealed five years later when Sir Leonard Hutton spoke at a ceremony to commemorate the restoration of the ground. The results on the field matched the endeavours of those who had fought long and hard to bring about the revival. In 1969, the club joined the Dales Council, ten purposeful years later it was in the Leeds League, and the enterprise was crowned in 1987 when it joined the Bradford League and won promotion to the first division two years later.

It was a remarkable feat of dogged perseverance. All Pudsey rejoiced in the renewal of the old cricket rivalry. Herbert Sutcliffe, in his old age, was among those who sent their greetings. His remembrances of his apprentice years at Britannia were undimmed. From his nursing home he wrote to express his delight at the restoration of a ground upon which he had first won his spurs as a cricketer.

3

A Yorkshire Welcome

'There were no limits to his ambition. I have never met anyone as determined as Herbert. He was a special and original man.'

Sidney Hainsworth

The newly commissioned young officer looked like a millionaire. Strongly built and strikingly handsome, Herbert Sutcliffe had the winning graces of a movie matinée idol. In his smartly tailored uniform, Second Lieutenant Sutcliffe, on leave during the First World War, headed the promenade of boys and girls in Pudsey on Sunday evenings.

The display of vanity did not appeal to everyone. 'There he is, lording it,' remarked the more envious townsfolk, as he marched up and down the town. 'Think on, he had nowt two years ago.' Another man was more in sympathy with the proud young officer steering his upward course. 'Herbert was immaculate,' he said, with the emphasis on the final syllable. 'There was a polish about him. His hair was lavishly brilliantined.'

Sutcliffe was called up for war service in 1915, first serving with the Royal Ordnance Corps, with whom he was stationed near York. He was then transferred to the Sherwood Foresters and, by his own account, took unofficial leave to play, under an assumed name, for Pudsey St Lawrence in the Bradford League. 'On Saturday afternoons I cycled the 20 miles from York to the Leeds tram terminus near Killingbeck, deposited my cycle there, and travelled on to Pudsey by tram.'

The wartime cricket excursions, which escaped the attention of the military authorities, were profitable interludes for Sutcliffe. Many renowned cricketers came north to play in the Bradford League. Jack Hobbs represented Idle, Frank Woolley was at Keighley, George Gunn and Cecil Parkin at Undercliffe, Fred Root at Bowling Old Lane, and the legendary S.F. Barnes exerted his command at Saltaire. The Bradford League ranks also included Yorkshire county players, among them Percy Holmes, Sutcliffe's future partner. Holmes represented Spen Victoria, for whom in 1915 he scored 640 runs, including a half-century against Keighley. One of his opponents in this match was Wilfred Rhodes. 'The opportunities of watching and playing against all these illustrious players counted for so much,' said Sutcliffe.

It was during the First World War that Sidney Hainsworth renewed his boyhood friendship with Sutcliffe. The association was to last throughout their lives. Hainsworth was his best man when Herbert married Pudsey girl Emily Pease in September 1921. Hainsworth's father, Moses, had been a cricket colleague of Herbert's father, Willie, with Pudsey St Lawrence in the Leeds League. Before the war, the young Sutcliffe had been an occasional weekend visitor to the Hainsworth family home at Farsley. Hainsworth, in later years a prominent businessman, recalled that his friend was a strong man in both physical and mental senses. 'There were no limits to his ambition, he was always perfectly turned out and conscientious about his cricket. Everything had to be subordinated to the way he thought the game should be played. He was one of those players whose career meant more than the social round and pleasures of the evening.' As chairman of Fenners, the power transmission engineers, Hainsworth travelled the world and came to know a wide variety of people. 'I never met anyone as determined as Herbert. He was a special and original man,' he said.

As the war advanced, Sutcliffe and Hainsworth were fellow members of The Green Howards (then known as the Yorkshire Regiment) and played cricket together for the Officer Cadet Battalion at Gailes in West Scotland. Hainsworth said he was one of two nominations (the other was Sutcliffe) as captain when the battalion team was formed. Sutcliffe won the election, much to the initial annoyance of the competing Hainsworth. The pique dissolved when he realised Sutcliffe's qualities as a leader. 'I would have been ashamed to be captain with Herbert under me,' conceded Hainsworth. There was a marked contrast in their batting performances as openers against Glasgow University and other leading Scottish XIs. Standing at the other end, Hainsworth knew for certain that he was well below Sutcliffe's class. 'I usually managed a painstaking 20 or so, while Herbert was moving to a half-century at least,' said Hainsworth. 'To my eyes, he was amazingly strong on the legside, placing boundaries with staggering accuracy between the fieldsmen.'

Sutcliffe was demonstrably the right choice as captain. He was popular as a cricketer in the army but he imposed a firm discipline. He would never let his teammates practise without being in cricket flannels. There was a special emphasis on fielding at these practices. Sutcliffe, who was to become a fine and fast outfielder with Yorkshire, won a trophy for throwing during his time with the battalion. 'Herbert had a splendid arm,' said Hainsworth. 'He could throw a cricket ball over 100 yards.' Sutcliffe was, in fact, a superb all-round sportsman, a powerful swimmer and a footballer, who attracted the attention of leading Yorkshire clubs. He was an outstanding centre half in the battalion soccer team and, in Hainsworth's words, 'ideal in this position, with the whole game pivoting around him.' Yorkshire cricket was to beckon more strongly. As Sutcliffe's cricket promise became evident, another sporting career would have been sternly resisted by Lord Hawke, the county president.

The joys of cricket for Sutcliffe and Hainsworth in wartime gave way to fears of a posting to the British Expeditionary Force in a military emergency in France. Bearing in mind the carnage of a terrible conflict, it was fortunate for both men that the draft was cancelled. When their turn did come to move to the front they were both commissioned officers. They reached Etaples on the day after the Armistice. 'It was sheer good luck that neither of us saw any fighting,' said Hainsworth. The current gossip in 1918 dwelt upon the lifespan of newly commissioned officers. The grim estimate was three weeks before they were either wounded or killed. One of the wounded was Sutcliffe's future brother-in-law, Reggie Pease. He was blinded on the last day of the war. Sutcliffe, remembering his own good fortune, was a kindly protector of his relative in later years. Theirs was a strong and lasting bond.

Herbert Sutcliffe ended his war service in The Green Howards at Salisbury, where his commanding officer was Colonel White, the brother of Sir Archibald White, a former Yorkshire captain. Sutcliffe sorely wanted to obtain an early release, so that he could resume his cricket career. Col. White told him: 'I am afraid you will not be able to get out of the army this summer. You see, Sutcliffe, we shall want you in the battalion cricket team.' Sutcliffe, disappointed at the response, was about to leave the office, when Col. White laughingly called him back. He was overjoyed to learn that his release was imminent. At the age of twenty-three, he had lost vital years to the war and he was anxious to press his cricket claims at the earliest opportunity.

On demobilisation, Sutcliffe was first contracted to play for the Allerton Bywater colliery club in the Yorkshire Council. He was also employed as a checkweighman at the colliery, a position he retained in the winters before establishing his retail sports outfitters, together with another Yorkshire cricketer, George Macaulay, in Leeds in 1924. In May 1919, batting against the bowling of Rhodes, Hirst and Roy Kilner, Sutcliffe hit 51 not out for the Yorkshire Colts against a full-strength county XI. It was the best individual performance by a Colts player. The *Yorkshire Post* reported: 'Sutcliffe's promise is distinctly high. He combines sound defence with a variety of scoring strokes expected of a class batsman.' Percy Holmes, playing for the county seniors, coincidentally scored 51 before the Yorkshire captain, D.C.F. Burton declared to give the Colts (and Sutcliffe) the chance to make their challenge for recognition.

Sutcliffe never played for the Colts again. After only ten appearances for the county Second XI, he made his Yorkshire debut against Gloucestershire at Bristol at the end of May. Kilner, with a century, and Rhodes put on 165 for the third wicket. Sutcliffe, batting at no.6, was out for 11, caught behind the wicket by the Gloucestershire captain, F.G. Robinson. He was one of Alf Dipper's four victims in the innings. He remembered how his partner, George Hirst, went out of his way to help him. 'There was something about George that encouraged and comforted me,' he said. Before long Hirst had noted Sutcliffe's unease against Dipper's tempting deliveries pitched well outside the off-stump. Between overs he talked to the Gloucestershire bowler. 'You know, Alf, this is the lad's first match. Why don't you bowl on the wicket and give him the chance to make a shot or two if he can?' suggested

Sutcliffe, the earnest young professional. (W.H.H. Sutcliffe)

Hirst. Dipper was not prepared to be generous against the debutant; the fretful Herbert lost patience and edged a catch and Yorkshire's last five wickets tumbled for the addition of 28 runs. Wilfred Rhodes, after his 72 with the bat, led the counter-attack as a bowler. He took 11 wickets in the match, including 7 for 47 in the Gloucestershire first innings, and Yorkshire won by an innings and 63 runs.

At Lord's, in the match against the MCC, Sutcliffe was again Hirst's partner. The master and the pupil were dogged in defence as they resisted a cock-a-hoop attack. Sutcliffe hit 38 and Hirst 41 in a stand of 67 for the fourth wicket, as Yorkshire were bowled out for 120. 'Sutcliffe's batting was the most encouraging feature of the innings,' commented the *Yorkshire Post*. 'He had to go in when steadiness was necessary to prevent an inglorious collapse, and he maintained his defence for an hour and 40 minutes before being bowled by Hearne. The Pudsey colt pleased all onlookers with his form.'

Hendren, with a double century, irrepressibly led the way as the MCC totalled 488. Yorkshire, after these humbling events, recovered their poise in the second innings. Holmes was dismissed for 99, off the penultimate ball of the day. Then, on the following morning, Kilner and Hirst rallied Yorkshire with batting of controlled aggression. They both hit centuries and scored at the rate of 80 runs an hour in adding 160 runs for the fourth wicket. Pride was restored as Yorkshire topped 500, and the match was drawn.

Sutcliffe's first year in championship cricket in 1919 coincided with experimental two-day matches. The hours of play were 11.30 to 7.30. Before the season was halfway through, the new arrangement was roundly criticised. 'Can there be a greater unreality in the championship than now exists?' questioned one observer of the quickly discarded programme. 'The public can see clearly enough that two-day cricket is a game for weak or unequal teams and bad wickets. Definite results are chiefly to be looked for when either or both combatants are weak, or when wickets have become difficult through rain.' The experiment, said another writer, threatened to alter the entire character of the game.

It would substitute timetable scoring, a form of slogging, for skilful and intelligent batting. The writer was properly indignant and he would have been aghast to learn that he was prophesying the future course of the game. 'In place of a pastime, which is essentially British in its characteristics, such as patience and determination, there might be set up an entertainment which would be calculated to "tickle the multitude" and draw gates.'

Herbert Sutcliffe, in the time at his disposal, was able to sketch an outline of his imperious temperament in a remarkable first season. His play against the troublesome bumpers of Derbyshire bowlers, Horsley and Bestwick, said the *Yorkshire Post*, was worthy of a veteran. 'Sutcliffe did not make a mistake until he reached 58, and in the conditions such a score was in moral value worth a trebled score on an easy wicket.'

Yorkshire, in 1919, were fallible in batting and bowling. Their resources had been severely sapped by the deaths of Major Booth and Alonzo Drake. They relied heavily on the undiminished skills of Wilfred Rhodes, then entering, at the age of forty-one, the third phase of his extraordinary career; and George Hirst. The talismanic qualities of Hirst, immensely reassuring as a player and coach, were richly evident. His was a brilliant swansong. At forty-eight, he had astonished the cricket world by scoring 180 not out against the MCC, 120 against Essex and 120 against Warwickshire. Early in the season he had almost single-handedly carried Yorkshire on his broad shoulders.

It was said of George Hirst that his face was like a harvest moon in seasons of glory and plenty. The indomitable man enjoyed a joke and one of my favourite stories about him occurred during his twilight years as a Yorkshire cricketer.

His cricket companion on a journey to Taunton for a match against Somerset was Schofield Haigh. Both Yorkshiremen were then in their forties. 'Schof,' said George, 'we're getting a bit old for this game; it's time we gave it up.' Haigh replied: 'Aye, George, you're right.' As they walked on to the ground, the man at the turnstile offered the query: 'Umpires?' Hirst and Haigh did not reveal their playing identities. With expressions of sadness, their forlorn voices in accord, they replied 'Aye, lad', and passed on into the field.

George Hirst, perhaps more than anyone, rejoiced when Sutcliffe and Percy Holmes came forward to show themselves capable of maintaining the high Yorkshire standards that he had worked so hard to establish. The turning point in Yorkshire's fortunes in 1919 came with the elevation of Sutcliffe to partner Holmes for the first time against Kent at Headingley at the end of June. Another propitious development, in the following match against Derbyshire, was the debut of Bradford bowler Abe Waddington. His introduction brought a welcome hostility to the Yorkshire attack.

The decision to promote Sutcliffe and relieve Rhodes of the batting responsibility was taken after consultations between David Burton, the Bridlington amateur and Yorkshire captain, and George Hirst. Holmes recalled talking to Rhodes after a match at Bramall Lane. The veteran had said that he thought it was time to hand over the position of opener to someone else. 'I remember it didn't take Herbert long to volunteer. George Hirst had suggested him for the job. It was one of those decisions you don't forget.' In the later years of the Holmes–Sutcliffe alliance, Burton said: 'How successful this change proved to be everyone knows, and I do not hesitate to express my opinion that there are no greater first wicket batsmen in the country. They gave us a great send-off on many occasions.'

The hopes of Burton and Hirst for the new Yorkshire partnership were soon fulfilled, despite an inauspicious start. Newly capped Holmes and Sutcliffe, playing in only his ninth first-class game, were troubled tyros against Kent. Holmes was dismissed for a duck; Sutcliffe struggled to 20 against Woolley and Fairservice on a bad wicket; and Yorkshire were all out for 64.

This opening lapse was erased within a few weeks. Before the end of July, Holmes and Sutcliffe had achieved the first of their century partnerships – a monumental 279 against Northamptonshire at Northampton. Sutcliffe, with 145, and Holmes, 133, excited the praise of 'Old Ebor' in the *Yorkshire Post.* 'It was,' he wrote, 'a performance reminiscent of the days of Tunnicliffe and Brown.' There was some hesitation in the Yorkshire dressing room before Burton decided to bat after winning the toss. The wicket was soft after recent rain and appeared likely to assist the bowlers. If any difficulties did exist, Holmes and Sutcliffe made light of them in their headlong pursuit of runs. There were 14 boundaries by the pair to hoist the first 100. The openers put on 102, despite a rain stoppage, in the two hours before lunch.

'Holmes was always scoring a little quicker of the two until both were in sight of three figures, when Sutcliffe went ahead with some brilliant hitting,' reported the *Yorkshire Post.* Sutcliffe had reached 94, when George Hirst, watching from the pavilion, said: 'He ought to hit a six now.' There did appear, as Herbert said, to be a kind of telepathy existing between himself and Hirst. Whatever the reason, Sutcliffe did complete his first Yorkshire century with a towering six off Ted Freeman. It was a quite magnificent strike and the ball soared into the tennis courts near the entrance to the Northampton ground. Sutcliffe was not prone to be frivolous as a batsman. The century flourish might have been a signal to the county committee. Between the overs he had made clear in chats with one of the home fieldsmen that his prime concern was to gain capped status, and so ensure an income from cricket during the winter. The coveted cap was awarded to Sutcliffe in August.

Before the end of the season, Holmes and Sutcliffe had ushered in their reign by compiling five century partnerships and
scoring five individual hundreds. Sutcliffe hit another century,
his second in consecutive innings, against Gloucestershire at
Headingley. He shared a double century stand, 237 for the
second wicket, with David Denton. Against Middlesex at
Lord's, he scored another 100 (103 out of 187), after Yorkshire
had lost five wickets for 23 runs. Sutcliffe's highest and best
innings of the season was his 174 against Kent at Dover.
Watching Sutcliffe at work was Tom Pawley, the Kent manager. Pawley said, in his unsolicited opinion, that Yorkshire
had discovered a true batting prospect, the best he had seen
for years.

It was the vigour of Sutcliffe's batting, which produced
21 boundaries at Dover, that won the praise of Pawley. E.R.
(Rockley) Wilson, the Yorkshire amateur and Winchester
College master, endorsed the verdict. Wilson, a knowledgeable
observer, said that Sutcliffe, in 1919, batted like a very good
public school player. What especially appealed was Sutcliffe's
penchant for attack and the majesty of his off-drive. Defensively,
Sutcliffe could be faulted, considered Wilson, but he added that
Herbert soon tightened up this part of his game. The embry-
onic stylist, with his 'picture postcard' shots, so called because
they finished as well as they began, took great pains to improve
his defence. Sutcliffe was to restrict the flowery touches and
adapt his play to that most likely to prove successful.

The greatest satisfaction for Holmes and Sutcliffe in an
eventful first season was their baptism in the cauldron of Roses
cricket. Cecil Parkin, with 14 wickets in the match, had spun
Lancashire to victory by 140 runs at Old Trafford. Sutcliffe,
then batting down the order at no.7, did his best to defy the
old enemy by scoring 53 out of 153 in Yorkshire's second
innings. Yorkshire made atonement for the defeat in the return
fixture at Sheffield. Lancashire were bowled out for 124, and

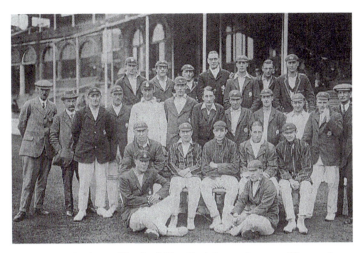

Yorkshire *v.* The Rest of England, The Oval, September 1919. The newly capped Sutcliffe is pictured third from right in the back row. Yorkshire colleagues in the group include Abe Waddington, Arthur Dolphin, Wilfred Rhodes, Percy Holmes, Emmott Robinson, Roy Kilner and George Hirst. (W.H.H.S)

Yorkshire replied with 253 before the first wicket fell. Holmes and Sutcliffe both scored centuries – their respective scores were 123 and 132 – and established a double record. They eclipsed the only previous three-figure stand of 115 recorded by Tom Birtles and Benny Wilson against Lancashire at Sheffield in 1914. It was also the first time that two individual centuries had been made by first wicket partners in a Roses match. Parkin, the dominant bowler at Manchester, suffered a fierce and salutary bombardment. He was left to contemplate figures of 0 for 97.

Holmes and Sutcliffe, brought together in a batting emergency, played key roles in Yorkshire's tenth championship in 1919. Both scored over 1,800 runs, Sutcliffe just heading his partner by a single run in the county averages. They were the new standard bearers, but it would be wrong to suggest that the honours were theirs alone. Hirst, Denton, Rhodes and

Roy Kilner all made over 1,000 runs. Waddington, in a mete-
oric start to his career and in little more than two months as
a member of the attack, took exactly 100 wickets. Above all,
there was the enduring Rhodes, who was inspired to greater
effort to compensate for the loss of Booth and Drake. Rhodes
bowled nearly 900 overs and obtained 142 wickets in the
championship at the beggarly cost of 12.42 runs apiece. The
Yorkshire maestro, with another eleven years of his career to
run and other England caps in the offing, bowled almost as
well as in his pristine years. His length was as unerring as ever,
and there were glimpses of the old, tantalising spin.

In the field, especially in the latter part of the season,
Yorkshire reached brilliant heights. Contributing to this resur-
gence was the debut of Keighley cricketer, Emmott Robinson,
then aged thirty-five, but a splendidly keen and alert recruit.
'Robinson's quickness gave to some of the other players the
"bucking up" that early in the season they needed,' commented the *Yorkshire Post*. 'It is the desire to seize the fraction
of a second in fielding which saves runs and prevents batsmen from taking liberties between the wickets.' Robinson
was a livewire in this department. He was also fearless in a
helmetless age. One amateur opponent suggested that fielding
so close at silly mid-on was carrying bravado beyond reasonable limits. 'Never mind me,' said Emmott, 'thee get on wi' thi'
laikin'.' The batsman did, and was promptly caught at the point
of danger.

Yorkshire responded to the fervour of Robinson to swoop
like vultures in the field. All the bowlers benefited from the
zest, around and away from the wicket. Any drifts into leth-
argy produced exclamations of withering scorn. George
Macaulay, as one of Yorkshire's greatest bowlers in the 1920s
and 1930s, did not hide his disgust at one sequence of shoddy
fielding. Sutcliffe, Holmes and Kilner, in strict rotation, once
put down three slip catches off Macaulay in one over. At the

end of it George, to whom anger always lent an enhanced fluency, delivered this rebuke. 'When Madame Tussauds want a set of slips,' he bellowed, 'I know where to find them.' Wilfred Rhodes, in relating the story, said: 'That made everywoon laff.'

It was not, though, a laughing matter; the fun was in Macaulay's droll banter: it also reflected a camaraderie which could shrug off occasional lapses in concentration. The jocular backchat did carry an implicit warning of the perils of a repetition of dropped catches. One may be sure that it did not go unheeded.

In its review of the 1919 season, the *Yorkshire Post* dwelt upon the versatility of a team accustomed to field in any position. Holmes was complimented as a first-class slip, while Sutcliffe earned praise as an improved outfielder. 'The way Sutcliffe took three catches in front of the pavilion against Middlesex at Lord's showed that he has a much safer pair of hands than one would have credited him with in the early weeks of the season.'

It was the deeds of Holmes and Sutcliffe as batsmen which were brought sharply into focus in the *Wisden* accolades. The two Yorkshiremen were selected as two of the Five Cricketers of the Year. 'Sutcliffe's record for a first season must be almost without parallel. The highest honours on the cricket field should fall to him in the near future.' *Wisden* intriguingly, and at some variance with their later development, added: 'By reason of his fine driving, Sutcliffe is perhaps a more attractive bat to watch than Holmes, but he may not yet be quite so strong in defence.' The judgement of *Wisden* was that Sutcliffe, by virtue of being a younger man, might have a brighter future before him. 'But Holmes has the sovereign virtue of playing with a perfectly straight bat, his defence is strong, and he has great patience and self-restraint. As regards hitting, he is best on the legside, but he is by no means deficient in either his driving or cutting power.' The exploratory verdicts could not foretell how the swings of fortune would reward either man. Sutcliffe was always adamant in his view that Holmes was a gifted cricketer of whom all Yorkshiremen could be proud. 'He had the technique, grit and fighting power.'

The two batsmen were, as time would prove, inseparable in their complementary strengths. In 1919, after a season festooned with high accomplishments, there was just a happy sense of wonder at the discovery of such talents. 'That Holmes and Sutcliffe would establish themselves as the best first-wicket pair in the country and set the cricket world talking of their achievements was not contemplated at the start of the season,' reported the *Yorkshire Post*. 'Yet, if an England team was chosen today, could either be left out?'

The sporting editorial could only be faulted on one count. Loyalty to their chosen men avoided a supplementary question: which of them would have the mettle or good luck to partner Jack Hobbs?

4

Holmes and Sutcliffe

'Holmes, with his brisk, light-infantry step towards the wicket, looked like a man going to the races, while Sutcliffe had the air of an alderman about to lay a foundation stone.'

The Times

The strange neglect by the England selectors of Percy Holmes is one of cricket's unresolved puzzles. The mystery deepens when one refers to the assessment by one eminent writer of Yorkshire's 'heavenly twins'. He judged Sutcliffe to be the perfect second string and subsidiary in a technical sense to the brilliant and mercurial Holmes. 'Percy was wonderfully free, a natural batsman, with strokes of genius,' said Sidney Hainsworth, a lifelong Yorkshire supporter, patron and benefactor.

Holmes, eight years Sutcliffe's senior, was born at Oakes, Huddersfield on 25 November 1886. The First World War, as with his great partner, curtailed his career. He was in his thirty-third year when he came to the forefront of Yorkshire cricket in 1919. In fifteen summers he scored 30,573 runs, registered 1,000 runs in fourteen seasons, and hit 67 centuries, including two not out totals of over 300 runs. With Sutcliffe, he shared 74 century stands, including 69 for Yorkshire. Of these, 19 exceeded 200 and four were over 300.

The impressive figures, as one writer commented, conveyed little of the true quality of his batting, which had the authentic sparkle of champagne. 'He was always up on his toes and dancing into the fray,' recalled Bob Wyatt. Another Yorkshireman, Bill Bowes, likened Holmes to a ballet dancer. 'He never fielded in boots, always pumps, and his dainty heel-toe walk gave him the appearance of bouncing over the ground. A century by Holmes was an experience to remember all your life.' Holmes took on the mantle of David Denton, a merry cavalier of Yorkshire batting of other years. What was said of Denton could have been said even more fittingly of Holmes. You might get him out, but you could never tie him down. Neville Cardus said there was a curious stable-boy air about Holmes. 'He seemed to brush an innings, comb it, making appropriate whistling sounds.' Roy Kilner, a cricket companion of an identical sunny temper, caught the flavour of Holmes in a lovely Yorkshire phrase, which means the best. 'Percy was a bobby-dazzler,' he said.

Harold Larwood, at the peak of his powers, attested to Holmes' courage as a batsman. Larwood greatly admired the gambling instincts of his Yorkshire opponent, and the darting footwork which sent many of his fastest deliveries scudding to the boundary. Holmes, like Sutcliffe, did not flinch under the fiercest barrage. At Trent Bridge he emerged triumphant from one bruising encounter with Larwood. 'Harold hit me 36 times before lunch,' recalled Percy. 'I was black and blue, but I stuck it out and by Monday I'd scored 285.'

The audacity, which confounded bowlers and charmed spectators, clearly did not commend him to the Test selectors. His single appearance against Australia was surely an aberration in judgement. The weight of runs ought to have confirmed his consistency and stature as a batsman. Holmes had confidence in abundant measure; but he did confess to one limitation. Bill Bowes said Percy marvelled at the restraint of Sutcliffe. 'As he watched Herbert striving for mastery, he would murmur: "If only I had his patience!"'

This was probably the key to the riddle. While Holmes was dashingly importunate, looking, as one observer said, 'like a man going to the races', Sutcliffe solemnly took root with the appearance of an 'alderman about to lay a foundation stone'. It was, however, a narrow thread which divided them in the quest for international honours. Sidney Hainsworth thought the difference between Sutcliffe and Holmes lay in the fact that 'Herbert was indisputably one of them at Lord's'. Hainsworth said Percy did not do anything wrong but he was not acceptable to the MCC hierarchy.

In later years, R.C. Robertson-Glasgow made an intriguing observation: 'There is a danger that Holmes may be forgotten except in Yorkshire, and that would be wrong. There were suggestions of greatness in his play. Only fate and the committee [the England selectors] made him an opening batsman during the long reign of Hobbs and Sutcliffe.' In other words, Holmes might have been the batsman to build excitingly upon their partnerships lower in the order, or as a counter should either of them have failed.

Andrew Sandham, another superb opening batsman for Surrey, was similarly overshadowed and neglected. His record at county level was even more impressive than that of Holmes. He hit 107 centuries and shared 63 partnerships of 100 or more with Hobbs, six behind those realised by Holmes and Sutcliffe for Yorkshire.

In the last of his fourteen England appearances, Sandham scored a triple century against the West Indies at Kingston, Jamaica in 1929.

Sandham, like Holmes, had to adopt a philosophical disposition. In one match, after Hobbs had been dismissed first ball, he rescued Surrey with an immaculate century. For once, it seemed, the spotlight would fall on him. As he walked out of the ground, he glanced at a newspaper placard. It read: 'Hobbs 0 at the Oval.' Sandham commented wryly to his companion: 'Well, I suppose you've got to be a pretty good player to merit a contents bill when you've got a duck.'

Monty Garland-Wells, the former Surrey captain, and Ronnie Burnet, who led Yorkshire in the 1950s, regarded Sandham and Holmes as possessing qualities which would have graced the England scene. Such was the dominance of Hobbs that Sandham was subdued to a point of near stroke-lessness when the great man was in full cry. 'If Hobbs was first out,' said Garland-Wells, 'Sandy flourished. He could then claim the crease as his own stage.' Bob Wyatt provided another reminiscence, which emphasises how Sandham regarded his subordinate role at the Oval. Wyatt said Hobbs would claim the bowling as of right in all conditions. Wally Hammond was another great batsman who would count the balls 'if the bowl-ing was not too rough at the other end.' As a young cricketer, Wyatt once batted with Sandham in a match in Ceylon. 'I played one ball, the last of the over, to deep mid-off for an easy single. When I arrived at the other end, he hadn't moved.' Wyatt said: 'Come on, Sandy, good gracious, we've time for two. Sandy just looked at me and replied: "If you don't hurry back, you'll get run out."' When the over was called, Sandham turned to his partner and said: 'Now, look here young man, I've spent a good deal of my life running no.6 for Jack Hobbs. I'm not going to do it for you.'

Herbert Sutcliffe never deviated from his view that Holmes would have been a tremendous success in Australia. 'I feel sure that Percy would have proved to be one of the outstanding successes in Test cricket had he been given the opportunity. He would have done as well as I was able to do.' J.M. Kilburn, the Yorkshire historian, thought Holmes was essentially a county cricketer, but he shared Sutcliffe's opinion and ventured further: 'With the slightest change in fortunes, the history of cricket would have made different reading. As it was, Sutcliffe's career became vastly more spectacular and it must remain for ever a matter for conjecture whether or not justice was equally done.'

Yorkshire's supporters, if truth be told, were probably content in the rewards of a magnificent county association. Ronnie Burnet hero-worshipped Holmes and Sutcliffe as a boy. 'Watching them walk out to bat was sheer delight. You did not fear anyone in any conditions.' Burnet was entranced as one batting feat followed another. A *Cricketer* profile in 1921 delightfully depicted the atmosphere on such occasions:

> There is usually a hum of expectancy when Holmes and Sutcliffe appear, their faces wreathed in smiles, and chatting happily together. They seem to be sharing some all-absorbing joke. Holmes, proudly wearing his Yorkshire cap, walks with quick, short steps, shoulders erect, and head in the air, doing his best to look as tall as Tunnicliffe. Sutcliffe has dark, glossy hair, and usually disdains the valued White Rose cap when batting. He strolls casually along by the side of Percy, keeping his weather eye open for the wicket-keeper's end, and the honour of taking the first ball.

It is interesting to reflect upon the merits of Holmes and Sutcliffe, as compared by *The Cricketer*, during the early years of their alliance. 'Sutcliffe is essentially a brilliant and stylish batsman, his driving on both sides of the wicket, when thoroughly set, being well-nigh perfection.' The writer drew attention to Sutcliffe's new emphasis on defence and said it was at the expense of his naturally free and easy methods. It was, in fact, a deliberate decision by the Yorkshireman. The efficacy of the change was to be shown in the years ahead. A flamboyance did lurk beneath the surface of Sutcliffe's batting. It was revealed in two memorable displays of hitting for Yorkshire. It is, however, as an unyielding lynchpin that he is remembered. In the early 1920s he was working on a blueprint for all situations. *The Cricketer* correspondent was, however, disapproving of Sutcliffe's bias towards defence. 'There are so few really fast-scoring professional batsmen today, that we shall welcome the speedy return of Sutcliffe to his 1919 form.'

Percy Holmes never changed, as a man or as a cricketer. He was engagingly impish, a dapper little man whose swift movements showed his relish for batting plunder. He had the happy reputation of playing to please. His was blithe spirit like, as someone said, that of a minor, but not very minor, Macartney. R.C. Robertson-Glasgow remembered 1925 as Holmes's finest summer. 'He was like an ostler inspired to cricket; nimble, quick in glance, bat and eye, jocular and stern in rapid alternation, excelling in the cut and in the eyebrow hook from imprudent risers, strokes which the Yorkshire coaches teach pre-eminently well.'

Rarely can a player have done more to show his calibre than Holmes in this season. Of his five centuries, a 'long series of triumphs,' as *Wisden* described them, three were obtained before the MCC jury at Lord's. In what must be regarded as the greatest innings of his career, Holmes scored 315 not out against Middlesex at the headquarters. It beat the 278 of William Ward whose score had stood as a record at Lord's for 105 years. Holmes' own record was not destined to gather the moss of antiquity. Hobbs beat it by one run in the following season.

'Those who saw that match in which the Huddersfield man made his highest score will never forget the beauty and strength of the innings,' wrote J.M. Kilburn. 'He scored all round the wicket – on the first day he cut well and was skilful with strokes on the legside, and on the second day he drove splendidly on both sides.' Holmes batted for six hours and

fifty minutes, without giving a chance, and he hit 38 fours.
Years later, when he reminisced about the Lord's innings,
Holmes said he could not account for it, at least not for the
first half-hour of his stay. He reckoned that he was 'morally
out' half-a-dozen times in the opening overs. One of the
Middlesex bowlers, who suffered at his hands, said he hadn't
'so and so' noticed any signs of insecurity. 'He never missed a
ball he intended to play,' he insisted. Holmes, batting at no.3,
also hit 92 for the Players against the Gentlemen at Lord's.
On his next visit, with Yorkshire, he scored a century against
the MCC. His detractors, on this evidence, were uncommonly
lacking in discernment. 'I regard Holmes as the least fortunate
of our Test players,' commented Sydney Pardon in *Wisden*.
'In view of what he has done since the war, one cannot help
thinking he is much under-rated.'

Ronnie Burnet recalled another innings by Holmes, in the
late 1920s and long before bodyline had been hatched, against
Warwickshire at Bradford. Holmes refused to be cowed by a
persistent leg-stump attack. 'Warwickshire set a completely
legside field and Mayer bowled bouncers at him all afternoon.
Percy never refused anything. He hooked and hooked, either
over the inner ring, or over the boundary, and he finished up
with 275.'

The Cricketer, in an early tribute, warmly greeted Holmes's
confidence and commented:

It is coupled with a sure defence and the straightest of bats.
He never neglects any opportunity of scoring and few men
execute leg strokes with such grace and precision. They are
his speciality, whether it be the glance, the placing shot, or
the full-blooded hook from the short rising ball on his nose.
To these he and Patsy Hendren add one almost entirely on
their own. It is a cross between the old-fashioned sweep to
square leg and a short-arm hook stroke. Both players move

slightly forward, and then pivot sharply round as the bat meets ball, using tremendous power of wrist and forearm. It is invariably a raking four.

The association of Holmes and Sutcliffe began on a Leeds tramcar upon which they travelled for their first trials at the Headingley nets. 'We recognised each other as cricketers by our bags,' recalled Percy. 'We began talking cricket and never stopped until the tram pulled up at Headingley.' It was a friendship which prospered both on and off the field. For many years they believed that they were born on the same day, 25 November, and exchanged greetings accordingly. The mistake was not spotted until Sutcliffe chanced to look at his birth certificate and discovered that he had been born on 24 November. In his years of affluence, Sutcliffe would pay the bill for a birthday dinner. It was a kindly gesture. He believed that it was his duty, as the wealthier man, to bear the cost of the celebration. It was only later that he learned that Percy was not without means. He had been bequeathed a legacy of several thousand pounds.

Percy Holmes, at fifteen, was an established member of the Paddock club in the Huddersfield League. His first professional engagement was with Spen Victoria in the Yorkshire Council, and it was through his batting for that team that he came to the notice of the Yorkshire cricket authorities. He made his county debut, with innings of 13 and 5, against Middlesex at Lord's in June 1913. In that season, he played in six championship matches, scoring 144 runs at an average of 16. His greater possibilities were revealed in a Second XI match in which he hit 162 not out. He made a slight advance for Yorkshire in 1914, but though he scored 61 against Gloucestershire at Bristol and 46 against Sussex at Hove, he was still, at twenty-seven, no more than a batsman of promise.

His subsequent form, on the resumption of first-class cricket in 1919, surprised even those who thought most

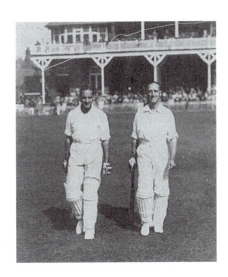

The run stealers: Sutcliffe and Percy Holmes, Yorkshire's illustrious partners, begin another innings against the MCC at Scarborough. (F.G. Jeavans)

highly of his batting. Tucked away in the margins of the sporting columns before the war was an unconsidered note. It reported the first century partnership of Holmes and Sutcliffe for Spen Victoria against a Keighley side, which included another redoubtable Yorkshireman, Emmott Robinson. Keighley batted first and totalled 104. Percy and Herbert were not separated as they hit off the runs in an hour and ten minutes.

It was a joyous little romp, the merest scratch in a scorebook but it carried significant portents for Yorkshire cricket. From the moment the two batsmen came together as openers, almost as an afterthought in 1919, there was an awareness that they meant business. They were a contrasting pair, but A.A. Thomson considered that 'it was a kind of optical illusion that Holmes so often appeared to be batting with more enterprise than Sutcliffe. His technique was never as massive as that of Sutcliffe, but it was ever on the move, and the cheeky strokes, like the hook and the very late cut, were his favourites.' In Lancashire, it used to be said that they feared Holmes more than Sutcliffe because he 'travelled the faster'.

Their running between the wickets rivalled, if it did not beat, the surety attained by Sutcliffe and Hobbs for England. Roy Wilkinson, the Yorkshire statistician, calculated that in all the fifteen seasons they batted together, one or other of them was run out only twenty-two times – an average of one and a half times a season. Holmes was the victim on four-teen occasions and Sutcliffe eight, a remarkable testimony to their rapport as partners. Sutcliffe would never differentiate between Holmes and Hobbs. With each, he maintained, it was a mutual understanding and trust. The fallibility of other great batsmen, notably Denis Compton, in running between the wickets often seems unaccountable. Wilfred Rhodes, another unerring judge of a run, was once asked to explain the secret. His droll response banished any mystique about calling. 'When I'm coming I say "Yes"; when I'm not I say "No".' In his view, it was a perfectly simple procedure.

Percy Holmes's star was in the ascendant in 1920. He achieved an aggregate of 2,254 runs in all matches, with an average of 50.08. He was sixth in the first-class averages. His tally included seven centuries, including two in one match against Lancashire; and his 302 not out against Hampshire at Portsmouth was the highest individual score of the season. The triple century, out of a score of 585, turned the tables on the southern county. Earlier in the season, on a brilliant sunny Saturday at Headingley, in June, the Yorkshire bowlers had been severely mauled. Brown and Mead both scored unbeaten centuries; Hampshire hit 456 for the loss of only two wickets and won by an innings. The domination was stunning. Nothing of this order had been seen at Leeds since Somerset's record assault of 630 in 1901. Compensation of substantial proportions was required to restore Yorkshire's esteem. At Portsmouth in August, Holmes and Sutcliffe, batting in equally favourable conditions, took Yorkshire to 347 before the first wicket fell. Hampshire were beaten by an innings and 235 runs. Rhodes, in taking 11 wickets in the match, completed the double for the eleventh time in succession. When congratulated on the achievement, he remarked: 'Fancy scratching for it until this time of the year.'

Holmes, after a season of high enterprise, was omitted from the MCC tour of Australia, under the captaincy of J.H.W.T. Douglas, in the following winter. It was an inexplicable decision. Sydney Pardon, writing in *Wisden*, could not understand why Lancashire's Harry Makepeace was given preference over Holmes for the tour. 'Holmes is not in any sense a spectacular batsman,' he maintained, at odds with the general view. 'But as to his class there can scarcely be any doubt.' The authors of *A History of Cricket*, H.S. Altham and E.W. Swanton, also considered that a place should probably have been found for the Yorkshireman. Herbert Sutcliffe, in later years, also frowned on the blatant disregard of his partner. 'The pity of it was that we who played with Holmes, knew that he had the big match temperament and was in every way equipped for an Australian tour.' Russell, of Essex, opened with Hobbs in the first Test at Sydney. He scored nought and five. Wilfred Rhodes, his replacement as opener in remaining Tests, thus renewed his association with Hobbs. But it was asking too much to expect the veteran to withstand the rampant Australians. England lost all five matches.

In 1921, the selectors did call upon Holmes. He made his one and only appearance against Australia in the first Test at Trent Bridge. His opening partner was Donald Knight, of Surrey. It was an inopportune time for an England debut. Three years later, Sutcliffe was able to settle his own claim in less arduous circumstances against South Africa. Holmes recalled the ferocity of Gregory and McDonald on a Nottingham wicket freshened by rain. 'The ball was flying about so much that I couldn't have reached the first one from Gregory with a clothes prop.' Knight was caught at the wicket by Carter off

Gregory for eight; but Holmes defied the Australian bowlers for an hour and a half. He was top scorer with 30, out of the England total of 112. In another humiliating procession, England were bowled out for 147 in their second innings, and Australia won by ten wickets.

Changes were assuredly needed after such a dismal display, but Holmes just as assuredly deserved to retain his place. The selectors were Pelham Warner – according to Holmes, his only supporter – R.H. Spooner and F.R. Foster. Holmes said that Spooner asked him on the morning of the second Test if he would mind standing down. 'I don't mind,' said Percy, 'if you think you're picking the right side. But are you?' Knight kept his place and Dipper, of Gloucestershire, was brought in to replace Holmes. Dipper's contributions were 11 and 40, and it was left to Frank Woolley, with two glorious nineties, to provide solace amid England's shame. Gregory and McDonald were the remorseless bowlers in a disheartening season. England shuffled their inadequate resources, picking thirty batsmen in the Tests and *Wisden* pointedly referred to the XIs as a 'series of scratch sides'.

Percy Holmes had to wait six more years before England turned to him again. By then he was forty-one and his batting had inevitably lost some of its lustre. In the 1927/28 series in South Africa, he opened with Sutcliffe in five consecutive Tests at Johannesburg, Cape Town and Durban. His scores were 0 and 15, 9 and 88, 70 and 56, 1 and 63, and in the fifth game of the series he was twice dismissed without scoring. Holmes played once more for England, opening with Sutcliffe against India at Lord's in 1932. His Test record of 357 runs (average 27.46) is a denial of his talents. The figures are a false representation of his true worth. He was a household name in Yorkshire, hugely prosperous as he totted up his runs season after season. It is certain that he would have been just as bountiful for England in other more propitious times.

In his old age, Wilfred Rhodes was once asked to make a comparison between Yorkshire's championship-winning teams during the years of his reign. He considered that the team which carried off the honours three times in the early years of the century was the best. Rhodes said that the record of his first Yorkshire side did not reveal the full strength of the county's batting roll call. 'It was not possible then for a team to declare until the third day of the match and our batsmen frequently when we had a good lot of runs on, threw their wickets away in order to get the other side in.'

Herbert Sutcliffe and Percy Holmes were among the legatees of the doctrine of efficiency established in Rhodes's formative years. From 1922 to 1925 they were members of a Yorkshire team which won the championship four times to equal the record of Nottinghamshire (1883-1886). Yorkshire's twelfth championship in 1923 was one of unparalleled achievement. 'Yorkshire had a wonderful season,' reported *Wisden*. 'Never since the competition reached its present dimensions has the championship been won in such an overwhelming fashion.' Meeting all other first-class counties, Yorkshire won 25 matches out of 32, and lost only one, to Notts by the margin of only three runs. Thirteen matches were won by an innings. Among other victories was an eight wickets' success over Lancashire at Bradford. The interest shown in the match at Park Avenue exceeded anything seen in the long history of the Roses series. The attendance was 26,000 on the Bank Holiday, but the gates had to be closed before the start of play, and it was estimated that around 50,000 intending spectators were turned away from the ground or stopped in the city from making a wasted journey. In their four championship years in the 1920s, Yorkshire lost only six out of 124 matches and recorded 81 victories. They were undefeated in 1925.

In 1923, Yorkshire had at their command the contrasting bowling talents of Rhodes, Macaulay, Roy Kilner, Emmott

Robinson and Waddington. The first three took over 100 wickets, and Robinson missed his century by only four wickets. These five bowlers took 594 wickets between them. Despite the fact that it lacked exceptional pace, it must rank as one of the finest attacks in county cricket. Kilner, as the slow left-arm bowler deputed to reduce Rhodes's burden, was judged by *Wisden* to possess 'pronounced spin. His good length bowling was combined with something of the imaginative quality that made Colin Blythe famous.'

It was not uncommon for Rhodes and Kilner to each bowl 40 overs in an innings and the accuracy of their bowling was shown in the number of their maiden overs. It was said during the season that it seemed curious Yorkshire should have two left-arm bowlers so frequently in action together. They were, though, different in their styles. Rhodes, with less finger spin than in his great years, could lock up one end with his masterly length. 'The effect,' said A. W. Pullin, 'with Kilner often bowling over the wicket, was to make a contrast with Rhodes which unsettles the batsman. It enables Kilner to slip in his fast "going away" ball by which many batsmen have been taken unawares, or to get them leg-before-wicket with an elusive straight one.' Waddington, before suffering a shoulder injury, also enjoyed days of astonishing success. There were occasions during his curtailed career when, it was said, he bowled with a bewildering swerve to recall George Hirst in his pomp. In four seasons, Waddington took over 470 wickets.

Sutcliffe, in the previous season, had demonstrated his blossoming command. 'After two disappointing seasons,' commented *Wisden*, 'he came into his own, fulfilling all the hopes inspired in 1919.' Cautiously, it added: 'He is a sound rather than a brilliant player, but his style is irreproachable.' Sutcliffe topped the Yorkshire averages and was eleventh in the national list. He exceeded 2,000 runs for the first time with an average of 46.97. His advancement gave rise to the view that he

Sutcliffe and Holmes with Pudsey sporting benefactor Richard Ingham.
(Richard Smith)

might have been blooded on the winter tour of South Africa,
especially as Hobbs had declined the trip. The selectors were,
as events would prove, wise to delay his promotion. It ensured
that Sutcliffe would have Hobbs as his influential guide on the
international stage.

Meanwhile, Sutcliffe and Holmes gathered their prizes with
Yorkshire. In the record season of 1923 they were associated
in nine century stands and took their tally to 25. It overtook
the previous Yorkshire record of 19 set up by Tunnicliffe and
Brown in nine seasons from 1895 to 1903. The new Yorkshire
pair reached their milestone in only five seasons. They began
their sequence of opening hundreds with 127 in the first
home match against Middlesex at Bradford. It was followed by
another of 238, without being separated, against Cambridge
University, and 119 against Middlesex at Lord's. Before the
end of June, there was another joint success against Sussex
at Leeds, where they scored 131 in two and a quarter hours.
There was another century stand against Warwickshire at Hull

a few days later. Then, in the next match against Somerset at the same venue, they vied with each other in a blaze of strokes. Sutcliffe was dismissed for 139 when the partnership was worth 274, and Holmes was caught just one run short of his double century. At the Scarborough Festival there was a stand of 120 against the MCC. The industrious pair crowned an amazing season by scoring 180 in two and three quarter hours in the Champions versus the Rest match at the Oval. Their opponents included the formidable bowling pairing of Maurice Tate and Arthur Gilligan.

In all matches in 1923, Holmes and Sutcliffe each scored over 2,000 runs. 'It was recognised long before the season ended that Sutcliffe had established his claim to be considered one of England's first-wicket batsmen,' wrote A.W. Pullin, the Yorkshire historian. He added, with pardonable irritation: 'It will also be difficult to convince the Yorkshire members and public that Holmes ought not to have been overlooked in the selection of all England teams since the war.'

Percy Holmes, in the words of Neville Cardus, was prepared to risk the mercy and indulgence of fortune. Herbert Sutcliffe, moving into a higher realm, was not so trusting; his iron will to succeed disdained caprice. His supreme confidence was to carry him along another spectacular route with Jack Hobbs.

5

Alliance with the Master

'Hobbs is undoubtedly the sauciest run-stealer in the world today. In Sutcliffe, he has found the ideal partner in the felony.'

The Cricketer

The greatest of opening partners began their England rule, in a whirl of indecision, again South Africa at Edgbaston in June 1924. A catastrophe loomed in the first over of the match. Herbert Sutcliffe, in a split second of chilling fright, was left stranded halfway down the wicket. He had made just two runs. Jack Hobbs, astonishingly, the injudicious caller, shook his head in dismay. Pelham Warner wrote:

Only eight runs had been scored when the gods pre-sented the South Africans with a rare opportunity. Hobbs had played the ball slowly past the bowler, Parker. Sutcliffe started for the run and the ball was picked up by Commaille at mid-on, with the Yorkshireman yards out of his ground. The fielder, with all three stumps as a target, took deliberate aim from short range; but throwing overhand instead of underhand, which is the better way in the circumstances, he missed the wicket; and Sutcliffe scrambled back.

The wicket was unguarded by the bowler, who had been unable to check his delivery stride. Even so, the ball missed the stumps by only a few inches.

The *Yorkshire Post* reported, with more than a hint of rebuke:

> It was not his [Sutcliffe's] fault that his wicket was endangered. Hobbs made the stroke and moved for the run, but when Sutcliffe responded he was sent back. In returning he slipped and the wicket should have been put down. Sutcliffe flung himself towards the wicket with the bat extended, and thus gained his crease.

George Parker, the South African fast bowler, looked back reproachfully at the hapless fieldsman. Parker, born in Cape Town and then playing as an amateur with Eccleshill in the Bradford League, had been recruited to strengthen the tourists' attack. It was his debut in first-class cricket. He was left to rue the folly of the first over. By the end of the day he had bowled 33 overs and taken five wickets for 138 runs. It was an exacting spell for the Test novice. He was so overcome by exhaustion that he had to leave the field before the close of play.

Herbert Sutcliffe, remembering the anxiety of his narrow escape in his first Test at Edgbaston, often pondered on the good fortune in later years. 'What would have happened had mid-on thrown the wicket down, as he almost did at Birmingham? Would I have had another chance? And if I had had another chance, would the first setback have upset my confidence to produce a second failure?' The reflections do provide food for thought: a host of quality players have been peremptorily discarded and given no opportunity to redeem themselves. The ways of Providence are strange, bestowing favours on one and not another, without apparent cause. Yet the impression persists that Sutcliffe was destined to rise above any misadventure. Jack Hobbs had no doubts about his partner's qualities, even at that early stage. 'None would have guessed from his demeanour that this was Herbert's first Test. He was so cool and naturally endowed with the big match temperament.'

At Edgbaston, England were sent in to bat by the South African captain, Herbie Taylor. Torrential rain had drenched the Birmingham ground in the two days preceding the Test. The wicket had recovered well and was reasonably dry and firm, but there were still damp spots on it, and the glass was rising. The promise of assistance for his bowlers clearly influenced Taylor's decision. Ronald Mason said that if Taylor had looked at the England pair a year or two later, he would have 'cut his own throat rather than send them in'. On this occasion, he could see after a few overs that he had 'sold himself bound and gagged down the river'.

Hobbs and Sutcliffe, after surviving the misunderstanding, upset South Africa's calculations with a century partnership. They added 136 in two hours and ten minutes. Sutcliffe was dismissed, yorked by Parker, ten minutes after lunch. His 64 included six fours and the flourish of a six which scattered the spectators on the square leg boundary. The *Yorkshire Post* enthused:

> There is a special reason for expressing satisfaction at Sutcliffe's success, for it can be assumed without reserve that he will be one of England's first-wicket batsmen for some time to come. Further, his cricket compared very favourably with that of his senior and experienced partner. He hit all round the wicket, treating each ball on its merits.

Wisden's verdict on the England debutant was that his first Test was 'nothing less than a triumph. He played flawless cricket, being especially strong on the legside.'

England, bolstered by her new opening pair, totalled 438. On the following day, Arthur Gilligan and Maurice Tate, another rampant combination for a regrettably brief time, bowled their way into the record books. South Africa were dismissed for 30, the lowest total in a Test in England. Gilligan took six wickets for seven runs in 6.3 overs and Tate four for 12 in six overs. Catterall scored a century for South Africa in the follow-on, but he could not deny England, winners by an innings and 18 runs.

Hobbs and Sutcliffe had, in fact, first come together as opening partners at the Scarborough Festival in 1922. They shared a century stand, 120, with Sutcliffe going on to reach his own three figures, for C.I. Thornton's XI against the MCC's South African touring team. Their next alliance, in 1923, for the Players against the Gentlemen at Lord's, was only moderately successful, but Hobbs and Sutcliffe gave a foretaste of their future renown when they represented an England XI against the Rest in a Test trial at Lord's in August. It was a rehearsal of their joint resource on bad wickets. They would unravel even more teasing knots in the future. 'The wicket had become quite nasty, the ball popping up in the most disconcerting fashion,' related *Wisden*. 'But Hobbs and Sutcliffe played superbly and overcame all difficulties. The greatness of what they did was hardly recognised until the other batsmen were seen against the same bowling.' They included Mead and Hendren, who both failed to score, and Woolley, who was dismissed for 11. Hobbs actually hit 43 in forty minutes as the first wicket stand raised 57. Sutcliffe, more dourly resistant, was the sixth man out after scoring 65. The substance of their innings can be gathered from the fact that they contributed more than half the England total of 206. They had two more profitable partnerships before the season ended. For the Players against the Gentlemen at Scarborough they made 70, Hobbs 39 and Sutcliffe 34, in the first innings. In the second innings, Sutcliffe was dismissed cheaply and his partner struck a majestic century.

A note in *The Cricketer* in 1924 drew attention to the growing understanding between Hobbs and Sutcliffe:

> Hobbs is undoubtedly the sauciest run-stealer in the world today. Yet saucy though these runs may be, his partner mostly seems to get home by yards. In Sutcliffe, Hobbs has found an ideal partner in the felony, for the Yorkshireman unhesitatingly responds to his calls, showing absolute confidence in Hobbs's judgement.

Les Ames, another England colleague, remembered the assurance of their running:

> Jack and Herbert would just play and run, sometimes when the ball had travelled no more than 15 yards away from the wicket. They were not especially speedy as runners. Herbert only strolled. It would have been undignified for him to rush as if he was trying to catch a train.

The placing of the stroke was the secret; it was so neat and precise that they could finish the run at almost a walk. Bob Wyatt, who opened with Sutcliffe for England in the 1930s, also recalled how Sutcliffe became as adept as Hobbs in garnering short singles. 'Herbert was a very easy chap to bat with. I cannot remember getting into a tangle with him.'

The inexperienced South Africans could not counter the ease and certainty of Hobbs and Sutcliffe in the second Test at Lord's in 1924. Catterall hit his second successive century as South Africa totalled 273. It was quickly revealed as a paltry target. By lunchtime on the Monday, England had cruelly exposed bowling almost wholly designed for the mat and help-less on turf. Hobbs and Sutcliffe did not spurn the gifts offered to them. Their command was crushing and calculated to break a bowler's heart. 'We both felt in tip-top form,' said Hobbs. 'We took all the risks in our stride, and yet we never seemed to be in danger. How thoroughly we enjoyed our run-stealing on that dove-grey midsummer morning.' It was a conquest of fearsome proportions. *Wisden* related: 'Seldom in a Test match has bowling been so mercilessly knocked about. The running between the wickets was daring to a point of audacity.'

In two and a half hours before lunch, Hobbs and Sutcliffe added exactly 200 runs. South Africa were offered just one chance to break the partnership. At 80, Sutcliffe lifted a ball from Blanckenburg to the legside, where a vacant space seemed to make the hit safe. Deane, at square-leg, made a valiant sprint to reach the ball but could not cling on to the catch. Hobbs reached his 107th century, his first against South Africa in England. Sutcliffe's 122 occupied three hours and twenty-five minutes, and was his first hundred in Test cricket. Their stand of 268 passed the previous best first-wicket part-nership of 221 against South Africa by Hobbs and Rhodes at Cape Town in 1909/10. When Sutcliffe mistimed his drive and chopped the ball on to his wicket, the torment of the South Africans was not finished. Frank Woolley was the next man in. He and Hobbs proceeded to slaughter the bowling. Hobbs reached his double century and Woolley his first Test 100 in England. The England pair put on 142 runs in 80 minutes. In a final flurry before Gilligan's declaration, the undefeated Woolley and Hendren added 121 in an hour. England totalled 531 for the loss of only two wickets and were subsequently victors by an innings and 18 runs.

Amid the riot of runs at Lord's Hobbs strode on, with a fine fury belying his forty-one years, to pass other milestones. He overhauled the 164 which had stood to the credit of Arthur Shrewsbury and Warren Bardsley in Test cricket at Lord's. He then progressed to beat Philip Mead's 182 at the Oval in 1921; exceeded his own highest Test score of 187 against South Africa at Cape Town; and finally equalled the 211 scored by W.L. Murdoch for Australia against England at the Oval in 1884.

Hobbs, as was his nature, was sublimely indifferent to the proximity of the record. The stroke that would have eclipsed the forty-year-old record was a casually lofted drive to cover. Taylor gratefully accepted the catch. In his brilliant 211, Hobbs hit 16 fours. The veteran had good cause to feel tired. 'Never have I seen a batsman so weary as Hobbs at the end of an innings,' commented one observer. 'You must remember, however, that he ran 90 of his own singles, around 40 of Sutcliffe's, and a good number of Woolley's, and he must have covered several miles during the innings.'

Just as wearying for Hobbs must have been the insistence of his admirers that he should score as many runs as possible. He often said that newspapers would do cricket a favour if they refrained from publishing the first-class averages. He did not usually linger long after making a 100. Of his 197 centuries, no fewer than 51 of them were scores between 100 and 110. Hobbs, when asked why he got out so quickly after making a century, said: 'Well, there are such a lot of good players to follow me.'

Bob Wyatt interestingly contrasted Hobbs with Don Bradman whose appetite for runs was unquenchable. 'With the Don,' said Wyatt, 'the completion of one hundred simply meant that it was time to start for another. This applied throughout his career in all matches. Bradman would always be looking to advance his score, as did Ponsford and most other Australians.' Wyatt believed that Hobbs, had he been similarly inclined, could have doubled many of his centuries. 'Jack would often have a go once he had reached his hundred.

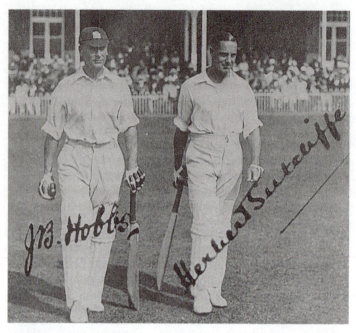

A striking accord: Jack Hobbs and Sutcliffe, England's greatest opening pair, who were associated in 26 century stands in nine years of wonderful attainment. (Brian Johnston)

Occasionally, if his score had moved on to around 160, he would take stock and say to himself: 'Well, I suppose, I might as well try for 200 now.'

Wyatt also made the point that Hobbs' reluctance to build big scores, except when the circumstances warranted them, was due at least in part to the fact that he did not want to lessen his batting enjoyment. The role of the automaton would have been alien to his nature. Hobbs, in the 1920s, was not a young man, and he had to pace himself in the daily round of championship cricket. But his achievements, including 98 centuries after his fortieth birthday in 1922 and over 35,000 runs in fifteen post-war seasons, are, by any standards, remarkable. When he reached his 100th century in May 1923 he had batted only once with Herbert Sutcliffe. When their partnership ended in 1932 Sutcliffe had also passed this milestone.

Herbert Sutcliffe, in a booklet published in 1927, doubted whether his England partner had an equal. 'As a batsman, he stands alone – the best I have ever seen – and if the great "W.G.", as is often claimed, was as good as Hobbs, then he must have been wonderful.'

Hobbs, like others of his time, was an instinctive cricketer. John Arlott said:

> He was the best kind of self-made man: independent, often making decisions alone; at need self-sufficient; yet too affectionate to be a solitary. No one taught him to play cricket; he never had an hour's coaching in his life, nor more than an occasional piece of advice. Yet he was, in every way, a complete batsman.

Bill Bowes, a fiery opponent on occasions, was astonished at Hobbs' ease, grace and confidence. Hobbs always laid great stress on quick runs at the outset of an innings. It was the means of asserting his authority over bowlers. Bowes recalled:

> The first time I bowled at him, he went down on one knee and hit me past the left hand of square-leg. The ball had pitched seven or eight inches outside the off-stump. My jaw dropped and George Macaulay at mid-on, shouted reprovingly: 'It's no good you peepin' – he'll do that three times an over when his eye's in.'

Hobbs was venerated as the 'Master', and his distinction actually led to a club, bearing that name, being formed as a tribute to him. At fifty, his technique was undiminished and perfectly intact. In 1933, he was goaded into a response when the West Indian fast bowler, Martindale, imprudently remarked that he thought the great man had run his course. When the tourists came to the Oval to play Surrey, Hobbs did not forget the accusation. He looked out of the dressing-room window and made an uncharacteristic forecast: 'I think I'll get a hundred today; that looks like a good wicket.' He did rather better, scoring 221 in six and a half hours. It was also an exercise in physical endurance. He was stiff for a week after the innings. As his tired muscles shrieked in protest, Hobbs permitted himself a modest chuckle at the apology of Martindale. 'Mister Hobbs,' said the West Indian, 'you are a great player.'

Jack Hobbs played in 41 Tests against Australia, and in 71 innings he scored 3,636 runs at an average of 54.26. The tally included 12 centuries, the first at Melbourne in 1911/12 and the last, at the age of forty-six, also at Melbourne in the 1928/29 series. No other Englishman has matched this feat. 'Figures,' commented one observer, 'can convey no idea of Hobbs, of his full-blooded hooking when he was young, of his driving on light, swift feet, of his peerless square-cut, of his leaning leg-glance, of the natural growth of his talents to a quite regal control and superiority.' Hobbs was supreme on all wickets, and the nonpareil when the struggle was hardest on brutish pitches. One writer said that it was Hobbs who excised the word 'unplayable' as a classification.

Herbert Sutcliffe treasured his association with Hobbs; they had from the beginning a friendly accord and were temperamentally in tune, despite the gap of twelve years in their ages. At the start, Hobbs assumed the guise of a reassuring elder brother. 'Come on, young fellow,' he said, with a cheering smile, as they walked out to bat in their first Test together at Edgbaston in 1924. Sutcliffe was serene and happy in their burgeoning alliance. He recalled the simple advice of Hobbs. 'Play your own game,' was the directive of the Surrey master. 'Four words – they counted for so much. They told me all I wanted to know,' said Sutcliffe. Hobbs was satisfied that if

Sutcliffe played to his normal standards he would prove good enough for Test cricket. Sutcliffe came home to an approving welcome, as the lauded junior, for the third Test against South Africa at Headingley.

There was, however, yet another running hiccup to jangle the nerves of the expectant spectators. The order of their calling, soon to become a byword, was not yet fully established. As at Edgbaston, there was a near calamity in the first over of the match. 'All order and principle vanished in a moment of expanding horror and agony,' wrote Ronald Mason. Hobbs played a ball to cover and began to run, but noting that the fielder, Deane, was shaping to make a quick return, he changed his mind and regained his crease. Sutcliffe, in the meantime, had crossed quickly. Both batsmen were at the same end when Deane impulsively shied the ball at the opposite stumps. The ball missed the wickets and sped wide of the bowler to the boundary. Hobbs, instead of being run out, was given a bonus of five runs.

It was, reported the *Yorkshire Post*, just one of many lamentable examples of indiscreet running in the match:

> Hobbs ought to have been run out, and could have blamed no one but himself had that been his fate. Then Ernest Tyldesley ran like a schoolboy in the first throes of exaltation when he had only Hendren's back view on going for a third run from his own stroke.

Finally, in the South African innings, Commaille made the unpardonable error of supposing that a shot to the prowling Hobbs at cover was worth a single, and paid the inevitable penalty.

Hobbs and Sutcliffe, suitably chastened after their first-over trauma, added 72 with no further alarms. Sutcliffe was restrained by the leg-theory tactics of the South African bowlers. But his innings of 83, out of England's match-winning total of 396, was judged the best of the day. 'He unquestionably held pride of place,' commented the *Yorkshire Post*. The newspaper referred to a 'calculated campaign of negation. The purpose of Nupen and Nourse was to bowl wide of the leg stump, with six, seven and sometimes eight fieldsmen on that side of the wicket, with the joint object of taking fugitive catches and keeping down the runs.'

Sutcliffe was not to be betrayed into rashness. For three hours he was impassive in his quiet contemplation of the restrictive attack. The *Yorkshire Post* reported:

> With masterly judgement, he picked out the balls which could be hit. The variety of his strokes and his resources against bowling of a kind, which does not allow a batsman to display his artistry, can be judged from the fact that of his 12 boundaries, five were off-drives, two were cuts, three were made by turning the ball sharply away behind the wickets on the legside, and two were hooks.

Sutcliffe, with 303 runs at an average of 75.75, shared the England batting honours with Hobbs and Hendren against South Africa. Along with Arthur Gilligan, reappointed as captain, he was one of ten players named in July for the tour of Australia in the following winter. The fee for the tour was £400 plus bonuses awarded on the basis of merit and discipline. In addition to the sea passage, railway fares, travelling expenses and accommodation, each player received personal expenses of £1 10s a week on board ship and £2 a week on land. On this journey, the first of his three tours of Australia, Sutcliffe crested the heights of fame. It also signalled a compelling landmark in the history of batsmanship, the flowering of his partnership with Jack Hobbs in an otherwise luckless time for England.

Events might have been ordered differently if Hobbs had adhered to his original intention not to make the tour. On first being invited he declined, because he was unwilling to leave his family and his business for the winter. He had missed the previous tours of South Africa and the West Indies for the same reasons. Before the issue was resolved Hobbs was approached by Lionel Tennyson and asked if he would join a private tour to South Africa that was being sponsored by Mr Solly Joel. The carrot being dangled before Hobbs was a free trip for his wife. It was a tempting proposition for the devoted couple.

As Hobbs was considering the offer, the news was relayed to the influential Lord Harris. 'If we arrange for Mrs Hobbs to accompany you, will you switch to the Australian tour?' asked Harris. Hobbs, having gained the concession, was typically loath to rob another player of selection. It was finally agreed that he should go out to Australia as an 'extra member' of the England party. Rumours doubtless abounded on the incentives which had forged the pact. Hobbs later vigorously made clear that the intervention of the MCC did not include financial assistance. 'The entire expense incurred on behalf of my wife was paid by myself, nor did I receive higher remuneration than any of the other players.' He did not tour without his beloved Ada again.

Hobbs's change of mind was, though, an important afterthought. It ensured that Herbert Sutcliffe was able to prosper mightily with a cherished cricket companion. A separation from Hobbs at this stage might have led to a parting of the ways. The England selectors, whether they knew it or not, had displayed an admirable percipience in maintaining this alliance. Hobbs and Sutcliffe won new friends and scaled fresh peaks in a momentous campaign.

6

Triumphant in Australia

'He is a cool customer and earnest to a degree. The way he set out to master the idiosyncrasies of strange wickets and hard bright lights marked him out as a player who must make good.'

M.A. Noble, the former Australian captain.

Emerging through the cats' whisker wireless in January 1925 was the barely audible news of cricket in Australia. The voice, gradually deciphered by one intent listener, broke through the airwaves to announce that Herbert Sutcliffe had rallied England once more. 'He's done it again,' was the message relayed by Pudsey enthusiast Frank Birks to the Sutcliffe family. 'What's he done?' asked Arthur Sutcliffe, eager to learn about his nephew's latest achievement. 'He's got another 100,' said Birks. 'Uncle Arthur', the Pudsey cricket gallant of other years, nodded his head in approval. 'Ah well,' he said, 'he can carry it, can ahr Herbert. It won't go to his head.'

Herbert Sutcliffe, at the age of thirty, reached his zenith as a cricketer, under the leadership of Arthur Gilligan, in this ill-fated series. After his selection for the tour, he said:

I feel very proud that my ambition to play for England has been attained. I have been fighting for it for nearly twenty years – ever since I started playing cricket at eleven years of age. I shall use every endeavour to uphold the highest traditions of English cricket and strive to bring honour both to Yorkshire and Pudsey.

Sutcliffe's honours in Australia were all the greater because he achieved parity with Jack Hobbs. They were the pillars of England's batting strength. Given better support for the openers and the indomitable Maurice Tate in the bowling attack, the tale of the series could have had a happier ending. The margin was 4–1 in Australia's favour; but as on Freddie Brown's tour twenty-six years later, when England suffered an identical defeat, the fluctuating contest merited a fairer outcome. As a matter of historical interest, each of the series served as preludes to an England renaissance, in 1926 and 1953.

The pairing of Hobbs and Sutcliffe in Australia in 1924/25 confirmed their precedence as England's opening batsmen. Ronald Mason considered that Sutcliffe was no longer a pupil in his association with the Surrey master. 'The unresting willowy genius of the one complemented the rooted and reliable oaken genius of the other.' Hobbs himself, in one affectionate recollection, provided an instance of their prospering comradeship. At Sydney, in the first of their four century partnerships on the tour, Hobbs took the first over against Kelleway, a bowler whose late outswinger could cause problems. Sutcliffe thought, perhaps rather impertinently, that his partner looked a little unsafe. Hobbs, in fact, had shown adroit judgement in playing out a maiden. At the end of the over the Yorkshireman came down the pitch and said: 'Best to leave the new ball alone, Jack.' Hobbs, in recalling the incident, commented: 'I knew then that we'd found the right opener for England.' By way of a return compliment, Sutcliffe also counted it a privilege to open with Hobbs. Without question, he was fortunate that their careers coincided. 'It was a source of strength for me to see Jack take his free and graceful stance at the wicket,' said Sutcliffe. 'When I walked out with him I gained confidence, and that confidence was increased by everything he did.' Sutcliffe described Hobbs as a 'scientific wonder'. 'Each stroke was a technical masterpiece, feet, body, shoulders, wrists and fingers working perfectly together, the whole controlled by a keenly alert brain.'

Before he gathered his laurels in England's magnificent uphill fight, Sutcliffe had confessed to difficulties in timing the ball in the piercingly strong light in Australia. It took him about six weeks to adjust to the conditions. The wickets, he said, were at least four yards faster than in England. He realised that the best plan was to play up and down the pitch. 'I sacrificed many of my shots, but it paid off in the end.'

His patience did, indeed, reap rich rewards, culminating in a sequence of unprecedented successes. Sutcliffe began with three consecutive centuries, including two – 176 and 127 – in the second Test at Melbourne. At Melbourne, in the fourth Test, he scored another century. He eclipsed the record of three hundreds in a series by Stanley Jackson in England in 1905 and Hobbs in Australia in 1911/12. There were two other 100s, one in Tasmania and the other against Northern Districts. In seven successive innings his scores were: 59, 115, 176, 127, 33, 59 and 143. His Test aggregate of 734 runs, at an average of 81.55, was nearly 20 runs higher than Hobbs' own formidable contribution. It placed Sutcliffe in the category of the world's leading batsmen.

A writer in the *Athletic News* described Sutcliffe as the wonder man of England. 'His is the noblest record of them all.' He reminded his readers of how Archie MacLaren and Ranjitsinhji had aroused jubilation by their early performances in Australia. Their feats, he said, did not produce the furore which had resounded in the ears of Sutcliffe and would glow in his memory all his life. Other correspondents waxed rhapsodically about Sutcliffe, bestowing the soubriquet of 'the pleasant face, the fascinating smile and a heart of oak.' One observer enthused: 'No Englishman, not even R.E. "Tip" Foster, with his record 287 at Sydney in 1903–4, has ever played such innings as those by Sutcliffe at Melbourne.'

The plaudits for Sutcliffe did, however, need to be coupled with the distinctions of Hobbs. 'It is Sutcliffe, to whom England will turn for cricket greatness at the wicket in the future, but to think that the career of Jack Hobbs is appreciably waning would be ridiculous,' wrote Capt. E.W. Ballantine from Melbourne. Hobbs, the reluctant tourist in 1924/25, was to share even greater feats with his partner in subsequent series against Australia. His reputation gained fresh lustre, while Sutcliffe pocketed the gleaming coins of his own admirable currency. 'For nearly ten years the cricket world offered Hobbs and Sutcliffe as one of its prime adornments on the twin levels of art and attainment,' wrote Ronald Mason.

In his early impressions of the 1924/25 tour, M.A. Noble, the former Australian captain, prophesied a largesse of runs for Sutcliffe:

> He is particularly good on the legside and pulls with great certainty and power. His backplay is safe and sure. None of the bowlers appear to trouble him, except the slow ones, against whom he betrayed a marked inclination to scratch forward. He is a cool customer and nothing appears to disturb him.

Hobbs and Sutcliffe had twice hoisted the 100 together before a more exacting challenge awaited them in the first Test at Sydney. Australia, batting first, took eight and a half hours to total 450. England's openers, studied and cautious against the bowling of Mailey and Gregory, replied with a stand of 157.

Hobbs obtained his seventh Test century. Sutcliffe hit 59 but, according to Noble, he was never at ease against Mailey:

> The fact that the acting Australian captain, Bardsley, placed a silly point, a silly mid-on and a square leg worried him greatly. The ball with which Mailey got him was a half-volley on the off-stump, going away. Richardson took an easy catch. Sutcliffe's downfall was a tribute to the strategy of Bardsley and Mailey. They had planned very carefully for that catch, and it would have needed a more experienced player than Sutcliffe to avoid it.

Sutcliffe severely chastised himself for an 'exceedingly scratchy knock' in his first Test innings in Australia:

> I was troubled most of the time by Arthur Mailey, who was then at the top of his form. He got my wicket in the end, for I fell into his 'booby' trap at silly mid-off. When it was all over, the best I could say about it was that, in my stay of two and a half hours, I had had a vast amount of useful experience. I had been able to weigh up the Australian attack. By the time my innings ended I had little difficulty in differentiating between Mailey's leg-breaks and his wrong 'uns.

Sutcliffe did have early problems with spin but he learned to counter it by his accurate assessment of pitch and line. Ian Peebles did not regard the Yorkshireman as a great picker of the googly. He remembered a match at the Scarborough Festival when Sutcliffe sought to 'read' the Middlesex leg-spinner, Walter Robins. Sutcliffe's concern was exceeded by Frank Gilligan, who was keeping to Robins for the first time. After conceding around 20 byes in three overs, an embarrassed Gilligan met Robins in the middle of the pitch and asked for a signal for the 'wrong 'un'. Robins said he would walk back with the ball in his left hand when he was going to bowl it. Gilligan was spared further bother as Sutcliffe, having settled down, did not miss a ball and scored freely from the googly. As they walked in at lunchtime, Robins said: 'You're picking it pretty well today, Herbert.' The undefeated batsman modestly acknowledged the tribute. At the pavilion gate Sutcliffe paused and gave his rival an impish glance. 'The next time you make an arrangement with your wicket-keeper,' he told Robins, 'you want to take a look to see who else is listening.'

Maurice Tate, his huge feet striding valiantly into the fray, took 11 wickets in the seven-day Test marathon at Sydney. His monumental effort could not disguise the limitations of the England attack. Australia scored 452 in their second innings, Taylor and Mailey putting on 127 in a last-wicket stand. England, with no realistic chance of victory, lost by 195 runs. Even so, their 411 was then a record for the fourth innings of a Test. Hobbs and Sutcliffe raised another century partnership, the Yorkshireman advancing to his own three figures in implacable style, and Woolley then charmed everyone with a serene century. England were heavily beaten but pride was restored in a brave, if unavailing, struggle against tremendous odds. The stage was set for gallantry of a higher order in the next Test at Melbourne.

There was, at first, the vision of an ignominious rout. Arthur Gilligan, after losing the toss, was heartened by the buoyancy of Tate, who swiftly sent back Collins, Bardsley and Arthur Richardson before the total had reached 50. It was a false signal of hope. England were just as quickly set back on their heels as Ponsford, Taylor and Victor Richardson, with massive aplomb, carried Australia to 600. Three of the England bowlers, Gilligan, Tyldesley and Tate, conceded more than 100 runs. Amid the weight of runs Tate, in both Australia's innings at Melbourne, accomplished the outstanding feat of sending down the equivalent of 104 English (six-ball) overs at a cost of

241 runs. S.F. Barnes, writing in the *Daily Chronicle*, considered this was great bowling. Tate had taken 20 wickets in the first two Tests, and he was to obtain 38 wickets in the series, on his first visit to Australia. He overtook Barnes's own record of 34 wickets in the 1911/12 series.

England's batting reply at Melbourne was a feat to match that of Tate in spirit and determination. On the Saturday, in an astonishing turn of events, the situation of the game was changed by one of the greatest achievements in cricket history. By the close of play, absurd as it may seem, there was the prospect of England gaining a tidy lead. In February 1912, Hobbs and Rhodes had established a record opening partnership of 323 for England against Australia at Melbourne. Now Hobbs was joined in the same arena by another equally resolute Yorkshireman, who relished defying the laws of improbability. Jack Gregory without, it must be said, his great bowling partner, Ted McDonald, was still a formidable proposition. Ian Peebles described Gregory as 'towering, tanned and powerfully lithe'; and it was said that the Australian's sheer speed frightened batsmen into submission. Charles Kelleway was the supporting fast bowler and the England pair also had to contend with the varying spins of Mailey, Hartkopf and Arthur Richardson.

Throughout the long January day of enervating heat, the two England batsmen travelled along a careful road to conquest. The eloquent figures of 283 – Hobbs 154, Sutcliffe 123 – shone brightly on the scoreboard at the close of play. A writer in *The Australian* reported:

> Never have I seen sounder, safer batting. Hobbs and Sutcliffe are not of the belligerent kind, preferring to make their runs in a more delicate manner; but as to their skill and touch there can be no two opinions. All through their big stand so masterly were their methods that only two mistakes were made, neither constituting a chance.

Monty Noble also commended a flawless display:

> It was English cricket at its best. You have only to remember the total that glared in the faces of these men as they went out to open the innings to realise the mental as well as the physical effort necessary to overcome the feeling of hopelessness. As a demonstration of perfect cricket it was probably unique, but as a spectacle it was more fascinating for its precision rather than its brilliance.

Herbert Sutcliffe remembered how Hobbs had urged caution against Gregory at the start of the England innings. 'If we can tame Jack, we might be there for a considerable time,' said Hobbs. This objective was duly achieved in a partnership which Sutcliffe rated as the second best of his career and only superseded by the awesome demands of the sticky wicket at the Oval in 1926. At Melbourne, said Sutcliffe, they appeared to be facing an almost impossible task. 'We defied every change in the bowling. Sometimes we were defending, sometimes in aggression, but always careful and confident.' The joys of the occasion were not because of their personal triumphs; but rather because 'our mental and physical effort had been the means of opening out a game, which had seemed fairly hopeless'.

One observer in *The Cricketer* commented:

> Such play these two gave us. They were content with ones and twos, stealing with complete safety scores of runs by perfect judgement. At one period, when Sutcliffe was about 40, he brightened, hit one or two balls with full vigour, but wisely took himself to task, and returned to the routine of the job.

Sutcliffe had clearly set his sights on overtaking the previous first-wicket Test record. On the Sunday following the

Melbourne feat he received a cable from the joint holder,
Wilfred Rhodes. Rhodes offered his congratulations and
wished the England pair luck on the resumption of play. The
partnership was broken by Mailey on the Monday morning.
'There was a gentle eleven o'clock breeze to the bowler at the
pavilion end,' reported one observer. 'We looked forward to a
repetition of Saturday. But such is cricket – Hobbs made no
more. In Mailey's first over, a yorker, almost a full toss, swinging down and with the help of the breeze, was not sent to
the onside for Saturday's habitual single, but hit the leg-stump.'
Hobbs remembered the ball which ended the partnership. 'I
tried to play it just wide of mid-on. I made a yorker of it.'
Sutcliffe had tried to persuade Hobbs to join him for a spell of
practice before the start of play. 'Herbert was desperately keen
for us to break the record,' said Jack. Hobbs declined the invitation. 'No, I shall be all right, Herbert.' Sutcliffe, chiding his
senior in the manner of an indignant parent after the abrupt
dismissal, said: 'But he wasn't all right.'

Records apart, Sutcliffe knew that England could ill-afford
the early loss of Hobbs; the subsequent decline to 479 all out,
after such a wonderful start, confirmed his suspicions. The
next best stand was 68 between Hendren and Chapman for
the fourth wicket and no other batsman advanced beyond
the thirties. Woolley was promptly yorked by Gregory; and
Sutcliffe alone, on his raft of defiance, retained his composure
to score 176. It was all deeply disappointing after the heroics
of the Saturday. Tate offered England a glimmer of a chance
of victory in taking six wickets for 99 runs in Australia's
second innings. Taylor's 90 was the decisive score on a wearing
wicket. England were beaten by 81 runs, and it was largely
due to Sutcliffe, with his second century in the match, that
such a small margin separated the teams. His 127, including
12 boundaries, was a model of coolness and restraint. It was
one of the supreme occasions of his career. In his two innings

he was at the wicket for thirteen and a half hours and absent from the field for less than an hour and a half. 'When Sutcliffe completed his hundred for the second time in the match a delightful incident followed,' reported his home-town newspaper, the *Pudsey and Stanningley News*. 'The crowd rose as one man to give him an ovation such as can never have been surpassed on a cricket ground. It was truly a wonderful scene of triumph.'

An Adelaide correspondent wrote:

> Had Victor Trumper achieved the same distinction, it would have been impossible for the Australian idol to have had a greater reception. The characteristic doggedness of Yorkshiremen was never more in evidence than with Herbert Sutcliffe. There was never a suspicion of selfishness throughout his long second innings. Heroism, courage and patriotism were written large during his tremendous efforts. Sutcliffe has proved himself just as capable of adapting to Australian conditions as Jack Hobbs did.

Monty Noble was one of many Australians captivated by Sutcliffe's qualities on the tour. 'He is earnest to a degree,' said Noble, 'and the way he set out to master the idiosyncrasies of strange wickets and the hard, bright lights marked him out as a player who must make good.' Noble said Sutcliffe never seemed to court popularity, 'yet there was something in his personality that compelled the admiration of great numbers of Australians'.

These engaging qualities aided Sutcliffe in his rapport with the barrackers in the 'scoring board squad' at Brisbane. Early in the game against Queensland the wags around the fences tested the Yorkshireman with their witticisms; but he returned their sallies with interest. Sutcliffe remembered the noise and the unrelenting banter of the barrackers. He soon realised that

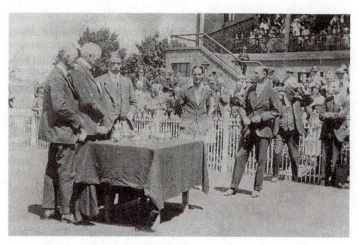

A presentation of silver tea and coffee services to Hobbs and Sutcliffe at Melbourne in 1925. (W.H.H.S)

the best thing to do was to joke with the crowd. In the first game at Brisbane he had been given out lbw although he had hit the ball so hard that the sound could be heard in the stands. The Australian captain had asked the umpire to reverse the decision. On the following day the newspapers dwelt upon the unjust dismissal. The erring umpire was then subjected to an even fiercer bout of barracking. On another occasion one English bowler had not been able to see the disquieting figures accompanying his name on the scoreboard. It was suggested that he should bowl from the other end, so that he could examine his analysis. Against the resistant batsmen the bowlers would be urged to 'Burn him out'. Others, who lingered tediously at the crease, would be told that they were 'wanted on the telephone'.

The friendship grew between Sutcliffe and the barrackers' squad at Brisbane in the intervals between the times when he was scampering round the boundaries to cut off the fours. The squad held a 'tarpaulin muster' to raise a collection for a case of pipes. It was a memento for 'Herbie', their favourite

Englishman whom, they declared, had been 'adopted' by them. Sutcliffe was called over the ropes to receive the gift. It was inscribed with the words: 'To H. Sutcliffe, from the Scoring Board Squad, in appreciation of his sportsmanship.'

Back home in Pudsey there was universal, rejoicing at the exploits of Hobbs and Sutcliffe. 'The town on the hill has its tail up because one of its sons has brought distinction on it by partnering Hobbs in one of the most brilliant displays ever given in a Test match,' reported the *Pudsey and Stanningley News*. 'Any town may reckon itself no mean hamlet when it can turn out a batsman who can share an opening partnership of treble figures in three successive innings and, in one of them, can bat all day against the cream of Australia's bowling.'

The crucial match of the 1924/25 series was the third Test at Adelaide where an injury-stricken England lost by just 11 runs after a courageous rally. Australia thus retained the Ashes but this was defeat akin to triumph. Arthur Gilligan described the chapter of injuries as 'astounding ill-luck'. Ryder hit 201 off the depleted England attack. Hobbs, once with the new ball, and Hendren were called upon to bowl in the absence of Tate, Freeman and Gilligan. Then torrential rain came to England's aid. Roy Kilner and Woolley shared eight wickets in Australia's second innings. Australia lost seven wickets for 39 in an hour and a half, and collapsed to 250 all out. England needed 242 runs to win but could not quite make it. Hobbs, after his first innings century, put on 63 with Sutcliffe. Sutcliffe, Whysall and Chapman (the latter pair adding 89 at a run-a-minute) all reached their half-centuries before the game moved to a thrilling climax. In a last-ditch struggle Gilligan, handicapped by a thigh strain, battled for two hours for his 31; and he and Freeman added 45 for the ninth wicket in a vain bid for victory.

Gilligan at last spun the coin correctly in the fourth Test at Melbourne as a prelude to England's first success against

Australia for twelve years. Hobbs and Sutcliffe put up 100 for
the fourth time in the series; and the Yorkshireman, having
been missed at nine, went on to score 143, his fourth century of the series. Australia followed on 249 runs behind and
Tate drove home the advantage, taking the last four wickets
for 21 runs, as England won by an innings and 29 runs. One
observer at Melbourne commented:

> We should have rejoiced to see Hobbs keep pace with his
> new partner and make another century. Hobbs has stood
> supreme for a long time as an artist batsman, the man who
> not only made runs but secured them in a perfect style. If
> the Surrey master's primacy is to pass, it could not move
> into worthier hands. Sutcliffe, too, is an artist, who displays
> his skill with a supple grace that comes of a sure command
> of his means and a temperamental delight in its exercise.

The writer was premature in transferring the baton to Sutcliffe.
Hobbs had still more runs in his locker; the rule would not be
drawn below his career for some time yet.

In London, lashed by gales and squalls of rain, the depression gave way to delight at the happenings in Australia.
Newspaper placards hailed the hero from Yorkshire. 'Non-stop
Sutcliffe', 'Sutcliffe, Chapter IV' and 'Sutcliffe's New Record'
were among the laudatory headlines regaling the crowds. In
Yorkshire, one enterprising Bradford tobacconist placed a
photograph of Sutcliffe in his shop window. He had a good
day's takings. The shop was besieged by people who gazed
with wonder at the picture of the handsome record-breaker.
The news of Sutcliffe's success brought sheaves of congratulations. From his birthplace in Nidderdale and the Dacre Banks
club came a cable which read: 'Heartiest congratulations on
your splendid achievement.' Sutcliffe acknowledged this trib-

ute, along with countless others, with a handwritten note of thanks, all penned in his immaculate copybook style.

A generous and overwhelming stream of gifts measured Australia's regard for England's premier batsmen. Before the start of play on the Saturday of the Melbourne Test, Hobbs and Sutcliffe were each presented with a silver tea and coffee service as mementoes of their batting feats. From Brisbane came a Q-shaped jewel, representing the state of Queensland, upon which were inscribed Sutcliffe's Test scores. In the Victorian town of Albury, en-route for Melbourne, his admirers presented him with a set of gold cufflinks bearing his two century scores in the second Test. Miners in Kalgoorlie gave him two gold nuggets, while in Adelaide other enthusiasts eulogised him in an illuminated address in ceremonial style. Sutcliffe's baby daughter, Barbara, was also remembered. A silver egg cup and spoon was sent to her; and Mrs Sutcliffe received a present of possum skins.

The surge of adulation almost inevitably brought a salutary tumble. The Australian tour ended on a note of anti-climax for Hobbs and Sutcliffe. At Sydney, in the final Test, England were rendered strokeless by the leg-spin of Clarrie Grimmett. Grimmett, a tiny gnome of a man, with his curious round-arm action, made his Test debut at the age of thirty-four. He took 11 wickets for 82 runs to leapfrog into the ranks of the world's leading bowlers. England were beaten, dismissively, by 307 runs. Grimmett was entitled to smile in his sleep for years to come. Hobbs's first-innings duck, after Oldfield had acrobatically held a catch from a firm glance yards down the legside, was followed by one by Sutcliffe in the second innings.

A spirit of good cheer did persist despite England's defeat in Australia. Arthur Gililgan, the buoyant campaigner, was convinced that the tide was turning. 'It was bad luck to lose the rubber, but we shall win in 1926.' *Wisden* was more guarded in its judgement. C. Stewart Caine, the editor, wrote:

The narrowness of the margin by which on two occasions the Englishmen lost, coupled with the ill-fortune experienced in tossing for the choice of innings, appears to have persuaded many that the actual difference between the sides was small, and that better times are in store... there is no gainsaying the fact that a strong belief is widely entertained that the dark days are coming to an end.

The grounds for optimism were not unfounded. England still had Hobbs, not yet contemplating retirement, and Woolley and Hendren. With Sutcliffe and Tate, the two indisputable young champions of the tour, on call the outlook was good.

Extraordinary sporting deeds fire the imagination and are fixed immovably in the calendar of a lifetime. The grandeur of such events, as we turn the pages of our memories, emerges with startling clarity. The salute paid to Herbert Sutcliffe, after his first triumphant tour of Australia, was a tribute to his gallantry. It was a valiant episode and it is still talked about with a fervour which allows no contradiction. Sutcliffe was, in modern terms, not a young man but he came to maturity as a Test cricketer in a time of adversity. It was in keeping with his character that he should succeed in such circumstances. He was at his best when the challenge was greatest.

Just after half past nine on a Sunday night in April 1925, Herbert Sutcliffe stepped off the train at Leeds Central Station. He and his wife, Emily, who had travelled down to Dover to greet her husband, were surrounded by eager porters competing to carry their luggage to a waiting car. It was a quiet, unannounced arrival; the tumult of the homecoming celebrations followed two nights later. An adoring crowd, estimated at around 15,000 people, roared their welcome at the Pudsey Recreation Ground. The reception committee included Richard Ingham and Ernest Walker, Sutcliffe's first cricket mentors. A posse of photographers and a Pathé

Gazette cinema unit filmed the proceedings. Five large horns carried the speeches to the rim of the field. As the bronzed and happy Herbert mounted an improvised platform of lorries, the Pudsey Brass Band played 'See the Conquering Hero Comes', and the applause redoubled in intensity. Messages of congratulations from admirers throughout the country were read out by the town mayor. 'Herbert, the inimitable', said one; 'Good old Sutcliffe', commented another from Kent. Another correspondent, writing from London, said: 'As one who had the pleasure of accompanying the MCC team in Australia, I should like to assure you of my admiration for Herbert Sutcliffe. His conduct on and off the field was a credit to your great county.' A cheque for £215 was sent to Sutcliffe from a Sheffield group. Ten Doncaster miners sent ten shillings to 'Pudsey's great batsman'. A Yorkshire newspaper set up a public subscription fund and another proposal was that the county membership should purchase a house for the Sutcliffe family at Pudsey.

Cllr Simeon Myers, the president of the Pudsey and District Sunday Schools League, recalled the words of an Australian, who had described Sutcliffe as the greatest 'commercial traveller' to leave England's shores that year. Cllr Myers said they were welcoming the return of a traveller who had delivered the goods, and the Pudsey people were well satisfied. As the league's tribute to their townsman, every boy who scored 50 runs, or took a hat-trick, would be presented with a photograph of Sutcliffe together with details of his achievements in Australia.

Mr J. Clifton Town, a former chairman of the Leeds Cricket, Football and Athletic Club, said that Sutcliffe had fulfilled his promise to give of his best when he was selected to tour Australia. 'Herbert is a record-breaker and maker of history. He has fully justified our confidence and returned with his reputation enhanced, honour unsullied, and covered with

Sutcliffe addresses the audience at a Pudsey civic reception after the 1924/25 tour of Australia.

glory.' Town said he rejoiced with all Pudsey people in welcoming home the best of their sons, and shared with them the earnest desire that he would prove in the days to come that he was even greater than they thought him that night.

In his response, Sutcliffe remembered the grim battles in Australia, three of which had lasted over seven days, the toll of energy and the strain imposed on the nerves. He paid tribute to the steady and inspiring influence of Jack Hobbs in their opening partnerships. He said that he would never forget the ovation at Melbourne after his second Test century in the match. 'The cheers were almost deafening. They went on for several minutes and were renewed at the end of the over.'

The homage paid to Herbert Sutcliffe on a memorable night at Pudsey was a recognition of his place in a nation's regard. It closely paralleled the reception afforded to his Pudsey and Yorkshire successor, Leonard Hutton. The peals of acclaim were no less welcoming for Hutton after his record 364 at the Oval in 1938. They rang out again for him, as a mature England captain, when the Ashes were regained on another famous Oval occasion in 1953. In Sutcliffe's, as in Hutton's triumphs, there was a surge of joy among his caring people. Herbert Sutcliffe did not forget those who had shepherded him in his cricket infancy. 'I am proud to be a Pudsey man,' he said.

7

The Aura of Authority

'Herbert never let cricket down in any way. He always behaved himself perfectly. He was the model example.'

Les Ames

The cultivated manner was motivated by a wish to make himself socially acceptable. The grand design of the self-made man was also, as many people have attested, governed by a desire to advance the cause of the professional cricketer. The refinement, painstakingly acquired, was, though, a rare act of moral courage among the broad-accented people of Pudsey. 'Getting on', in that sense, for Herbert Sutcliffe, invited ridicule; but the former cobblers' apprentice was not to be deflected from his single-minded pursuit of prestige.

As an officer in the Green Howards Regiment in the First World War, Sutcliffe had first worn the plumes of distinction; and when he was established as a sophisticated man of the world even the plainest and bluntest viewed him with increased pride and admiration. Sutcliffe, in his cricket sovereignty, was still 'Our 'Erbert' for his most devout admirers in the Grinders' stand at Bramall Lane, Sheffield. They relished his majesty, and especially his vivid jousts with Australian fast bowler Ted McDonald in Roses matches. Beneath the dignity, as they shrewdly perceived, was the fine passion and grit of a Yorkshireman. Sutcliffe did not enjoy the easy affection afforded to Bill Bowes and Maurice Leyland. But his relationship with the Yorkshire supporters was close enough for them to rebuke him. Unnecessary passiveness brought a swift reprimand, even for the lordly Sutcliffe. He once stonewalled at Old Trafford for half an hour, almost without scoring. It was a stiflingly hot afternoon, and as Neville Cardus related, 'a huge multitude sat in silence. Suddenly a voice addressed Sutcliffe, not critically, but with a simple honest inquiry: "'Erbert," the voice solicited, "'Erbert coom on; what dost tha think thi are, a bloody war memorial?"'

Cardus described Sutcliffe's self-assurance as an 'asset beyond mortal estimation'. He considered that this was the largest ingredient in Sutcliffe's success. Another contemporary attributed to the Yorkshireman a massive commonsense which, he said, outweighed the allegations of conceit. 'Herbert was a man of integrity, punctilious in discharging his obligations. He deserved to be admired.' Stuart Surridge thought that Sutcliffe's efficiency, his immaculate presence, and the fact that he had made the grade produced envy among undiscriminating people. 'Herbert was never pompous; he was guiltless in this respect; it was one of the last things he could be accused of. There was no fault in the way Herbert presented himself to the public.'

Sutcliffe's powers of concentration served him well as a cricketer and as a businessman. He had an amazing ability to put his life into compartments. This was best reflected in the story of a Test match at Lord's. Watched by a capacity crowd, Hobbs and Sutcliffe were in commanding mood against Australia. The pair were undefeated at lunch. 'Herbert,' said Sutcliffe's son, Bill, 'ordered a cup of tea and a sandwich, opened his briefcase to deal with his business correspondence. At 2.05p.m. precisely he returned the documents to his case, snapped shut the lid, and put on his pads again. Jack put his head round the dressing-room door, and called out: "Five minute bell, Herbert."' The affairs of business were dismissed and Sutcliffe walked out into the sunshine to resume his duel with the Australians. This mental agility was helped, according to one close friend, by Sutcliffe's study of Pelmanism. 'Herbert said he benefited very much from this course in mind-training.'

Sutcliffe, within his family circle, strictly censured slovenly speech. Even his wife was taken to task if she slipped into the broad, round vowels of Pudsey. None of the family can ever remember their father speaking with a pronounced Yorkshire accent. Herbert's youngest son, John, believed that the speech discipline stemmed from a total professionalism. 'He was not doing it in a snobbish way; he was aiming to show that he was as good as or better than the amateurs with whom he was associated as a cricketer.'

E.M. Wellings, the former London cricket correspondent and an Oxford University rival in the late 1920s, described Sutcliffe as a businessman cricketer. 'He shed his Yorkshire accent, doubtless as an aid to business, and was accordingly inclined to pomposity, which caused a few smiles from others in the Yorkshire team, though he was widely respected and liked.' Sutcliffe had an acute sense of public relations. At Oxford, in 1929, the Yorkshire captain arrived in a large, black limousine, with Wilfred Rhodes as his distinguished passenger in the back seat. In the following season Sutcliffe arrived at the Parks in an even more imposing limousine. The car might have been the capacious Studebaker which, with a market value of around £1,000, was evidence of Sutcliffe's increasing affluence.

The precise, clipped speech, a kind of drawl redolent of a country gentleman, was remembered by one friend at Pudsey.

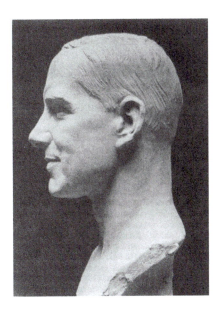

A profile in sculpture: an expression of dignity and authority. (W.H.H.S)

His assertion that Sutcliffe took elocution lessons was refuted by another townsman. 'I am sure that Herbert had the gumption to know better than to neglect disciplining himself to speak the King's English,' he said. The style of Sutcliffe's talk did attract the attention of Lord (C.P.) Snow, the novelist and physicist, at a Cricket Writers' dinner given for an Australian team at the Fishmongers' Hall in London. Philip Snow said that Sutcliffe, as one of the speakers at the dinner, regaled his audience with a speech that was as polished in accent as it was in content. It greatly impressed his brother, Lord Snow, who had long admired Sutcliffe's *sang-froid* as a cricketer.

After the dinner, an introduction to Sutcliffe was effected by Bill Bowes, one of the Yorkshire guests. 'Charles was always specially deferential to cricket professionals, who had been the heroes of his adolescence and early manhood,' recalled Philip Snow. In his conversation with Herbert, Lord Snow wasted no time in coming to the point, as was his custom. 'Mr Sutcliffe,' he said, 'that was a splendid speech, and I say that as one who has made a lot of them in my life.' He expressed his curiosity as to how Sutcliffe had achieved his equally splendid diction, without a trace of a Yorkshire accent. 'One would never know that you had not been to a public school or Cambridge.' Sutcliffe's reply was immediate:

> You are quite right, Lord Snow. Coming up into the Yorkshire team, I would, of course, speak totally like them. I knew no other way. It was when I became a member of the England team and mixed with amateurs, especially on long tours, that – at first I suppose unconsciously – I tried to speak to their standard. Then eventually my adoption to their way of talking, to my pleasure, was complete and I found that it helped me along socially with comfort.

Despite this explanation, Lord Snow and his brother were still intrigued by the comparison with the strong Yorkshire accents of Bowes and Brian Close, other members of the dinner group. Comparing impressions afterwards, the Snow brothers found it remarkable that Sutcliffe had seamlessly established such an absolute mastery of accentless diction. As a pose, it would have been instantly detectable, or at least wavered under duress. By dint of heightened perception, he had assimilated the alien speech patterns until they tripped unerringly from his lips.

Les Ames presented another example of his England colleague's excellence as a speaker in the august surroundings of the Guildhall, London. The occasion was a dinner hosted by the Lord Mayor of London after the 1932/33 tour of Australia. 'Herbert was asked to propose a toast, and he did it quite magnificently. I cannot think of another member of the MCC party, amateur or professional, who could have done it anything like as well.' Ames always considered that Sutcliffe did more for the professional cricketer than any other player. Of the speech at the Guildhall, he said: 'It really did raise the tone of our profession.' It was, said Ames, characteristic of Sutcliffe's attitude as a sportsman. 'He never let cricket down in any way; he always behaved himself perfectly. He provided a model example.'

Another admirer, a South Shields man, remembered the fluency of Sutcliffe in a speech given at Tynemouth. His judgement was:

> Voice pleasant (I should want you as a tenor in my choir); manner: easy, simple, not overdone; material: copious, picture always moving along; fair and full of judgement, recognition of others and generosity to critics. It was altogether just the ticket – discreet, good-humoured and expert and the best lecture I've heard for a long time.

As a meticulous man, one can be sure that Sutcliffe prepared himself thoroughly as a speaker. He obeyed the cardinal precept of well-timed discourse, rarely risking the indulgence of his audience. On one occasion, as a broadcaster at a Test match at Headingley, his sense of timing did desert him. Rex Alston, as the commentator, recalled that Sutcliffe was given a five-minute slot at the lunch interval. 'I did notice during the morning that Herbert was scribbling away.' Alston made his introduction at the interval, expecting that Sutcliffe would ad-lib his impressions. 'Suddenly, after two or three minutes, his comments came to an end. He didn't realise that this was a "talkie-talk". He had written a script. He hadn't anything more to say.' Sutcliffe was not alone in being defeated by the radio microphone. Bob Wyatt and Gubby Allen, two other equally articulate men, were also lost for words. Their thoughts, as with Sutcliffe, required more tranquil contemplation, or the promptings of a professional interviewer.

The integrity which marked Herbert Sutcliffe as a man of stature was coupled with a careful husbandry of his resources in business as well as cricket. 'He was always a man of economical

mind, but also charitable and generous,' said one relative, John
Varley. Sutcliffe, early in his career, quickly sensed the value of
his cricketing prestige, and lost no time in capitalising on it. An
advertisement placed in the *Pudsey and Stanningley News* at the
end of his first Australian tour announced that he had gone into
partnership as sports outfitter in Leeds and Wakefield with his
Yorkshire teammate, George Macaulay. It read: 'Macaulay and
Sutcliffe (Yorkshire and England XI's). Players and Providers
of Practical Cricket Equipment. Stockists and Distributors of
the famous Herbert Sutcliffe Extra Special Autograph Bat –
the bat that beat all records in the 1924–5 Australia *v.* England
matches.' Macaulay's interest in the business waned and their
collaboration was dissolved twelve months later. Sutcliffe persevered with his new challenge to become one of the leading
sports retailers in the North of England. The shop was housed,
following a Leeds town centre redevelopment, in King
Edward Street. It was until its closure in the 1990s managed by
Sutcliffe's son, Bill, who had followed in his father's footsteps
to become a Yorkshire cricketer.

Alf Gover, the former Surrey and England bowler, related
one telling story of the elder Sutcliffe's acumen as a businessman. It was a piece of advice that served Gover well in his
own business career at Wandsworth. Gover said he once found
Sutcliffe poring over his balance sheets during a rain stoppage
at the Oval. Herbert said: 'Just doing my accounts, Alfred. If
you ever work for yourself, do your own ledgers, because then
you'll know where the money is going.'

John Varley believed that it was Sutcliffe's thrift which enabled him to buy Woodlands, the mansion residence on the
brow of the hill at Pudsey, in the mid–1930s. Before moving
to Woodlands, Sutcliffe lived in a tall terrace house called
Lyncroft, approached by a steep flight of steps from the busy
Stanningley Road, and facing Gott's Park at Armley. It was
only a short distance from his next home at Southroyd House,

a double-bay detached property at Pudsey, which was rented from a local mill owner.

Sutcliffe's march to prosperity was sealed when he acquired Woodlands, which was built by Thomas Banks, nephew of James Banks, the owner of Fartown Mill, over 100 years ago. The Banks were an old Pudsey family whose origins dated back to the seventeenth century. At this time they specialised as blacksmiths. During the next century the Banks were increasingly involved in woollen cloth manufacturing. The brothers, Joseph and James Banks, arrested the slump in the family fortunes by taking rooms at Claughton Garth and Union Mills. In 1858, Joseph was killed when he fell over the railings at one of the mills. James continued to maintain the expansion of the business. In 1879, the firm occupied most of the Claughton Garth Mill. The family suffered a setback when the mill was devastated by fire, but in 1881 James Banks bought and rebuilt the ruined property. He renamed it Fartown Mill. Banks led a relatively modest existence at West House. When he died, in 1899, he left over £35,000. His nephew, Thomas, in the palatial surroundings of Woodlands, died in 1882, eight years after building his splendid home. The extent of his style of living, as detailed in the West Riding Registry of Wills, was reflected in a bequest of under £1,000. By 1908, the house had passed into the ownership of James Banks's son, William Henry. The Banks company enjoyed a last flourish of activity during the First World War before slipping into decline. By 1929, only thirty people were employed at the mill and the firm went into voluntary liquidation.

In the 1930s, when Herbert Sutcliffe purchased Woodlands, his investment was £2,000, a princely sum in a decade of depression. As a former mill office clerk, he must have enjoyed immense personal satisfaction at the gain in his fortunes. Even allowing for his eminence as a cricketer and the financial rewards which he had accrued, it was a remarkable accomplishment. From the lounge windows of the venerable stone building, he could look out over the valley from Fulneck School towards Tong village, and take in a view that vies with the Dales. There was not a mill chimney in sight, only wide green pastures, with a graceful church spire on the horizon.

Woodlands stood in grounds of about seven acres, bordered by a large circular drive. It included rose gardens, orchards, centrally heated greenhouses and a stable block, which was later converted into three mews houses. On the large lawn in front of the house the Sutcliffes held annual garden parties, special events in the town's social calendar, in aid of the local church funds. Sporting interests were not, of course, neglected. In addition to a tennis court, there was a concrete cricket pitch upon which Sutcliffe's son, Bill, and their close neighbour, Leonard Hutton, were tutored as young batsmen. The lounge at Woodlands was a large, comfortable room, with cream walls and a soft green carpet. On one wall was a cabinet housing Sutcliffe's cricket trophies. The house had three splendid and colourfully tiled bathrooms, a feature which greatly impressed Sutcliffe's daughter, Barbara. There were four main bedrooms, two with adjoining dressing-rooms, and another smaller bedroom. On the ground floor was the dining room and a cosy snug (where the Sutcliffes relaxed with friends in the evening). Out on the terrace on the long summer evenings, Herbert would exchange reminiscences with his cricket guests, including tourists from overseas. After dinner, perhaps as a refuge for more boisterous banter, Herbert would take the illustrious cricketers down to the nearby Regent pub. Here he would introduce the Test celebrities to the customers. The talk would become even more convivial as they ordered the rounds of strong Yorkshire beer.

Sutcliffe's study, bedecked with imposing souvenirs of great cricket occasions, was the most fascinating of all the rooms at Woodlands. His daughter, Barbara remembered the large, magnificent desk built into the study. When she was a little girl the takings from the Sutcliffe shop were brought home each night and there was the ritual of the counting of the money on Herbert's desk.

Emily (or Emmie as she was known in the family) Sutcliffe brought her skills as a qualified book-keeper to help with the shop accounts. She also typed Herbert's business letters and, as a dutiful cricketer's wife, laundered his cricket shirts and flannels. Emmie, a Pudsey Grammar School girl, was the 'bright lass of the family, good-looking, quick-tempered and very popular', in the words of her cousin, John Varley. She was personal secretary to the millowner, Richard Ingham (Herbert's first cricket benefactor). This was the link which brought Emmie and Herbert together. Frank Parker, the father of Roland Parker, a later Pudsey St Lawrence club captain, was the contending swain. Parker lost the contest for her affections; and Herbert and Emmie were married at Pudsey Parish Church in September, 1921.

Emmie's upbringing was not dissimilar to that of her future husband. One Pudsey nonagenarian, Frank Birks, who attended the same elementary school at Littlemoor, possessed a picture of Emmie in her best Sunday dress at a Whitsuntide photo-call at the school. She was the daughter of William and Polly Pease. Her mother, originally from Islington in London, came north to take up a post as a children's nurse to the Butler family, owners of the Stanningley foundry. She married William Pease, then a coachman for one of Pudsey's manufacturing families. The Peases also owned a small-holding and eked out a modest living with hens and pigs. In later years, when Emmie and Herbert were away at cricket, Mrs Pease occasionally visited Woodlands to assist the maids in looking after her grandchildren.

The image of a masterful father, who liked to be regarded as the head of the family, is presented by Bill Sutcliffe. 'His word was law, especially with the boys, my brother, John and myself. Herbert perhaps showed the better side of his personality outside the family.' One example was Sutcliffe's kinship with the hero-worshipping John Witherington from Sunderland. They were correspondents for many years until Witherington, as a Royal Air Force bomber pilot, was killed attempting to land his badly damaged aircraft in Lincolnshire in September, 1941. Sutcliffe was the only non-member of the family to attend the funeral. Herbert Witherington remembered his brother as Sutcliffe's most devoted admirer. Copies of letters reveal the extent of their comradeship and present Sutcliffe as a gracious character who watched the progress of his friend with the fondness of a parent. In a letter only a few weeks before Witherington's death, Sutcliffe congratulated him on passing his pilot's examination:

> You are in for thrills galore and no doubt you will be in many tight corners. I know you won't take risks when they aren't necessary. Don't think I'm too awful in giving this advice. It is, as you know, because I want you to come through this war unscathed. We can't afford to lose too many of the 'Cream of England'.

Another correspondent in Australia remembered the human-ity of Sutcliffe during the MCC tour in 1928/29. His father was a general practitioner in New South Wales. At the time he had under his care a Yorkshire exile, who was seriously ill and close to death in hospital. The patient had no relatives or friends in Australia. The doctor asked Sutcliffe if he would visit the hospital to meet his fellow Yorkshireman. Sutcliffe read-ily agreed. It was a poignant little interlude. The dying man was unaware of the arrangement. As Sutcliffe approached his bedside, his eyes lit up with delight. He instantly recognised the great cricketer. 'Sootcliffe,' he cried out. It later transpired that he was a native of Summerbridge, Sutcliffe's birthplace.

The family man: Sutcliffe, with his wife, Emmie, and baby daughter, Barbara. (Richard Smith)

They had played together as children in the Nidderdale village. Sutcliffe seated himself beside the bed and gently held the man's hand until he lapsed into unconsciousness and died.

The genial side of Sutcliffe's nature also surfaced in his relationship with his daughter, Barbara. She remembered Herbert as a loving and caring man although she acknowledged that, unlike her brother, she did not have to work with him. 'He was very conscious of the long periods of separation when he was on cricket tours and gave up much time to entertain us at home.' Friends of the family also recall Sutcliffe's charm with children. 'He would tease you quietly and nicely,' said Roland Parker, a close neighbour at Pudsey. Sutcliffe's godson, Richard Smith, who lost his own father at an early age, also provided a glimpse of a kindly guardian. 'Herbert took his duties as a godfather very seriously. He could be very stern; if I departed from the straight and narrow, I expected and received a telling off.'

Stuart Surridge recalled how, as a small boy, he incurred Sutcliffe's displeasure. He was upbraided by his father when he eavesdropped on a game of billiards at his home:

> I happened to be standing beside one of the pockets on the table. I was watching Herbert play a shot. He just stood, with the cue in his hand, and didn't make a movement, or say a word. My father called out: 'Get out of the way, young man, you're disturbing Mr Sutcliffe's line.'

Sutcliffe always encouraged a sense of adventure among his own children. For Barbara and Bill there were early swimming lessons; they were taught to skate on Yeadon tarn; there was tennis on the court at Woodlands; and there were exciting, plunging scrambles over the rocks and heart-stopping climbs in the hills above the Yorkshire Dales. Emmie, their dazzlingly feminine mother, did not take part in these athletic pursuits. She was at her best in an elegant social setting. Her tomboy daughter perplexed her greatly. Barbara recalled: 'Herbert would take Bill and myself to Ilkley by car. We used to climb the Cow and Calf rocks. Mother just sat in the car and dithered with impatience.' Emmie much preferred the theatre outings and the spectacle of pantomime and musical comedy in Leeds. Seats were almost invariably reserved in the Royal Box. The Sutcliffe elders usually chose the more sophisticated panto at the Grand Theatre before Francis Laidler's homely Christmas romp at the city's Theatre Royal. One of Herbert's favourite musicals was 'The Desert Song', then enjoying a tremendous vogue in the theatre. It must also have made a big impression on the children, for it was estimated that he made twenty-eight visits to the show. 'Herbert revelled in "The Desert Song",' said Barbara. 'I think he fancied himself as one of the characters, the "Red Shadow".'

Both Bill and Barbara, after their primary education at Fulneck, went to boarding schools. Bill was a pupil at Rydal,

Colwyn Bay, the rugby nursery of Welsh internationals, Wilfred Wooller and Bleddyn Williams. Barbara attended Hunmanby Hall School, near Filey. 'Herbert took a great interest in my schooling,' she remembered. 'He encouraged me in my intellectual activities. He bought me beautiful copies of A.A. Milne and Rudyard Kipling books.' As a self-confessed timid child, she is grateful to her father for his help in achieving independence.

Herbert was, though, as a meticulous man, an unsparing taskmaster. Barbara remembered, as a young girl, weeding the gardens at Woodlands throughout one long day during the war. She was exhausted after her labours and left a small patch of weeds. Herbert exploded with anger when he examined the incomplete work. Emmie had to come to Barbara's rescue. As Herbert fumed, she told him: 'Well, she has done it all day.'

There was also the affair of the willow tree and the elm tree, up which Barbara used to climb to the topmost branches. Herbert's decision to fell the trees because they spoilt the view left Barbara in tears. At the end of his life, he had not forgotten her distress at the execution. In a gesture of remorse, he exclaimed: 'I did the wrong thing in felling those trees at Woodlands.'

The closeness of Herbert and Barbara was perhaps, in a curious, way, partly derived from her lack of interest in cricket. This was a source of great amusement to her father. It also meant that he was freed from one obsessive topic of conversation, and could relax and talk of other things. Barbara remembered being admonished by her mother for failing to concentrate at county matches. When Herbert was batting she was not even allowed to go to the lavatory. Childhood outings to Harrogate are an uneasy memory. Connie Leyland, wife of Maurice Leyland, the Yorkshire cricketer, was often given the custody of Sutcliffe's unruly children during matches at Harrogate. Barbara and her brother, Bill would sit on Mrs Leyland's knees after their mother had grown tired of their antics. Pieces of treacle toffee were handed out to the children as a bait to still their voices. 'She was very stern and cross,' recalled Barbara. 'She was the only one who could keep us quiet. I was frightened to death.'

The bond between Barbara and Herbert was especially nurtured by a love of solitude, nature – and dogs. Boxers, engaging and slobbering with affection, were Herbert's particular favourites. He idolised them with a devotion bordering on fanaticism. One of the most amusing stories related about Herbert and his dogs came from a Headingley fish shop proprietor. It also demonstrated Sutcliffe's quiet humour. The trader related:

> He used to park his Rolls-Royce, with two great dogs in the back, outside my shop. He would come in for an order which never varied – haddock and chips with just a sprinkling of vinegar and salt – and two fish, wrapped separately with no seasoning. One day I asked him about this order and he told me: 'I drive up the road towards Otley and stop outside the Parkway [a large residential hotel]. The dogs have a fish apiece and I eat my haddock and chips and sit looking at the Parkway, wishing they could serve food as good as this.'

The droll anecdote counters the sober image; the illustrious cricketer is revealed in human terms, hearty and mocking in his Yorkshireness.

Bill Sutcliffe recalled two other instances to show how his besotted father indulged his dogs, even when they misbehaved. 'Master' and 'Sam' were allowed to slip their leashes when they accompanied Herbert, in his presidential year, to the Scarborough Festival. 'It was a lovely summer's day and the ladies were in their finery in one of the marquees,' said the younger Sutcliffe. The dogs roamed among the guests and, in an effusion of friendliness, uncoiled their tongues to lick the dresses of the parading women. Then, without a care for disgrace, 'Master' galloped out to the wicket and proceeded to urinate on the stumps.

On the next occasion, at the Sutcliffe's Leeds shop, Bill was less than pleased at his father's indifference when a young customer took exception to being accosted by one of the dogs. Bill was cross at the lack of courtesy to the girl. He was even more angry when Herbert declared: 'If she doesn't like dogs, then we don't want her in the shop.'

Sutcliffe's authority was under serious threat in the shop interlude. At other times, on and off the field, it had a mesmeric spell. The ladies, even those with little or no interest in cricket, were captivated by his debonair manner. The presence was enhanced by his sartorial dignity. Consignments of silk were ordered from Thailand and made up into cricket shirts. They were sold in the Sutcliffe shop and worn by Herbert and other Yorkshire players. Herbert retained a bronzed complexion after his travels abroad and he cut a suave figure in his fluttering silk shirt and immaculate flannels. In Yorkshire, especially, Herbert, with his glossy black hair and twinkling, deep-set eyes, was worshipped by the girls. One correspondent remembered that his Aunt Martha, who was completely uninterested in cricket, had a dream of partnering Herbert in the heel-tapping rhythms of the Charleston in the 1920s. Sutcliffe basked in an admiration to match that of Clark Gable or Gary Cooper on the cinema screen.

The magnetism of Sutcliffe's presence dominated gatherings on social occasions. 'If he came into a room and you had your back to him, you did not need to turn round to know that he was there,' commented one admirer. John Varley, less romantically, presented another view at variance with the version of a paragon of glamour. Varley, as a family friend, respected

Woodlands, the Sutcliffes' imposing mansion home on the brow of the hill at Pudsey. (W.H.H.S)

Favourite companions: Sutcliffe, his sons, Bill (left) and John and a bevy of boxer dogs. (John Sutcliffe)

Sutcliffe as he would have done an elder brother. 'Herbert did have an air of authority, but I am sure that he never regarded himself as infallible. He was essentially a very private man. He knew his own mind and knew what was expected of him.'

Sutcliffe's attractions for women, lingering into old age, did, inevitably, lead to roguish stories of his conquests. He did enjoy female company, which is not to say he was a philanderer. His attentions were never objectionable, and his gallantry in the company of the ladies was of the order which inspires affections. In later years, young family friends responded to his flattering sallies with the merriment they might have afforded a favourite playful uncle.

Les Ames recalled incurring Sutcliffe's wrath on tour in Australia. It was a terrible gaffe. Ames conceded that he was at fault in a contrite apology to his England teammate. The incident occurred during dinner at their hotel. Herbert was sitting at a table with two attractive girls. As he passed the table, Ames congratulated Sutcliffe on the century he had scored earlier in the day. He was introduced to Herbert's companions. Before he could still the words on his lips Ames said: 'Where there is a pretty lady, you will find Herbert.' It was a tactless outburst which was met by a stony silence. 'Herbert didn't say anything then,' said Ames, 'but he ticked me off later. He thought I had been ill-mannered in making such a remark.' Bill Sutcliffe remembered one conversation with his father, which dwelt upon the charms of Australian girls. 'Herbert said: "Never get married until you've been to Australia because you will find that the girls are absolutely magnificent."' The younger Sutcliffe said that he was never good enough as a cricketer to check out the claim.

One Western Australian correspondent recalled Sutcliffe's charm and courtesy when she inadvertently invaded the Yorkshire members' enclosure during a visit to a Test match at Headingley in 1968. She wanted a photograph of Sutcliffe to take home to her father, who was one of the Yorkshireman's great supporters. In a conversation with a former county player, she was persuaded that Sutcliffe, who had arrived on the ground at lunch, would be delighted to pose for a photograph. The picture was taken and a copy was later sent to Sutcliffe. It elicited the following acknowledgement:

> This is to thank you for your kind letter, couched in perfect English – which I always note and love – and for the excellent photograph.
>
> Had I known you had 'gatecrashed' I would have invited you into the holy of holies – the Board of Control seats – and for lunch because I have the greatest possible admiration for Australia and Australians.

In his letter Sutcliffe apologised for not taking a note of the name of another Australian featured in the photograph. 'It surely must have been your vivaciousness which was responsible for my brain not functioning properly,' he added.

Running an impish eye over Sutcliffe in the 1930s was Arthur Wood, Yorkshire's jovial and wisecracking wicket-keeper. He described, with delicious irony, his colleague and friend as 'Beautiful Herbert'. Arthur was not at all abashed by one misunderstanding in the field, which resulted in a painful disturbance of Sutcliffe's handsome features. Herbert was fielding at first slip as the ball flew sharply between them. Arthur shot out a glove and the ball nipped off his right thumb and knocked out Herbert's two front teeth. Sutcliffe was furious at the unexpected dentistry.

Arthur said he could not comprehend the disquiet. 'I could nivver understand why he was so bloody mad about it, cos after all I did apologise.'

8

Conquerors on a Gluepot

'It was the worst sticky wicket I ever saw – and without
doubt Hobbs and Sutcliffe put up the best performance I
have witnessed in such conditions.'

      Sir Donald Bradman on the Melbourne triumph

Herbert Sutcliffe unflinchingly faced the examinations set
by bad wickets. He especially, perhaps above all great batsmen, excepting his, equally obdurate partner, Jack Hobbs,
relished the extremities of alien conditions. Sutcliffe paraded
the bruises sustained in torrid action like the decorations of
a bemedalled war veteran. His resilient spirit moved Neville
Cardus to express one of the finest tributes ever paid to a
sportsman. 'I would choose Sutcliffe to play for my life, taking
out, as I chose, a long life assurance annuity policy,' said Cardus.

Stuart Surridge, the former Surrey captain, recalled
Sutcliffe's quiet joy after he had emerged triumphant in one
gruelling contest. Sutcliffe, a lifelong business associate and
friend of the Surridge family, was spending the weekend at
their farm in Surrey. Herbert had taken a bath and was dressing

for dinner when the following conversation took place. Percy Surridge, Stuart's father, winced as he looked at the ravages of the day's cricket. The stain of an ugly bruise covered the length of Sutcliffe's thigh. Percy asked: 'Is it really worth it, Herbert, to stay out there and take such a battering?' Herbert, with a smile of content, replied: 'Ah well, Percy, you know I'm *there* for Monday. It will be better then.'

Drawing the venom of a wicket poisoned by rain was an accomplishment savoured by Sutcliffe. It was the benchmark of excellence in batting technique. At times, notably on the brutish pitches in Australia, a batsman was called upon to display almost superhuman qualities of resource and courage. Another Yorkshireman, Leonard Hutton, an adroit batting master on difficult wickets, always maintained that he would be a poor sort of player if he did not set out to score a century, whatever the conditions. He once said that if he was given a corrugated iron sheet to bat on he would still be intent on his three figures. 'All I would have to do would be to exercise more care,' said Hutton. 'You can't get hundreds having a swing at a ball that is going all over the shop.' He added that everything that was given to the bowler, placed an extra responsibility upon him.

Herbert Sutcliffe and Jack Hobbs had accepted this burden many years before, in what are acknowledged as two monuments of batting achievement. At the Oval, in 1926, they overcame the odds with a partnership of 172 runs against Australia, which enabled England to regain the Ashes after fifteen years in the doldrums. The previous four matches in the series, all played over three days, had been drawn; and the deciding Test was played to a finish. The preliminary skirmishes had been distinguished by the batting grandeur of Charles Macartney, who scored three hundreds in succession. Macartney was popularly known as the 'Governor General' and his most exciting feat was at Leeds. He was dropped by Carr off Tate from the fifth ball of the innings. The reprieve enabled him to play one of the classic innings of all time. The England bowlers could not staunch the flow of runs as Macartney scored a century before lunch. One writer described the Australian as a 'swift and brilliant stroke-player, who always, it seemed, was on the point of surrendering his wicket to some crowning impertinence, yet never allowed his genius to outstrip the bounds'. At Lord's the Australian opener Warren Bardsley hit 193 not out and carried his bat through the innings. It was the highest Test innings at the headquarters until Don Bradman annexed the honour four years later. Hobbs and Sutcliffe were just as impressive in their batting command. They shared two century stands, one at Lord's and the other at Leeds after England had been forced to follow on.

So the outcome of the series, with time eliminated as a factor, rested on the events at the Oval. Percy Chapman, at the age of twenty-five, was installed as England captain for the game, following the abrupt dismissal of Arthur Carr. One of the young captain's advisers was Wilfred Rhodes. Rhodes, co-opted along with Hobbs on to the Test selection committee, was persuaded to return to the fray. He was then aged forty-eight, and had played Test cricket before some of the current team were born. All the way back to his daughter's home in Leicester he had agonised over the recall. He wished he had declined the invitation. His anxiety was to prove unjustified. 'I played and I have never regretted my return to Test cricket for just one match,' said Rhodes. 'My fear was that I might let the side down. A man's nerves do not improve with age, and I was getting on for fifty.'

Rhodes' enduring skills did prevail to drive home the advantage secured by England's opening batsmen. Sutcliffe had provided a welcome ballast with a dogged 76 in the first innings total of 280; but Australia recovered alter losing four wickets for 60 to lead by 22 runs. Hobbs and Sutcliffe calmly cleared the deficit and looked forward to a period of consolidation on the following morning.

Overnight a violent storm broke over South London. The Oval was lashed by unceasing rain. 'When the spectators began assembling on the Tuesday morning the wet seats were smoking in the warmth,' wrote Ronald Mason. 'The storm had passed and the sun was beginning to break through. The feeblest imagination saw that stretch of grass as a potential cauldron of unholy hates. The confidence of last night had gone down the swollen gutters of Kennington.'

Neville Cardus reported Sutcliffe's surprise at the deluge; the Yorkshireman's sleep had been undisturbed; but Hobbs, whether he was awakened or not, knew the perils which lay ahead. 'Pity it rained in the night,' he remarked to Sutcliffe, as they settled down to take the strike. It was a classic understatement. Both Hobbs and Sutcliffe knew that the match and the rubber would be decided within the next few hours. They had to gain a foothold on a sluggish pitch before the elements of sun and wind stirred the potion. By midday, an hour after the start of play, the sun was beating down on a drying wicket. From then until lunch, the ball bit viciously, rising sharply as it turned. 'If it could not be "killed" at the pitch, it had to be followed and, if possible, left alone by the means of the last moment dropping of the wrists at which both batsmen were masters,' wrote E.W. Swanton and H.S. Altham in their recollections of the enthralling duel.

The Australian attack was in the hands of five bowlers: Gregory, Mailey, Grimmett, Arthur Richardson and Macartney. Gregory was not the awesome fast bowler of old; he had been handicapped throughout the season by a persistent leg strain and could not bowl long spells. In addition, the greasy run-ups posed problems for fast bowlers. The renowned leg-spinners, Mailey and Grimmett, had carried the weight of the bowling in this rain-affected season. *Wisden*

considered them a 'strange pair to take the places which
Gregory and MacDonald had filled in the Australian team in
1921'. Because of the uncertainty of his pitch Mailey was said
to bowl like a 'millionaire', while his partner, Grimmett was
judged the 'miser' as he begrudged every run. Both bowlers
were at their best on hard wickets. They shared six wickets in
England's second innings, but conceded 236 runs. Australia's
need at the Oval was for a slow left-arm bowler of the calibre
of Rhodes or Blythe. Either, armed with the seductive ball
which leaves the bat, would have probed more searchingly to
find a loophole in the batsmen's watchful defence. Macartney,
chosen primarily as a batsman, was Australia's left-hander. The
judgement by Australians was that Macartney was underesti-
mated in England. According to Arthur Gilligan, Macartney
and the offspinner Arthur Richardson were the two most
accurate bowlers in England that summer. Pelham Warner
admired Richardson's economy as a bowler. Both Australians
bowled over 500 overs in 1926 and took nearly 50 wickets.
Richardson averaged 19.71 runs per wicket and Macartney
conceded fewer than 18 runs per wicket. They could not,
therefore, be dismissed as negligible bowlers.

The technique of Hobbs and Sutcliffe stifled the accuracy
of Arthur Richardson, who was charged with adopting the
wrong method of a round-the-wicket attack. In the words of
one writer, 'he made the elementary error of bowling his off-
spinners at the middle and leg stumps.' Cardus thought the
Australians missed a rare chance before lunch:

> The pitch was unmistakably sensitive after the night's storm.
> Richardson caused the ball to break back sharply. But he
> did not give his attack wise direction. Surely, with the turf
> definitely unpleasant, he ought to have bowled his off-break
> on the off wicket, making it come back to the leg wicket
> and within the danger zone.

Australian leg-theory: Hobbs and Sutcliffe (the non-striker) stifled the accuracy of Australian off-spinner, Arthur Richardson and both scored centuries in the epic struggle of the Oval 'gluepot' in 1926. (W.H.H.S)

Another account suggested that Richardson's length was often inclined to be defensive and too short to take advantage of the conditions.

There was yet another story that Hobbs feigned discomfiture for over after over to persuade Collins to keep Richardson on. Hobbs always denied that he perpetrated a bluff. 'The fact is that he was bowling so well that I couldn't get him away.' Talking later about Richardson's direction, Hobbs maintained that nothing could have been more taxing than the decreed line of attack. His method was to take guard nearly a foot wide of his leg stump, so that the bowler could not range on his pads. Then, when he had judged the length and pace of the ball, he glided and sometimes ran into position to make a stroke.

Another observer, a former Test captain, considered that on a wicket made for bowlers, there was not a side in the world that could have made 100 runs on it against a well-conceived attack. Elaborating his opinion, he pointed out that what was required was good length bowling on the off-stump, and the wicket would have done the rest.

The emphasis, said another writer, was on keeping the runs down:

> At one point Richardson, bowling from the Vauxhall End, sent down ten overs for a single. His field was curiously set, seven being on the legside, but it was not a pitch for leg-theory while Hobbs and Sutcliffe were together, and all that happened during the two hours that Richardson bowled was that runs were reduced to the minimum.

The disputations over the Australian tactics, which were to suffer further criticism at Melbourne two years later, could not diminish the outstanding control of Hobbs and Sutcliffe on the Oval wicket. Most reports concurred that it became ill-natured after twelve o'clock, when a light breeze sprang up and the sun slipped through the clouds. It was especially angry in the last hour before lunch. Frank Chester, who umpired in the match, described it as 'the worst sticky wicket I have ever seen.' Match accounts referred to how the ball alternately squatted, popped, turned almost at right angles, and sometimes cut straight through. Pelham Warner handsomely praised Hobbs and Sutcliffe. 'They did not fail us at a time of desperate crisis. Never has English cricket known a more dauntless pair. Had either failed we might well have been dismissed for less than 200.'

Monty Noble, the former Australian captain, wrote:

> When Hobbs and Sutcliffe began their quest, even the most sanguine of England's supporters did not antici-pate the complete batting triumph which followed. How they did it, rose to the occasion and played through the

wicket's wet stage, then overcame the worst period until its gradual return to normal conditions, is recognised as one of the finest exhibitions of resourceful batting ever seen. Hobbs's innings was a model of patience and judgement. He left nothing to chance. On a rain-affected wicket he showed all the qualities of a great player, getting right back to the dangerous breaking ones, or waiting for those that were overtossed.

It was an innings worthy of a great batsman, and it put England in a winning position.

Hobbs and Sutcliffe, improbably in the circumstances, raised the century stand. It was their third in the series and their seventh in Test cricket. At lunch England were 161 for 0, 112 having been added in the morning session. Hobbs soon afterwards reached his 11th century against Australia before being bowled by Gregory. Sutcliffe's 161 rewarded a devoted vigil, extending over seven and a quarter hours. He was bowled by Mailey in the last over of an eventful day. The vexation at his dismissal so late in the day led to the reported comment that he was distracted by the movement of members leaving the pavilion enclosure. 'If Sutcliffe never makes another century, he has every reason to be proud of this one,' commented Noble. 'As a combination of cautious watchfulness and well-applied aggression, it was a masterpiece.' *The Times* correspondent referred to Sutcliffe's 'subordination of self to side, and his almost uncanny wisdom'. At the end of his innings Sutcliffe walked in with as firm a step as he had walked out in the morning. 'There he was,' said Jack Hobbs, 'and not a hair out of place.' Among the welcoming crowd was one jubilant Yorkshireman. He had tied a handkerchief to his walking stick and waved it like a flag. He said: 'I've come 200 miles to see this match and I don't care if I have to live on bread and water for the next three months.'

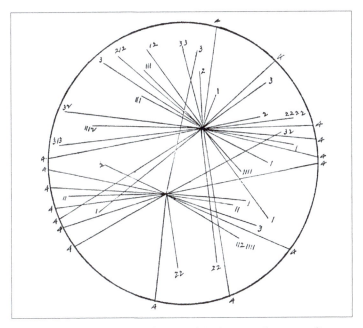

A diagram of Sutcliffe's runs in his second-innings marathon, extending over seven hours, at the Oval. His 161 included 16 fours, 10 threes, 18 twos and 31 singles.

Forty years after the epic struggle, Herbert Sutcliffe, in an article submitted to *The Cricketer*, remembered his partner's magnificent battle on the Oval 'gluepot'. Hobbs, said Sutcliffe, rated his performance in the match as the finest of his career:

The wicket was a real bitch from the start, and it continued to be so for hours. To play on such a brute of a wicket calls for courage, patience, skill, strategy and self-control. Many batsmen would have been overcome by the apparently hopeless task; but not so my great partner who, by his super scientific defence, coupled with his ability to take advantage of any scoreable ball and at the same time to execute the stroke with the grace and skill of a master, reached a memorable century. It more or less ensured our first rubber win since before the First World War.

Sutcliffe said the intervening years had not dimmed his memory of the occasion. 'Jack's century was full of grit, determination and unsurpassed skill. He displayed a terrific fighting spirit.' Typically, he added: 'The fruits of victory are so much sweeter when there is the satisfaction of having fought so tenaciously for several hours under adverse conditions.'

The criticised Richardson was judged by Sutcliffe to have bowled his offbreaks perfectly to a densely packed legside field.

Hobbs had had to acknowledge this accuracy by playing out ten consecutive maidens. Sutcliffe was also pinned back in defence by Grimmett and Macartney. He recalled:

I took over forty minutes to add to my overnight score. When Jack did manage to get away from Richardson's end, I was tied down by that great bowler for eight consecutive overs.

We both longed to 'have a go' but we just could not afford to take the risk. Our business was to stay there until the wicket eased and enabled us to produce our scoring strokes. We did surmount the difficulties and each of us had the pleasure of scoring a century.

Sutcliffe remembered the tumultuous ovation given to Hobbs, after he had reached his century, by over 30,000 spectators at the Oval. He often wondered whether this tribute relaxed Hobbs' concentration, leading to his dismissal by Gregory off the next ball:

Jack must have known, as he retired to the pavilion, that his masterpiece of an innings was responsible in a big way in making possible a great victory for England.

We scored 436 on that vile wicket, leaving our opponents to score 415 to win. On the last day there was still a little moisture in the wicket and, as the top had been severely mutilated, we had little difficulty in disposing of Australia for 125 runs.

Wilfred Rhodes, in his last Test against Australia, and Harold Larwood, on his England debut, shared seven wickets in this summary execution. Rhodes overcame his unease to exert his authority. 'When I was put on to bowl for the first time I was a bit jumpy,' he recalled. 'But the warm welcome of the crowd heartened me and, after two or three balls, the nervous feeling passed away, and for the rest of the match I was as cool as I have ever been on a cricket field.'

In Australia's first innings Rhodes had spotted a worn patch at the Vauxhall end where Grimmett had roughened up an inviting piece of turf adjacent to the middle and leg stumps. He took full advantage of the tempting target. He said:

I started with a maiden and then with the fifth ball of my third over I got Woodfull out. It was one of my lucky wickets. Woodfull played on. He had been cutting me, so I bowled a slightly faster one in an effort to push the ball through before he got there with the bat. He edged it into his wicket.

Rhodes took four other crucial wickets in the second innings, those of Bardsley, Ponsford, Collins and Richardson, to finish with four wickets for 44 runs. Yet he felt that his figures should have been better. 'That pitch was getting better all the time. They should have put me on sooner.' Recalling the exploit, he said the Australians had two left-handers (Bardsley and Gregory) who were able to play him. 'If they had been right-handers,' he remarked sadly, 'I would have had a better average.'

A writer in *The Cricketer* saluted the guile of Rhodes in his glorious swansong:

> There must have been many schoolboys at the Oval, and I hope they watched the great Rhodes carefully. They should have noted his easy action, his length, his spin and, above all, his cleverness. Ulysses earned a worldwide reputation for cunning, and Rhodes is the Ulysses of modern cricket.

The marvels of Hobbs and Sutcliffe at the Oval in 1926 were superseded by gallantry of an even higher order at Melbourne two years later. This was a series dominated by Wally Hammond, who emerged as England's greatest discovery since Sutcliffe and one of the most majestic batsmen in the history of the game. In this, his finest tour, Hammond achieved a first-class average of 91 and a Test average of 113. Bradman's own merciless brand of run-making later edged him ahead of the Englishman. Without such opposition, Hammond's astonishing tally of 905 runs in the Test series would remain unchallenged to this day.

England, again led by Percy Chapman, had marshalled a team of acclaimed names, alongside which two young recruits, Les Ames and Maurice Leyland, were being groomed for future stardom. It was Jack Hobbs' last tour of Australia; and it was opportune that he was able to step up on to this stage for a farewell triumph. England resoundingly won the first two Tests, by 675 runs at Brisbane, and eight wickets at Sydney, before the drama of the third and conclusive Test at Melbourne. An absorbing match, extending over seven days, drew record crowds. On two consecutive days at Melbourne there were attendances of over 60,000. The total for the match was 262,487 and it produced receipts of £22,561.

Jack Fingleton, the former Australian opening batsman and cricket writer, said no other ground, not even Lord's, could compare with Melbourne in the stark intensity of its Test match atmosphere. 'It drilled into your back as you walked out of the gate to take the first ball of a Test against England. Australians who make a century against England, never forget the enveloping crash of thunderous noise that greets the ultimate run.'

The Melbourne ground is set in the middle of a large park alongside the Yarra river, about three minutes from the centre of the city by rail. The massive stands bear the great names of Australian cricket. At the time of the MCC tour in 1928/29 there was an old members' pavilion surmounted by a huge clock. The clock stood about 50ft above the pitch and W.G. Grace was reputed to have fissured its face with a towering straight drive. The two highest innings totals in first-class cricket were achieved at Melbourne. They were 1,107 by Victoria against New South Wales in 1926/27, and 1,059 by Victoria against Tasmania in 1922/23. In the latter match, Bill Ponsford scored a then world record 429 to follow his 352 in the earlier marathon. One writer recalled meeting the weary Ponsford after this innings and said that his boots had to be cut off his swollen feet. The Melbourne ground also holds the unenviable record of the smallest total. Victoria were dismissed for 15 by the MCC in the 1903/04 season.

As a setting for cricket thrills and spills, this was an arena which Herbert Sutcliffe had good reason to regard as his favourite ground. He had assumed his full majesty there on his first tour of Australia in 1924/25. Melbourne beckoned again, this time with an evil glint in its eye, on the January day in 1929. His bad-wicket technique was to undergo its fiercest test on a pitch infamous as the worst in the world after rain and under a hot sun.

Gubby Allen, the England captain in the 1930s, was an appalled eyewitness of its behaviour. The decision to impose a worldwide covering of wickets – a regrettable impoverishment of cricket as a contest – was a direct consequence of events in Australia. Allen emphasised the futility of cricket in circumstances prevailing there after torrential rain both before and after the Second World War. In normal conditions, he said, the average Test total in Australia was around 350. 'But if you were confronted by a dirty wicket, you would do damned well to get 60.'

Allen recalled one instance of the malign influence of rain in a match against an Australian XI at Melbourne on the 1932/33 tour. Don Bradman was one of the uneasy batsmen as the ball reared with the sickening velocity of a roller-coaster car at a funfair. 'I bowled one at the Don; the ball flicked his glove and cap, and carried beyond the wicket-keeper,' said Allen. Pelham Warner, the MCC manager, was a distraught observer of this preposterous wicket. After the match was abandoned, Warner said: 'It was fortunate that the rain stopped the nonsense. It was the best thing that could have happened. Someone was going to be killed.' Allen added: 'The Australian wickets were murderous when wet.'

The third Test at Melbourne in 1929 provided a striking parallel with the earlier Oval triumph. After three and a half days, thanks chiefly to a double century by Hammond, England had gained a lead of 20 runs. In the Australian second innings Woodfull accumulated a characteristically careful 100, and the young Bradman celebrated his Test debut with a century. The wicket was, though, showing ominous signs of wear. A devastating storm in the early hours of the Friday morning seemed likely to exclude an England victory. Australia, with a lead of 327, awaited their chance to overthrow their hitherto dominant rivals. The only concern for them was whether play could be resumed. The persistent overnight showers did indeed make this problematical. But what threatened to be a spoilt day turned out beautifully fine.

Clem Hill, a famous Australian of other years, looked on as the first gleams of sunshine flecked the sky. He had been patriotically optimistic before the rains; and he discarded any doubts afterwards. 'On a wet Melbourne wicket when the sun is shining, the odds of ten to one against an England success would be generous,' he declared. Other experienced observers looked on sagely at the wicket baking in the gathering heat. They concluded, with a nod of acknowledgement to England's impressive batting line-up, that a total of 80 runs might just be possible. It was, in the words of one Australian spectator, 'all over bar the shouting'.

Play did not begin until nine minutes before one o'clock. Australia's last two batsmen added only four runs, and England were set a target of 332. Hobbs and Sutcliffe, grim-faced amid the dire predictions, must have hoped at best to retain their pride. Percy Fender wrote:

> From lunch until tea one of the most amazing batting feats imaginable was put up by Hobbs and Sutcliffe. In the first over after lunch Hobbs gave an easy catch to Hendry at slip, but the chance being declined, they lasted out the whole hour and three-quarters until tea, and what is more, got 78 runs in the time.

Fender said the wicket behaved as badly as it possibly could, and brought out every trick in its bag:

> England's opening pair fought on without flinching in the face of tremendous odds. About three balls in an over hopped up head or shoulder high, some turning as well, and all stopping almost visibly as they hit the ground. The batsmen were hit all over the body from the pads to the shoulder, and in two or three cases even on the neck and head, all from good, or nearly good length balls.

Fender, like Bradman, thought that Sutcliffe looked safer than Hobbs in the uphill struggle:

> His dead bat play was a masterpiece. The fighting spirit was manifest throughout, dogged defence combined with an occasional pull of the most ferocious type. He seemed calm, cool and collected all through the crisis, judging his strokes and his runs with unerring audacity.

Bradman recalled:

> It was the worst 'sticky' I ever saw – and without doubt Hobbs and Sutcliffe put up the best performance I have witnessed in such conditions. We didn't think any team could have batted two hours on it. The ability of the England openers to play with a dead bat, or better still their judgement as to which balls to let go, was incredible.

Bradman's testimony, conveyed in a letter to the author, seems ample proof of the state of the wicket. Sutcliffe himself said that before lunch it was a 'nightmare'. By three o'clock, he said, 'with the hot sun beating down, it was a terrifying, vicious, murderous thing, and ten times worse.' Yet Les Ames considered that the Melbourne wicket, upon which Wally Hammond made a near miraculous 32 (out of 76 for 9) in the 1936/37 series, carried greater hazards. As on Chapman's tour, Australia were the beneficiaries of rain and they had to win to save the Ashes. The weather relented and the mature Bradman made amends for previous failures in putting England to rout. Morris Sievers, at medium pace, was the unplayable bowler on this later tour. In his only Test he showed a proper regard for line and length on a wicket upon which the ball rose almost vertically. He took five wickets for 21 runs.

It is tempting to reflect upon whether Hobbs and Sutcliffe could have stemmed the tide, as they did at Melbourne eight years earlier. Both Bradman and Ames stressed their admiration for the England pair in the 1928/29 series, but considered that the Australians bowled and fielded badly. Bradman thought that the home bowlers were 'rather inept and totally unsuited to the conditions'. The Australian attack comprised Hendry and A'Beckett (medium pace); Oxenham (slow medium); Grimmett (leg-spin); and Blackie, the offspinner, at forty-six, the oldest player to represent Australia for the first time against England. Ames believed that Blackie should have been the destroyer at Melbourne. 'Jim Laker would have revelled on such a pitch. Had he been playing for Australia we would not have made 100.' Ames recalled that Hobbs, perhaps as an agreed policy, took most of Blackie's bowling. 'Jack shielded his partner for a long time. But when he got out Herbert took over completely. It was really all down to Hobbs and Sutcliffe. They did all the hard work and stayed there until the wicket became easier.'

A writer in *The Australasian* reported curiously that the rain defeated Australia:

> Before the rain came it was still a splendid wicket for run-making, but the wearing of the nap on the hard dry pitch was just the class of wicket that Blackie required for his bowling. While he could break on it at will, he would be able to come off the hard surface at a pace that would have taken an immensity of playing.

Monty Noble again put forward misguided tactics as the cause which aided England:

> The policy should have been to force Hobbs and Sutcliffe to play forward and hit at the ball. Blackie did not exploit

his slower ball, which would have been a tempting delivery in view of the state of the pitch. Foolishly, he crossed to bowl round the wicket, as Arthur Richardson had done at the Oval in 1926. Australia's greatest handicap was the absence of a left-hander, for the batsmen were impervious to the assaults of Ryder's combination.

Arthur Mailey more trenchantly observed:'We were presented with a gun and did not know how to use it.'

None of the post-mortems can disarrange the facts of a partnership which negotiated the perils and yielded 105 priceless runs. Hobbs's 49, paltry on paper, was worth many a hundred. 'He had weathered the storm during a period when the entire side might have been outed; and he definitely left the wicket a great deal easier than he had found it,' commented Percy Fender.

Sutcliffe, in the finest innings of his career in his own estimation, set the future course of the match. His work was by no means finished when he lost his partner. At the close of play on the Friday England still needed 162 to win, with nine wickets in hand. The position appeared secure but the mutilated wicket placed a question mark over the proceedings. Fender feared for the result in the morning. 'Patches completely bare, and as big as my outstretched hand, were numerous, a good dozen each end, all clustered round the good length.' Ben Travers, the playwright and cricket enthusiast, who had accompanied the England team, also inspected the wicket. 'It was like concrete with great holes in it,' he said.

It was, as expected, a protracted and stern struggle on the Saturday. England won by three wickets to retain the Ashes; but they faltered dangerously in the closing stages. 'Fortunately for England,' wrote Reuter's correspondent, 'the weather was in good humour, and the effects of its fickleness of yesterday were pressed out of the turf by the roller. The cracks were sealed up and the worn patches healed.' The pleasures

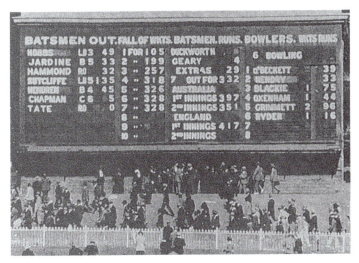

Hobbs and Sutcliffe again mocked the odds in another amazing batting feat in the third Test at Melbourne in the 1928/29 series. The scoreboard shows the victory margin of three wickets. (Melbourne Cricket Club)

of batting were revived; but Australia were also restored in spirit and determination. 'When the tide had definitely turned against them,' reported *The Australasian*, 'they were once again a convincing body of men in the field.' Jardine, sent in ahead of Hammond, on Hobbs' instructions on the previous day, was bowled by Grimmett. He had scored 33 in nearly two hours. One Australian writer commented:

> Well, this British team plays true to nationality. Jardine bats just as you would expect a Scotsman to do. He is most deliberate, apparently never flurried, with caution marking every action. Hendren, on the contrary, sparkles as one would expect of a cricketer of Irish descent, while Sutcliffe is a true example of English (Yorkshire) steadiness.

There were flutters of anxiety for England in a thrilling finish. The batting hysterics in a tumble of wickets at the end gave

Australia a faint chance of victory. Hammond, after escaping one stumping chance off the wily Grimmett, was the victim of Oldfield's agility. As he attempted a drive, the ball spun off his bat in the direction of the slips. Hammond moved out to run but the Australian wicket-keeper pounced with the certainty of a predatory cat to whip off the bails before he could regain his crease. Hendren survived a sharp chance to Bradman at long-on before being bowled by Oxenham; Tate was run-out in a heedless scamper; and Chapman, going for the winning hit, was caught at cover.

All ended well for England but Sutcliffe was lbw to Grimmett after a teasing duel. He was the fourth man out with only 14 runs required for victory. He had richly deserved the honour of carrying his bat after a match-winning innings. In scoring 135 in six and a half hours, he was the heroic and unyielding pilot who had carried England to the brink of an historic triumph.

'His patience was monumental,' related one observer, 'and the deft way he countered the craft of all the bowlers, and especially Grimmett, was beyond praise.' Sutcliffe once again proudly wore his badge of courage. 'I carried on my body for

Sutcliffe, the century-maker, fails to spot the wrong 'un and is lbw to Grimmett after a teasing duel. (Melbourne Cricket Club)

many days afterwards the marks of the ball which did such fearsome tricks on that rain-ruined Melbourne wicket,' he said.

In 1930, Jack Hobbs was in his forty-eighth year and Herbert Sutcliffe was nearing his thirty-sixth birthday. The sunset of a great association coincided with the shining dawn of the young batting emperor, Don Bradman. The English veterans, partners for the last time against Australia, were ill-supported as they sought to counter an unexpected challenge. They were twice associated in century stands, at Nottingham and Manchester but thereafter Hobbs' fortunes faltered, and it was left to the unyielding Sutcliffe to display his prowess in the conclusive Test at the Oval.

The notes of the impending discord between the two countries were sounded in this series. The cause of the alarm was the withering command of Bradman in a momentous first tour of England. Bradman's magnificence confounded those observers, including the Australian captain, Bill Woodfull, who had doubted the ability of his young tourists to win the series. Woodfull feared that Australia would be at a psychological disadvantage after their heavy defeat four years earlier.

Bradman dispelled the doubts, as he triumphantly led the march to victory. He surpassed Hammond's seemingly unassailable record of 905 runs in the 1928/29 series. In seven Test innings, the rampant young Australian achieved an aggregate of 974 runs at an average of 139.14. In the first Test at Nottingham he was modestly restrained with 131; at Lord's he became the ferocious reveller with 254 out of Australia's 729, then the second highest total in a Test match. His record score of 334 followed at Leeds to be succeeded by 232 as Australia won by an innings to regain the Ashes at the Oval. In all matches he scored 3,170 runs and averaged over 99.

Bradman's authority was briefly muted at Nottingham. He was dismissed by Tate for eight in the first innings and then, in the second innings, after completing his first Test century in England, he was defeated by Robins'googly. He did not attempt a stroke. Another leg-spinner, Eric Hollies, was to similarly baffle him on his last appearance at the Oval in 1948. Hobbs and Sutcliffe shared a century stand – 125 in less than two hours in the second innings – as England, favoured by the conditions, won by 93 runs. A thumb injury compelled Sutcliffe's retirement after he had completed his half-century at Nottingham. He was absent from the second Test at Lord's. His replacement was the veteran Frank Woolley, still in prolific form for Kent. In a tall-scoring match Australia won by seven wickets. Their batting plan was for Woodfull and Ponsford to undermine the England bowling and set the stage for Bradman. The method worked perfectly. Bradman went on the rampage with a double century. The only consolation for England was the enterprise of Duleepsinhji, in his first match against Australia, and Chapman. Both scored centuries of distinction.

Sutcliffe, amid England's increasing bewilderment, maintained his own poise through a wretched summer. Yorkshire, third in the championship behind Gloucestershire and Lancashire, sorely missed his presence in half their games. Sutcliffe provided a foretaste of the trials ahead for Essex. He twice scored centuries against them at Leyton and Dewsbury. His obduracy also averted greater humiliation for Yorkshire against the Australians at Sheffield. After the intervention of rain, the wily Grimmett bowled with remarkable accuracy to take 10 wickets for 37 runs. His triumph followed an opening stand of 59 by Sutcliffe and Holmes. Sutcliffe was third out for 69 after batting for two hours. The last seven wickets went down for only 35 more runs. Yorkshire were dismissed for 155 and only Wood, of the other batsmen, reached double figures. Bradman compounded Yorkshire's misfortune with a brilliant 78 out of 107 in less than two hours.

Despite his prolonged absence from the Yorkshire team, caused by his injury and later Test priorities, Sutcliffe scored nearly 1,000 championship runs. His overall aggregate was 2,312 runs at an average of 64.22 and he was the leading batsman in England. He also headed the English averages in the Tests, with 436 runs at an average of 87.20. In conditions made for his developing craft, an imposing Yorkshire newcomer, Hedley Verity, provided a signal of his quality. He joined Sutcliffe in a notable double achievement, heading the national bowling averages with 64 wickets at 12.42 runs apiece. As a thoughtful cricket apprentice, Verity watched the inexorable progress of Bradman in 1930. Before long their rivalry would become one of the marvels of sporting combat. Verity's name as a potential menace would soon be linked with one other only – Harold Larwood.

The genius of Bradman dominated the headlines in 1930, but Herbert Sutcliffe was a worthy adversary. In the drawn Test at Manchester he was associated with Hobbs in their eleventh and last century partnership – 108 – for England. Hobbs, handicapped by a groin injury, was for once overshadowed by his Yorkshire partner. 'One may question if, in any of their previous ten century stands, Hobbs was so signally outshone as he was by Sutcliffe's brilliance,' reported the *Yorkshire Post*. *Wisden* praised a 'dashing exhibition of strong and certain forcing cricket'. Sutcliffe hit one six and 10 fours in his 74, scored out of 115 in two and a quarter hours. Hobbs was forced to play a supporting role following an injury sustained before lunch; and Sutcliffe, in his turn, was struck a fierce blow on his left elbow. It meant that he also had to nurse his resources after one of the brightest displays of batting he had produced in Test cricket.

Duleepsinhji, with a scintillating half-century, matched Sutcliffe. 'Both Sutcliffe and Duleepsinhji brought Grimmett to subjection,' commented the *Yorkshire Post*. 'They made McCabe seek safer quarters than are to be found at silly point when batsmen are able and disposed to hit.' Sutcliffe's dismissal from a remarkable catch by Bradman quickly followed the departure of Hobbs. Having struck a full toss from Wall for four, he was presented with a long hop by the Australian bowler in the same over. It invited a six over the square-leg boundary. Sutcliffe did not quite gauge the distance. Bradman, the alert scout in the deep field, took the catch high up and just inside the ropes. He clung on to the ball before falling back among the spectators reclining on the grass behind him.

The much criticised demotion of Percy Chapman, England's popular and charismatic leader in the last Test at the Oval, was presumably based on erring management against Bradman. There were precedents for a change of captaincy during a series. Johnny Douglas had given way to Lionel Tennyson in 1921 and Chapman himself was hailed as an inspired choice when he deposed Arthur Carr in 1926. Bob Wyatt, the replacement captain in 1930, exuded a quiet efficiency. The twenty-nine-year-old Wyatt was a product of Coventry and North Warwickshire club cricket and he had first played for Warwickshire in his early twenties. He was a member of the MCC teams which had toured India, South Africa and the West Indies. He was an all-round sportsman, an accomplished ice skater and hockey player, and a keen motorist and aviator. Of Wyatt it was said that he was one of the most modest men ever placed in the limelight. One observer remarked: 'It is not a modesty that springs from shyness because he does not hesitate to express any opinion he holds, or from aloofness, for he has no time for anything resembling snobbery. In every way he is a good-natured and common-sensed young man.'

Wyatt was presented with an insoluble task against Bradman as he was when he was recalled as England captain in equally unpropitious circumstances against Australia in 1934. In both series he shouldered an unenviable burden. Ronald Mason concluded that it would have needed two cricket teams of world class to have contained Bradman in 1930. Wyatt did, however, bring a welcome solidity to England's middle order

at the Oval. The gain in batting strength was endorsed by
the crowd when he went out to aid England's recovery. The
applause was redoubled in an enthusiastic reception in front
of the pavilion at the close of play. It was a recognition of his
fighting spirit and a rebuke for those critics who had questioned his appointment.

Australia, replying to England's 405, scored monumentally
for the second time in the series at the Oval. The toiling Larwood, Tate and Peebles conceded 489 runs between
them; Bradman, ravenous in his pursuit of runs, compiled
another double century out of a total of 695. Australia won
by an innings and 39 runs. Sadly, Hobbs could only provide
a glimpse of his majesty before his devoted followers on his
last Test appearance. His perky enterprise brought him 47 runs
and he raced ahead of Sutcliffe in a stand of 68 for the first
wicket. But what was required was a vintage 100 to stem
the Australian advance. Whysall succumbed quickly to Wall.
Duleepsinhji, with a spectacular half-century, did not endure
long enough for England's needs. Hammond, the beleagured
champion in one of his least accomplished years as an England
batsman, again failed. Five wickets had fallen for 197 runs by
tea. Sutcliffe and Wyatt, divided by years but sturdy compati-
bles, were equal to the crisis. They came to the rescue with a
stand of 170 for the sixth wicket and their work did not end
until the following day. Wyatt was the eighth man out after
scoring 64 in three hours of valiant cricket.

Sutcliffe exactly duplicated his 161, scored in an even more
exacting situation and with greater reward in the epic battle at
the Oval four years earlier. It was his seventh century against
Australia. There were nine fours in his marathon innings
extending over six and three-quarter hours. The early restraint
of Sutcliffe and Wyatt was succeeded by sparkling batting after
the tea interval. The third hundred was raised in eighty-five
minutes. Despite England's precarious position, the average

scoring rate was 54 runs an hour. 'Sutcliffe was the dominant man of the day,' reported the *Yorkshire Post*. 'It has really been a great display of self-suppression. He knew above all things that he could not make a mistake and that it was his duty to keep one end intact until the bowling had been mastered.'

With this act of unavailing defiance, Sutcliffe was obedient to his batting code. By the end of the series he was the custodian of a tradition that he had shared for so many glorious years with Jack Hobbs. Their travels together were not quite finished. In 1931, at the Scarborough Festival, they shared two double-century partnerships for the Players against the Gentlemen and for H.D.G. Leveson Gower's XI against the New Zealand tourists. They came together for the last time for the Players at Lord's in 1932. As if he sensed the mourning at his impending retirement, Hobbs chose this occasion to play one of his stateliest innings. He revived the memories of his great years in carrying his bat for 161. It was his sixteenth century in these fixtures and he beat the record of W.G. Grace for the Gentlemen.

It was the end of a magnificent association. Ronald Mason wrote:

Behind them were nine years of wonderful attainment, 26 opening partnerships of 100 or more; a legendary technique and repute unequalled by any other pair; the lean, active quizzical Hobbs and the neat, wiry imperturbable Sutcliffe, who set a standard that can serve as a guide, but defied all attempts at emulation.

9

The Captaincy Furore

'Although Wilfred Rhodes and Percy Holmes were his seniors, it was Herbert who had the vote of the whole Yorkshire team. He was our representative all the time and never let us down.'

Bill Bowes, the Yorkshire and England bowler

The denial of the privilege of leading Yorkshire must be regarded as one of the few setbacks suffered by Herbert Sutcliffe during his long career. He recognised the immensity of the challenge but not the dissension his selection would cause; and his overthrow by the amateur diehards within the county was an unanticipated blow.

The captaincy controversy, extending over several weeks in November 1927, was a colossal piece of misjudgement by the Yorkshire committee. The esteemed Sutcliffe and Wilfred Rhodes, who was then in his fiftieth year, were the unwitting and distressed victims of a leadership campaign waged in the local press. It was a struggle from which neither could emerge as a winner. An army of correspondents had paraded

their views in the *Yorkshire Post*, some reverentially advocating
the confirmation of Rhodes as the rightful captain, and others,
equally vociferous, supporting the claims of the younger man
at the height of his fame. The upshot of the pressure was that
Sutcliffe 'gracefully declined' the invitation and declared that
he was willing to serve under any captain. Captain William
Worsley, from Hovingham Hall, was the man chosen to fill
the breach.

Sutcliffe had known before departing on the winter tour of
South Africa that he was being considered as a future captain
in succession to Major Lupton. His election, confirmed at a
meeting of the Yorkshire committee at Headingley, seemed
likely to provide a stimulus for the county. It was an attempt
to place at the helm a player of standing after a succession of
tactically ineffectual amateurs. Yorkshire, in this decade of brilliant successes, had, in any event, maintained their command
through the professional stewardship of Rhodes and Emmott
Robinson. Their resources were considered strong enough to
carry amateur captains, who were judged almost entirely on
their disciplinary qualities rather than prowess as players.

Sutcliffe was on board the SS *Kenilworth Castle* en-route
for South Africa when the Press Association correspondent
relayed the news of his appointment. 'Sincerest thanks for your
congratulations on my appointment as captain of Yorkshire – it
is the biggest honour of my career,' replied Sutcliffe. 'It will be
my earnest endeavour to emulate the greatest of all Yorkshire
captains, Lord Hawke, and I shall do my utmost to uphold the
best traditions of Yorkshire and England cricket.'

It must have appeared to Sutcliffe, in his elation at the
announcement, that the prize was a salute to his zeal in
advancing the status of the professional cricketer. His candi-
dature was deserving and carried no blemish. Derek Hodgson
has said that he 'cloaked his hard professionalism in an amateur's lifestyle'. J.M. Kilburn considered that Sutcliffe gave

to professional cricketers 'the credit card status that Henry Cotton gave to professional golfers'.

Bill Bowes admired and respected Sutcliffe's belief in the honour of professional cricket. 'Although Wilfred Rhodes and Percy Holmes were his seniors at Headingley, it was Herbert who had the vote of the whole Yorkshire team. He was our representative all the time and never let us down.' As a young cricketer, Bowes was gently taken to task by Sutcliffe during a match against Hampshire at Portsmouth. 'In those days,' recalled Bowes, 'we went off for lunch in a marquee on the edge of the ground. The Hampshire players, mostly amateurs, would walk off the field and straight into the tent. I did the same and went into the tent in my shirt sleeves.'

As he did so, Sutcliffe intervened and quietly said: 'Be a good chap, Bill, go and put on your blazer.' Later, in the Yorkshire dressing-room, he explained the reason for the instruction. 'If you were an amateur, you could please yourself. But as a Yorkshire professional you have to do everything better than an amateur. Your manners must be better and, if possible, you must speak and dress better, too.' Brian Sellers, as the president of the Scarborough Festival in later years, was equally zealous on the question of suitable attire. He once ordered four England players out of the festival marquee, because they were not wearing their blazers. 'You're not coming into my tent,' said Sellers, 'until you've learned how to dress properly.' Conduct and appearance were matters of paramount importance to Sellers and Sutcliffe.

Sutcliffe, the poor boy from Pudsey, had become the epitome of the well-bred gentleman. His supposed haughtiness (in reality, a manifestation of his unabashed self-confidence) did lead to confusion and irritation. He ruffled the feathers of the amateurs at Lord's and even posed problems for some of his fellow Yorkshire professionals, who were disinclined to disturb the status quo. Monty Garland-Wells, the former Surrey

captain, believed that Sutcliffe placed himself on the same foot-
ing as the amateur. 'Herbert was very much a gentleman. He
had the looks of a gent. He did not think it wrong to call amateurs by their christian names. On one occasion, at the Oval
in the late 1930s, Sutcliffe and Garland-Wells were the first
two players to arrive at the ground. Sutcliffe strolled over to
the Surrey dressing-room to say good morning. 'Hallo, Monty,
how are you?' he said. Garland-Wells said he was surprised but
not offended, although he was accustomed to being addressed
as 'sir' or 'Mr'. Jack Hobbs accepted the division between the
amateur and the professional. 'Jack always called me "sir",' said
the Surrey captain. 'It used to worry me to death.'

The distinction now seems a laughable charade but it was
strictly observed and even admired as a mostly benevolent
paternalism during Sutcliffe's career. He was stirring a hor-
net's nest in attempting to bridge the amateur–professional
divide. He was straying beyond his limits. Sidney Hainsworth
has defended Sutcliffe's mission. 'Herbert was the first of a new
generation of professionals who made it clear that their skill
and social standing must be taken into account. He was calm
and efficient and able to mix in any company.' In Yorkshire this
meant that Sutcliffe resisted the rule of officialdom when he
thought it was acting in an overbearing manner. Hainsworth
remembered one incident at the Scarborough Festival
when team selection was being vigorously discussed for a
Gentlemen versus Players match. H.D.G. Leveson Gower, an
august and influential amateur patron, was among those debat-
ing choices. Sutcliffe insisted: 'Percy Holmes has to go in with
me.' Hainsworth said that Sutcliffe's advocacy won the day and
Holmes was his partner in the match.

The decision to appoint Sutcliffe as Yorkshire's first professional captain for forty-four years was soon to be overturned.
The firmly entrenched amateur tradition was to prevail for
another thirty years. Sutcliffe was perhaps unwary in not

insisting at an early stage on a canvass of the Yorkshire membership. But he could hardly have anticipated such a backlash against his proposed captaincy in 1927. He had, though, some cause to be aggrieved by the indecisiveness of the Yorkshire committee.

Sutcliffe must have thought, in his professional fervour and as an acclaimed England cricketer, that he was well equipped to direct and counsel a team which had prospered in a graceless fashion in earlier years. Yorkshire had, in the words of J.M. Kilburn, looked 'in danger of becoming social outcasts.' E.W. Swanton commented: 'It was a pity that the properly antagonistic demeanour of Yorkshire on the field occasionally grew so openly hostile as to jeopardise relations with other counties.' The arrogance, which can emerge in an era of unchallenged supremacy, may have been at the root of the conflict. A talented Yorkshire side, as in another tempestuous period in the 1950s, required strong leadership. Geoffrey Wilson, the Leeds amateur captain, was in the eye of the storm in 1924 when the troubles flared in the match against Middlesex at Sheffield. In the earlier game at Lord's, Yorkshire, without Holmes, Sutcliffe, Kilner and Macaulay, playing in a Test trial, had been overwhelmed in a dispiriting manner. They were dismissed for 192 and then belaboured by the Middlesex amateurs. Dales and Stevens both hit centuries before Middlesex declared at 465 for eight wickets. Frank Mann also scored 79 and struck four sixes off Wilfred Rhodes. Yorkshire were beaten by an innings and 152 runs.

Kilburn described the return fixture at Bramall Lane as a 'sorry exhibition of ill-feeling and bad manners'. It was in the nature of a revenge match although neither side gained an advantage and a draw was always the likeliest outcome. The unpleasant atmosphere developed on the first day. The spectators became so objectionable that the umpires, Butt and Reeves, sent a written protest to the MCC, stating that the attitude of Abe Waddington, the Yorkshire fast bowler, had incited barracking. Yorkshire asked the MCC to set up an inquiry into the allegations; but before this had been done Middlesex declared that they were cancelling the fixtures for 1925. Middlesex's displeasure was cooled by the MCC report, which confirmed both their complaints and the umpires' report. A warning was issued to Waddington, who sent a written apology, and there was no break in the matches between the two counties. The quarrel did, however, simmer for many years afterwards, and one neutral observer blamed Middlesex for allowing the feud to continue. In August there were London newspaper reports of other unsavoury incidents in the match against Surrey at the Oval. These were probably exaggerated since there were no complaints from Surrey. Kilburn reported, without elaboration: 'The general atmosphere did not, however, add to the happiness of the season, and there can be no denying that Yorkshire's reputation was not at its highest in 1924.'

Geoffrey Wilson resigned in the autumn after winning three championships during his three years as captain. He subsequently alluded to the problems of leading a strong, all-round XI. In common with other Yorkshire amateur captains of the period, he had to defer to his senior professional, Wilfred Rhodes. Rhodes's presence was undoubtedly formidable and the wisdom of the veteran always required careful consideration. Wilson said: 'One of the chief difficulties was to make a decision that is considered the correct one in the opinion of the majority of the team, not only in the judgement of one's "chief adviser".' In 1930, Wilson, as an Old Harrovian, acted as an intermediary in arranging a coaching appointment for Rhodes at Harrow.

As the Yorkshire captain, Wilson probably felt, in some part, culpable for the turmoil of the Sheffield match; and his resignation was perhaps an attempt to bring about better relations with Middlesex. In his impressions of his time with Yorkshire, he made clear his distaste for belligerent tactics. 'I feel personally that any match, however serious it may be, and however much may depend on the result, should be played in a friendly spirit. The result should be second in importance.' Wilson's departure signified the need for a stronger hand at the tiller; and Lord Hawke, who had used his influence to keep the peace at Lord's, may also have requested a change of captain. Hawke's loyalty to the team remained intact. Whatever his private feelings, he rallied to their defence. 'You never met a rotter in those post-war days. They were good, straight fellows, some of the very flower of the land.'

Wilson's successor was Arthur William Lupton, an army major, who took over the captaincy at the age of forty-six, although he had made his county debut as long ago as 1908. His task was to restore discipline and harmony to the Yorkshire team. He very wisely left the cricket affairs to the joint supervision of Rhodes and Robinson. Major Lupton's captaincy and batting at no.10 (where he achieved a career average of just over ten runs) were modest contributions as Yorkshire finished as champions for the fourth consecutive year. Lupton did present a dignified facade to veil the wilder elements within his team. He earned the affection of his rough-tongued charges. Emmott Robinson was particularly fond of Lupton and was once heard to remark: 'He's too nice a gentleman to 'ave to play cricket.' The influence of Robinson and Rhodes gave rise to a number of apocryphal stories which, in the words of A.A. Thomson, 'moved Yorkshiremen everywhere to their particular form of grim smile'. The images of the amateur's dependency upon the wily Yorkshire veterans were especially fostered and relished by Neville Cardus, in his audacious forays into the 'higher truth'. According to one Cardus legend, Yorkshire had reached over 400 and Lupton, batting at no.9, struck the ball neatly past cover and started to run. Suddenly there was the ringing of the bell in the pavilion. Dolphin, the Yorkshire wicket-keeper batting at the other end, raised his hand and said: 'I shouldn't bother, Major. Wilfred's declared.'

There was also another story of an indignant Yorkshire attack confronted by two disrespectful young batsmen, newly promoted to the First XI. The unlikely marauders hit a spate of boundaries from all parts of the bat except the middle. They survived one hairsbreadth escape after another. Yorkshire's frustration mounted as the youngsters gleefully profited from their good fortune. The language, with George Macaulay among the more outspoken, was charged with ripe expletives. It produced a peevish protest from one of the umpires, who said it was like trying to keep order in a parrot house. 'How can I hear your appeals with all this jabber going on?' The raconteur telling this story was interrupted by a perplexed inquiry from someone innocent in the ways of Yorkshiremen. 'Why didn't the captain stop it?' he asked. The question was greeted with a tolerant smile and the reply: 'How could he? Wilfred had sent him into t'deep to spare his blushes.'

Other Yorkshire amateur captains were of sterner mettle in later years. They would not have permitted such buffoonery. Among them was Sheffield-born Alan Barber, an allround sportsman, who had captained Oxford University in 1929. Barber led Yorkshire in Wilfred Rhodes's last season in the following summer. He was regarded by Sutcliffe as a 'great captain'. E.M. Wellings gave credit to Barber as the disciplinary pioneer who paved the way for Yorkshire's magnificent reign in the 1930s. Barber, regrettably, could spare only one summer from his scholastic duties, but it was sufficient to impress many observers. He had, by many accounts, the potential to join the small elite of Yorkshire amateurs who were judged players of quality rather than just figureheads. Had circumstances been different, Barber might have taken his place alongside two men in this category, F.S. Jackson, who led the county but was never the official captain, and Norman Yardley.

Wellings recalled that Barber benefited from a slight stammer. It might have been a handicap but in the Sheffield amateur's case the speech hesitation had the effect of investing his commands with an authoritative emphasis. 'Not even Rhodes,' said Wellings, was proof against Barber's determination. The showdown was brief but crucial. At the end of one over Barber intimated that he wanted Rhodes to field at short extra cover. Rhodes, however, continued his journey to the peaceful haven of mid-on, which he regarded as his preserve. 'When he arrived and turned round, Barber was standing in the middle of the pitch. "W–Wilfred," he said, "short extra o-o the pavilion." Rhodes chose short extra.'

Wilfred Rhodes, in this instance, accepted the instruction of his captain. If he flinched under the rebuff, he kept his thoughts to himself. The same pattern of command existed under Brian Sellers. In the Sellers conception of captaincy, wrote J.M. Kilburn, decisions had to be firm, clear and unquestioned and command by example unceasing. Sellers came to distinction as an inspirational leader because he cultivated a uniformity to which he himself subscribed. 'Common service meant common undertakings. Early attendance on the first day of the match included Sellers. Wearing of the county colours on county occasions applied to Sellers. Acceptance of the conventional in the condition of flannels, boots and pads devolved on Sellers. His pride was to be one of the Yorkshire cricketers.'

Kilburn said that Sellers won the trust of his seasoned professionals because he maintained a predictable code and enlarged a common outlook. Herbert Sutcliffe was his model senior professional, at least after he had curbed the excesses of Sellers' discipline. Sutcliffe decided to teach him a lesson. On one embarrassing occasion, after he had left the amateur gate to lead the team on the field, Sellers was left standing in the middle with the two umpires and the batsmen. There was a short, agonising pause before Sutcliffe and the rest of the Yorkshire team, having made their point, joined their captain.

Pride was restored in the relationship between the Yorkshire captain and the players, but it was not long before Sellers dealt his riposte. After Yorkshire had won yet another championship, he presided at a discussion on bonus payments. 'Now let's talk about the share of the money and also about rebuilding the team for the future,' he said. Looking at Sutcliffe, he added: 'But before we do that, let's get one thing straight. You are my senior professional but you are also the man who is leading the opposition to me. So you won't get a brass farthing by way of a bonus.' Sutcliffe had to concede, if rueful at his exclusion from the cash distribution, that his captain had countered him in the most direct manner possible. From that point on he became Sellers' most loyal ally. Together, they became an unfaltering and merciless duo and fashioned triumph after triumph. Bill Sutcliffe, commenting on this relationship, said: 'ABS did a marvellous job in the 1930s but he was totally backed by my father, the best senior professional of his time. For someone who was such a great player, I would doubt whether he was excelled in loyalty.'

The maintenance of the amateur captaincy tradition in Yorkshire throughout Sutcliffe's career was in one sense a blessing in that it enabled him to conserve his energies, mentally and physically, as a premier batsman. Others like Leonard Hutton, less strongly endowed, found the responsibilities of leadership a severe trial and a draining task. It is also instructive to reflect that Hutton's successes as a captain were obtained with England and not Yorkshire. The words of Bill Bowes, in his heyday as a Yorkshire professional, were attuned to the intense competition within his own team. 'None of us would be good enough to captain Yorkshire,' he said. Bowes was not denying the tactical expertise of his colleagues. He was astutely acknowledging the problems of detachment by a professional in such a situation. Sutcliffe, with his cosmopolitan outlook and rigorous professionalism, might have surmounted the obstacles. In later years he regretted that he had withdrawn his acceptance of the Yorkshire captaincy. Sidney Hainsworth also regarded his friend's second thoughts as a mistake. 'Herbert was a great disciplinarian and he would have made a fine captain.'

At the time of the Yorkshire captaincy conflict in 1927, Charles Crane, the president of the Craven Gentlemen CC, dwelt upon the drawbacks of professional leadership. He thought the committee had not taken into account the prospect of jealousy among the players. 'It is a psychological fact that an eleven cannot work amicably together, and especially when they are always in each other's company. There must be some outside influence, not force, to keep them under control.' Crane also urged the committee to consider the question of the mental strain imposed upon a professional:

> It is not right to appoint a man as a leader who has to earn his living by cricket. It is adding too great a burden and responsibility. So long as Yorkshire are winning this burden might be light but let them begin to lose, and the public would soon begin to barrack him.

The dilemma facing Herbert Sutcliffe, across the world in South Africa, was compounded by the fluctuating debate among the Yorkshire membership. It was widely considered that the committee had made a hasty decision and that they had placed themselves in an awkward and undignified position by adopting an irregular and casual procedure. Adding to the consternation was the fact that Sutcliffe's appointment had not been a unanimous decision. The first proposal to give him amateur status had been defeated by nineteen votes to five before the appointment was carried by a margin of two votes – 13-11. In a cable from Cape Town on 10 November, six days after his enthusiastic shipboard response, Sutcliffe said: 'I have not yet received by mail an official offer from the Yorkshire authorities of the captaincy of the Yorkshire team next season.' He declined to make any further statement until he had received the offer.

Contemporary accounts said that the president (Lord Hawke) and the secretary (F.C. Toone) had disclaimed any knowledge of the matter. There was, in fact, an intriguing meeting between Toone and Wilfred Rhodes at the Yorkshire club's offices in Leeds before the start of the 1927 season. At the interview, Toone said he thought that it was time Rhodes took things more easily. He asked Rhodes to write a letter to the committee, suggesting that someone else should be appointed to relieve him of the onerous responsibilities of senior professional. Rhodes said that he would require time to consider the proposal. He returned home to discuss the matter with his wife. She warned him that there appeared to be elements of a plot and said that he should watch his step. Rhodes then wrote to the Yorkshire secretary and said that he had reached the conclusion that 'it would be very ungrateful on his part to do anything of the kind' indicated in the proposal. He genuinely felt that after all Yorkshire had done for him, and all the years he had spent with the county, he would be guilty of ingratitude if he, as he thought, deserted now. In the view of one observer, the approach to Rhodes was a signal that Yorkshire wanted to clear the deck before being free to appoint a captain of their own choice.

The sequel to the meeting was the appointment of Sutcliffe as captain, without consultation with Rhodes. It led to allegations that the decision had been prematurely disclosed by an unknown party to the press, with the object of rushing the committee into the acceptance of a particular nominee.

Power beneath the gentility: Sutcliffe relished the hook shot, which was of the nature of 'hard Pennine rock and the relentless strength which his native hills and native people alike embody.' (W.H.H.S)

The verdict of one correspondent was that certain amateurs, in recent years, had not been given a fair trial. He considered that the attitude towards amateurs had neither been cordial nor encouraging. 'Of course, we all want our team to win, but wish for something more, and that is bright and light-hearted cricket, which the majority of amateurs play, and desire cricket to be played as a game and not as a business.'

As the campaign mounted in ferocity, Wilfred Rhodes was drawn into a public rebuttal. Rhodes said the captaincy had never been offered to him. He had known nothing about the matter until he had read the news of Sutcliffe's appointment, 'being apparently passed over my head'. He later contra-dicted newspaper statements that he was unwilling to captain Yorkshire. 'I have not announced my retirement from cricket and that could not have been the reason why the captaincy was not offered to me.' The veteran, in a sharp rebuke and with a measure of hurt pride, said his own views had not been sought on the matter. 'Sutcliffe's appointment was a great surprise to me. I am a tremendous admirer of him, for he is a splendid cricketer and a good fellow.' However, Rhodes thought the selection ill-judged, particularly as there were several professionals (Holmes, Emmott, Robinson and Oldroyd) who were senior to Sutcliffe in the Yorkshire ranks.

Reflecting on his long reign with the county, Rhodes added: 'One cannot help thinking that after playing so long the committee would have given me first refusal of the captaincy. It almost looks as if my services are not appreciated.' Rhodes, like Roy Kilner, disagreed with the recruitment of a professional captain. 'I think it is a great pity that there is not an amateur to follow Major Lupton, who was very popular with us.'

Other correspondents raised their voices in sympathy with Rhodes. One Headingley man threatened to withdraw his membership subscription if the decision was not rescinded. 'What a graceful act it would have been on the part of the committee to have offered the captaincy to our Wilfred, a gentleman and the best all-round cricketer the world has known, as the crowning honour of his career.'

Another member from Morley, signing himself 'disgusted', said the Yorkshire committee had cast a slight upon Rhodes:

> After all he has done for Yorkshire and England cricket, to be passed over at this time, when the opportunity arose for him to reap the rewards of his long and faithful service, is utterly unworthy of Yorkshire traditions. I cannot see how the appointment of a younger man, however much we admire him as a player, over his seniors can be expected to work smoothly.

The situation, he said, was exacerbated by Rhodes being superseded by Sutcliffe. 'Rhodes has been the captain's right-hand man for years, and his knowledge of the game is unsurpassed.'

Another correspondent in the south wryly apologised for his intervention in the affair. He said that he was saved from 'utter obloquy by a considerable infusion of Yorkshire blood'. 'Although I appreciate Sutcliffe as a very gallant cricketer and gentleman, I shall not have the heart to be present at Lord's or the Oval this coming season, unless the Olympian Rhodes, in default of an amateur, leads the team to do battle for Yorkshire.'

Other writers considered that Sutcliffe's appointment should be heralded with enthusiasm. The threats by members to cancel their subscriptions were described as juvenile and bound to hurt Sutcliffe's feelings. The critics were asked to pay heed to C.B. Fry's remarks on old 'fossilised traditions'. 'It does not matter who captains the side as long as he is a gentleman by nature, has tact and leadership ability. I am certain that Sutcliffe possesses these qualifications,' commented one man. A county member in North Yorkshire applauded the decision as a means of strengthening the team:

> The honesty of making a professional the captain, still as the professional, appeals to me infinitely more than making an amateur the leader by means of creating an assistant secretaryship or treasurership, the holder of which is enabled to play as an amateur and captain the side by reason of the salary attached to the post.

At a meeting of the Leeds League a resolution was passed wishing Sutcliffe every success and offering congratulations on the honour conferred upon him. 'I have always thought,' said the Pudsey spokesman, 'that Herbert Sutcliffe was one of nature's gentlemen. I am quite sure that he will do credit both to the Yorkshire team and himself as captain.' He struck a cautionary note, a proviso shared by others, with the remark: 'I only hope that the appointment will not have a deleterious

effect upon his batting.' Another representative at the meeting gave, as his view, that there were many other professionals
who were worthy of being entrusted with the captaincy of
their counties.

In December, a circular and postcard, marked 'private
and confidential', was sent out by Mr S.E. Grimshaw to
Yorkshire's 7,000 members. Grimshaw sought their votes
in a poll on whether or not they approved of the appointment of Sutcliffe. The circular posed one question: 'If it is
not possible to secure a suitable amateur, whom are you in
favour of: Wilfred Rhodes or Herbert Sutcliffe?' A supplementary question asked whether the members would prefer
an amateur or a professional captain. Grimshaw responded
to allegations of 'mischief-making' by outraged correspondents. He said there was nothing unconstitutional or disloyal
in seeking the views of his fellow members, if he believed
that the county committee was not carrying out its duties
satisfactorily. Jack Hobbs, he said, had endorsed his question:
'Why not Rhodes?', and other cricketers had put forward an
identical inquiry. 'My quarrel,' said Grimshaw, 'is with that
section of the committee who have dared to oppose Sutcliffe
to Rhodes.'

Bill Bowes recalled the background to this early display of
Yorkshire democracy:

> Sid Grimshaw was a retired schoolteacher who was mad
> about cricket. He had only been a moderate player in the
> Leeds League but he helped George Hirst in coaching
> youngsters at Headingley. He got to know all the players
> and he felt it was wrong that Herbert should be approached
> as a possible captain before Wilfred. It looked at that stage,
> as though the job might go to a professional, and Grimshaw
> was determined to make sure that Wilfred's claims (and
> pride) were not overlooked.

Grimshaw's pressure prevailed and the result of the poll was as follows: In favour of the amateur – 2,264; In favour of the professional – 444. The first vote was a clear indication that the membership wanted to retain the amateur tradition. The second vote gave Rhodes (2,007) an overwhelming majority over Sutcliffe (876). After the count Grimshaw said: 'I think I ought to point out that many of the votes recorded for Sutcliffe and a professional were owing to the fact that he had already been selected by the committee.'

The conclusions of the backstage tussle doubtless reflected Lord Hawke's views on the matter, although he had affirmed his loyalty to the committee when the earlier decision had been announced. Yorkshire were emboldened by the result of the members' poll to send Sutcliffe a cable asking if he would consider withdrawing his acceptance of the captaincy. The weight of opinion against him in Yorkshire really left him with no other choice. Sutcliffe said that he had now carefully considered the question and expressed his thanks for the great honour; but regretted that he had to decline the offer. In another conciliatory message, Lord Hawke thanked Sutcliffe and recorded the committee's appreciation of 'your loyalty to the club'.

An editorial in the *Yorkshire Post* on 10 December also welcomed Sutcliffe's acquiescence in mollifying terms:

> The previous decision of the committee to appoint a professional captain was such a departure from the county's traditions that a conflict of opinion regarding it was inevitable, though probably most cool-headed observers will hold the view that this conflict has been carried to unreasonable lengths… Sutcliffe has taken a wise and dignified course in declining an honour which a message sent by wireless when he was on his way to South Africa suggested he was prepared to accept.

The leader continued:

> The first thought of a true cricketer is the success of his
> team. So Sutcliffe stands aside and indicates his readiness
> to play under the captaincy of another, thus showing that
> sportsmanship does not depend on amateur status. The
> honour of leading Yorkshire was a big thing to refuse, and
> no Yorkshireman will forget that it was refused by Sutcliffe
> in what he believed to be the best interests of the team.

The news of Sutcliffe's decision was received during a specially
convened meeting of the Yorkshire committee in Leeds to discuss the captaincy crisis. Capt. William Worsley, who had refused
the post because of farming commitments three years earlier,
was unanimously chosen as the new captain. He was the fourth
captain in nine years. This was destined to be another short term
appointment, lasting only two seasons. Capt. (later Sir) William
Worsley was to confer distinction on the club by becoming
its president; and his daughter, as the Duchess of Kent, would
bestow another honour as the Yorkshire patroness. In 1927,
Capt. Worsley, then aged thirty-six, fulfilled the ambition of
his father in succeeding to the Yorkshire captaincy. At Eton, he
had been a contemporary of the Hon. Lionel Tennyson, who
was later to achieve fame with Hampshire and England. One
of Capt. Worsley's most esteemed cricket exploits, occurred in
the match against Harrow on a bad wicket at Lord's in 1908. He
struck a valiant 42 to save Eton from an innings defeat. In his
cricket in the Army and at the family home at Hovingham, near
Malton, he was regarded as a punishing batsman. One instance
of these powers was an undefeated 135 (out of a total of 187)
against the Yorkshire Gentlemen. He was, by general consensus,
a cricketer of more than local accomplishment.

By one of those ironic tricks of fortune, Bill Sutcliffe gained
the honour, which had eluded his father, when he succeeded

Norman Yardley as the Yorkshire captain in 1956. He had had a long and gruelling cricket apprenticeship. One of his earliest cricketing memories was of arriving at Rydal Junior School in North Wales. He remembered being taken out to a soggy practice wicket in September to demonstrate his credentials, as the son of the great Herbert. While still in his early teens he opened with his father for Pudsey Britannia in a wartime charity match. Herbert Sutcliffe insisted that the opposing bowlers, including the formidable George Pope and Morris Nichols, should bowl at full speed instead of easing up to make things more comfortable for his son. At Rydal, Bill Sutcliffe played for the first eleven for four years, scoring liberally, with many of his runs coming from the hereditary hook shot. After service with the Coldstream Guards in India, he entered his father's sports business in Leeds in 1948 and also began his first-class career with Yorkshire. Sutcliffe deeply resented the jibe of some critics, who said: 'He's only in't team because his father is on the committee.' The criticism would be reinforced when he struck a bad patch. 'My contemporaries, players like Doug Padgett, Ted Lester and Vic Wilson, did not have the label or incur the same disfavour when they were out of form.' Sutcliffe did struggle to bridge the gap between club and county cricket. But in 1952 he revealed his growing confidence and mastery against the best of attacks. He scored 952 runs at an average of 41.39, and was fourth in the Yorkshire batting averages. At Canterbury he was in dominating mood against Kent and was undefeated with 181. One of his very best innings for Yorkshire was a dogged 41 against Lock and Laker on the vilest of Oval wickets.

In the 1950s, the belief still persisted that Yorkshire had an inalienable right to the championship pennant. The triumphant march of Surrey, seven times champions under the leadership of Stuart Surridge and Peter May, only served to heighten the criticism of the team. Herbert Sutcliffe, then a

member of the county committee and proud in his memories
as a distinguished Yorkshire and England batsman, could not
accept the ill-considered abuse heaped upon his son as captain.
He had never known failure and considered it a disgrace that
Yorkshire should finish second or third in the championship,
even to such a gifted team as Surrey. In 1957, Bill Sutcliffe's
second and last season as captain, Yorkshire did achieve third
position, an improvement of four places on the previous
season. *Wisden* reported: 'During the two years that Sutcliffe
held the captaincy he tried his utmost to infuse new life into
the team, but it must be said that he did not always receive the
support he deserved.'

Sutcliffe believed that his tenure as Yorkshire captain should
have lasted longer. His father insisted on his resignation. It was
a decision which rankled in his memory. Herbert's word was
law in the family. As the master of the household, he would
not brook disobedience. Two strong personalities were in conflict in this dispute. Bill Sutcliffe would soon take over as head
of the Leeds sports outfitters established by his father. But at
the time of the disagreement over the Yorkshire captaincy he
was intent on pursuing his cricket career. He also knew that
his future livelihood was at stake. It was a terrible dilemma
for Bill, who would become proud of his later achievement
in expanding the family business. Herbert's harshness in this
dealing with his son does seem an aberration, a departure
from his usual generosity. He might have been more forgiving
had he been above the fray and not subject to criticism from
members as a Yorkshire committeeman. Bill Sutcliffe himself
said the fact that his father was on the county committee did
place him at a disadvantage. 'I could put up with the grumbles
among the members because I knew that we were beginning
to establish ourselves as a good team. I was only thirty-one. I
gave up too young. Herbert made me sit down and write a
letter of resignation.'

He was denied a role in advancing the Yorkshire cause as the county moved into another thrilling championship decade. Herbert Sutcliffe, in his distress at the criticism of the team, issued what amounted to an ultimatum. 'If you don't resign, I shall sell the business,' he said.

10

Peerless at the Summit

'He enjoyed a season that would have been remarkable
once in a lifetime, but as it followed upon the magnificence
of 1931 it approached the phenomenal.'

J.M. Kilburn on Sutcliffe's batting feats

The high drama of Yorkshire's first championship for five
years in 1931 coincided with Herbert Sutcliffe overcoming
an injury setback to reach the second triple thousand runs
of his career. A thigh strain, attempting a quick single against
Middlesex at Lord's, was judged a fitness deterrent by the
England selectors. Sutcliffe was omitted from the Test against
New Zealand. His displacement, on the grounds of impaired
fielding mobility, ignited the fires of his batsmanship. In the
next ten days he hit 620 runs against Hampshire, Kent and
Somerset to add to the 120 he had scored at Lord's before the
injury forced his retirement.

By the end of the season, Sutcliffe's tally of centuries
totalled 13, including nine for Yorkshire. He headed the
national batting averages for the second consecutive year

with 3,006 runs, exceeding the next highest aggregate of Duleepsinhji by over 300 runs; and his average of 96.96 was then the highest ever recorded by an English batsman in England. It was hardly surprising that Sutcliffe considered his accomplishments in a wet season to be the best of his career. J.M. Kilburn said Sutcliffe's 'general consistency was almost past believing'. The *Yorkshire Post* enthused: 'To Sutcliffe the season brought the full flowering of his grave classical art. Great as he has been in the last seven years, he has never before been unapproached, but we may hope in the next seven he will take his place with Hobbs and "W.G." himself.' *Wisden* also reflected on Yorkshire's indebtedness to Sutcliffe. 'He rarely or never failed his side, while his numerous triumphs were nearly always the result of masterly skill and sound judgement.'

Yorkshire's surge towards their fifteenth title under their new captain, Frank Greenwood, was incontestably in tune with Sutcliffe's resilient spirit. His release by England, in circumstances which seemed to reduce the county's hopes, was the start of a bold revival. By late June, with practically a third of their fixtures completed, Yorkshire had taken only 56 points (out of a possible 135) and were eighth in the championship. They had trailed through a succession of games ruined by rain, eighteen days in all, and it looked as though their championship hopes had been washed out. Even Emmott Robinson, the inveterately buoyant campaigner, had labelled their chances as slim. Perusing the table and fixture list on the train journey to London, he had to confess that his optimism faltered when he thought of the points which the weather had taken from his side. He could not see how Yorkshire were going to make up the ground that had been lost.

Sutcliffe, as he limped painfully to his 1,000 runs against Middlesex in the welcome sunshine at Lord's, could scarcely have foretold that his century and Yorkshire's subsequent innings victory in two days would mark the turning point. In rapid succession on the southern tour Hampshire, Kent, Somerset and Surrey were all defeated by an innings. A draw with Nottinghamshire was the only interruption before Yorkshire embarked on another run of five consecutive successes. In less than a month they moved up to head the championship by a considerable margin. From June until the middle of August, Yorkshire played fifteen matches, won thirteen and drew two, and took 205 points out of the 225 at stake. Ten out of the total of sixteen victories were by an innings, two by ten wickets, and three by nine wickets.

At the heart of Yorkshire's revival was the massive batting of Sutcliffe and the bowling of the impressive new combination of Bill Bowes and Hedley Verity. Their contribution in taking 247 championship wickets was a significant omen. Verity, after his dazzling coup of all ten wickets in an innings against Warwickshire at Headingley, took 138 wickets at an average of only 12.34 runs each in his first full season; and Bowes's 109 wickets were obtained at a cost of 15.29 runs apiece. 'Those who have seen the side at work day after day, know that while Sutcliffe, Verity and Bowes have had the distinction of being able to give the lead, they have had the team behind them all the way,' reported the *Yorkshire Post*. 'The season has been graced by the happiest team spirit, and in the creation of this the enthusiasm and ability of the young captain has always been the telling factor.'

Before these events unfolded, Sutcliffe passed a fitness examination to his own satisfaction, if not that of the England selectors. He scored a century, his fifth of the season, against Hampshire at Portsmouth in the match immediately preceding the first Test at Lord's. He shared a stand of 131 with Oldroyd for the second wicket. If he was worried by the leg strain, it did not show as he secured his 100 (out of 166) in ten minutes short of three hours. He struck the ball in punishing style in an innings which included 11 fours and a six. A telegram was sent to Lord's by Frank Greenwood, the Yorkshire captain, immediately after the innings against Hampshire. It read: 'Sutcliffe's leg definitely not fit; although played brilliantly was conscious of strain. I suggest leave definite decision until later after fielding.' The selectors' reply, received by Sutcliffe later in the day, said: 'Most sincerely regret, but as your strain is not quite recovered, the committee is unable to play you on Saturday.' In a later published statement the MCC committee declared that they felt they could not risk a breakdown and play a man who might require a substitute in the field. Sutcliffe was obviously disappointed at losing his England place. He wrote to Pelham Warner, the chairman of the selectors, expressing his personal regret that more time had not been conceded before the decision was taken. The consequence of his omission was that England had two untried opening partners. Hobbs had retired from international cricket in 1930 bringing to an end his association with Sutcliffe. The new combination against New Zealand was Arnold, of Hampshire, and Bakewell, of Northamptonshire. Sutcliffe's experience was sorely missed. Arnold made nought and 34 and Bakewell nine and 27, and England were held to a draw.

The exclusion of Sutcliffe must have caused the Kent supporters to raise their eyes in disbelief as they watched him maltreat their bowlers on a day of grilling heat at Folkestone. As Sutcliffe beat the path to a double century, the news was flashed around the crowd that England had lost their first three wickets for 30 runs at Lord's. Around the boundary curious voices were repeatedly heard commenting on how a batsman who had scored over 400 runs in his last three innings could be left out of the Test team. Adding to their consternation was the fact that Sutcliffe's replacement at Lord's was Frank Woolley. Woolley, busily repairing the damage done by New Zealand's bowlers, was debarred from countering Sutcliffe at Folkestone.

Sutcliffe, with his leg heavily bandaged, only decided to play on the morning of the Kent match. He showed signs of discomfort but his batting was unaffected. The innings was one of his best. He reached his third successive 100 (out of 173) in two and three-quarter hours and completed the double hundred in just over another two hours. Among Sutcliffe's 24 boundaries was a string of half a dozen off Freeman. 'He had no more devastating stroke than the square cut, which he used so freely and unerringly at the ball which Freeman sent up just outside the off-stump,' reported the *Yorkshire Post*. 'Always Sutcliffe moved easily, always his bat flashed decisively, and always the ball sped to crack the fence in front of the covered stand.'

Freeman, untiring in his spinning quest on a pitch as firm as concrete, at length won his duel with Sutcliffe. The Yorkshireman was stumped by Levett off the Kent leg-spinner. He had scored 230 (out of 379) and the subsequent tumble of wickets amply reflected his command and Freeman's mastery of lesser opposition. Sutcliffe and Oldroyd (93) added 258, but of the rest only Robinson and Macaulay scored more than 30. Yorkshire totalled 467 to win by an innings; but Freeman's hard work had a mead of consolation when, against the later batsmen, his spin was able to exact its toll.

In the following match against Somerset at Dewsbury, Sutcliffe eclipsed two records and narrowly failed to achieve another, falling 17 runs short of a double century in successive innings. He became the first Yorkshireman to record the distinction of four consecutive hundreds. The previous record of three successive centuries for the county was jointly held by Hirst (1899), Denton (1910) and Rhodes (1911/12), although Sutcliffe had himself accomplished this feat for England in Tests against Australia in 1924/25. Sutcliffe, with his sixth century of the season, also passed David Denton's county record of 61 hundreds.

Percy Holmes was again Sutcliffe's ally against Somerset. Their three-figure first- wicket stand of 130 runs was their 62nd for Yorkshire, and the 67th in all matches. Sutcliffe's achievements would have been remarkable for a man in full fitness, and it was a testimony to his courage that he made light of his injury handicap in his magnificent progression in 1931. The severity of the injury compelled him to use a runner, Arthur Wood, when he had reached 96 against Somerset. It did not prevent him on a cold and gloomy day at Dewsbury from raising his century and then accelerating to hit another 50 in under an hour. The irony of the run-out dismissal, with Sutcliffe as the helpless onlooker, could not have been lost upon a batsman whose sharpness between the wickets normally confounded the opposition. At 183, he hit a ball from Young towards mid-off. Wood went for the single, but Earle displayed an agility to belie his size, and threw down the wicket from close range. Sutcliffe had had to refuse a number of singles because of his injury. He knew that the only cure was rest and, having established the Yorkshire title challenge, he sensibly withdrew from the games against Surrey at Bradford and the New Zealanders at Harrogate.

Sutcliffe's restoration to fitness was confirmed by his century against New Zealand in the second Test at the Oval. It was his fourteenth hundred for England and *Wisden* commented that he 'clearly showed what a great difference to the side his presence means'. New Zealand were dismissed for 193 and 197 and England won by an innings.

The welcome which greeted Sutcliffe's recovery gained in fervour at Bramall Lane. Sutcliffe always revelled in his rapport with his Sheffield admirers, and this was his favourite cricket ground. An August Bank Holiday crowd watched Holmes and Sutcliffe combine to realise their highest partnership against Lancashire – 323 in four and a half hours. It was the biggest stand made for any wicket by Yorkshire against Lancashire, easily beating the 280 scored by Louis Hall and Fred Lee at Bradford in 1887. It followed another triple century partnership (309) against Warwickshire at Birmingham. In Lancashire's ranks was Sutcliffe's esteemed adversary, Ted McDonald, playing his last match against Yorkshire. He was given a plumb wicket to bowl on, and the Yorkshire pair were almost invincible in such conditions. Holmes hit 125 and Sutcliffe was even more implacable, striking 21 fours in his 195.

The onslaught at Sheffield was without precedent in Roses matches. In an hour after lunch, Sutcliffe and Holmes hit nearly 100 runs to all parts of the field. In a gargantuan feat, 50 runs were scored in the first hour, and the 100 was hoisted 50 minutes later. Sutcliffe led the way all the time. Holmes, not easy with his form at the start, was content to plod along in the wake of his partner. He was still in his fifties when Sutcliffe reached his century, scored out of 165, in two hours and twenty-five minutes. The Yorkshire pair arrived at the double hundred mark in five minutes short of three hours. Holmes completed his century (out of 286) in three hours and fifty-five minutes; and the 300 was hoisted a quarter of an hour later. Sutcliffe's innings was ended by a miraculous catch by Paynter off Hopwood on the deep square-leg boundary. He had earlier just failed with two other drives for sixes. Paynter flung himself forward, held the ball low and rolled over and over, with a brilliant catch safely made.

One Yorkshire supporter, then a ten-year-old, recalled the joys of a thrilling day:

> The quality of the batting was quite superb and the marvellous understanding of Holmes and Sutcliffe in their running between the wickets; the patience and controlled aggression of the openers, leading up to almost 400 runs by the close of play, made it a day to remember, especially against the old enemy.

This observer was particularly impressed by one phase of the partnership. 'With McDonald pounding in from the football end, and dropping the ball short and wide, Sutcliffe carved him away to the third man boundary three times in one over. Peter Eckersley, the Lancashire captain, tried in vain to plug the gaps.' He recalled the expectancy of the crowd as Sutcliffe approached his double century:

> He hooked the ball hard and high – it seemed a certain six – towards the Shoreham Street boundary. With the crowd rising to acclaim his 200, a small figure raced along the boundary and took a wonderful, tumbling catch. That was the first (but by no means the last) time that I had cause to remember Eddie Paynter.

It was, in fact, Paynter, the sure-footed Lancastrian who baulked Yorkshire with an unbeaten 87 in Lancashire's second innings. 'He was Yorkshire's bane for six hours,' wrote Neville Cardus. 'He came to the wicket when failure of head and heart was losing Lancashire the match.'

The vivid impression of Sutcliffe's innings in 1931 produced an important gain for the Yorkshire correspondent. Sutcliffe would have been gratified to learn that his batting had inspired an adoring schoolboy towards academic success. 'That day's cricket had quite an influence on my life because in the following year I was due to undergo a student's nightmare – the 11 plus examination.' He had been accused of lack of imagination in his essay work. 'Imagine my joy when among the story titles for the examination was "A Sporting Occasion",' recalled the Yorkshire supporter. He pounced on the subject with alacrity. The events of a dramatic cricket day at Sheffield were related in compelling style and won over his examiners. 'I feel sure that this was a great help towards gaining a grammar school place, which later led to a teaching career.'

Gloucestershire, enterprising opponents and championship runners-up in 1931, were among Yorkshire's victims in
the exciting march towards the title. Vital points were at stake
in the match at Bristol. Hot sunshine beating down on a
drying wicket offered substantial rewards for spinners. On
the second day 17 wickets went down for less than 12 runs
each. After the home captain, Bev Lyon, had declared at
182 for nine, Yorkshire were thrust into the grip of Parker
and Goddard. At 21, Holmes skied a ball from Parker and
was caught at cover and only 13 runs had been added when
Mitchell was lbw to Gloucestershire's veteran left-hander.
Leyland and Sutcliffe briefly gained the advantage before
rain stopped play. The shower only lasted ten minutes but
it was a telling interruption as the sun broke through again.
Yorkshire were in the toils as Parker bowled a baffled Leyland,
and Goddard swiftly took the wickets of Barber, Greenwood
and Robinson. 'Sutcliffe fought on as brilliantly as he can in
such circumstances, and he batted two hours and 10 minutes
for his 58 runs,' reported the *Yorkshire Post*. He was seventh
man out, with the total at 105, superbly caught at long-on
by Barnett. Parker and Goddard, with their enticing and
complementary spins, shared the nine wickets. Yorkshire,
also looking for profit, declared 64 runs behind on the first
innings. Verity obtained the prize wicket of Hammond, and
Gloucestershire lost three wickets for 12 runs in a palpitating
last half-hour.

On the next day it was an inspired Macaulay who whirled
into action to overwhelm Gloucestershire. They were dismissed for 70, and Macaulay, with Robinson as his determined
partner in arms, showed such command of length and spin that
the batsmen were treading the path to the pavilion in a bewil-
dered procession. Macaulay secured six wickets for 27 runs in
13.3 overs; and Robinson three for 13 in 13 overs. Macaulay
took the last two wickets with successive balls, and four in the

morning for eight runs in 33 balls. Gloucestershire's last six wickets went down for 12 runs.

Yorkshire were set a target of 135 but it was by no means an easy task on a badly worn wicket. There was also the threat of rain behind the glowering clouds. Sutcliffe coolly took charge of the situation. He survived one lbw appeal in an uncomfortable over from Parker. Had this appeal been upheld, Yorkshire might have struggled just as much as their opponents. 'Sutcliffe stayed to demonstrate his greatness,' commented the *Yorkshire Post*. 'It was the defiance of his bat that hammered the heart out of the Gloucestershire bowling.' Sutcliffe was undefeated on 78. Leyland was equally resolute in defence, and the pair stole the initiative. Their partnership produced 107 runs in eighty minutes, and Yorkshire were victors by nine wickets.

Yorkshire were so far ahead of the rest that they were heralded as champions by the end of July. Their final points tally of 287 gave them a lead of 68 points over the second-placed Gloucestershire. The defiance of Douglas Jardine and Bob Wyatt denied Yorkshire's attempt to emulate the feat of their 1905 side in defeating the Rest of England at the Oval in September. Bowes and Verity bowled 71 overs between them at the cost of only 129 runs and shared eight wickets in the Rest's second innings. Duleepsinhji, Jardine, Wyatt, Hammond and Paynter, a formidable batting quintet, were all overthrown by the newly bonded Yorkshire bowlers, who were to dovetail their talents in a decade of peerless conquests. Jardine baulked Yorkshire with a century and one observer commented that only a player possessing his temperament and immaculate defence could have withstood the unceasing threat of the Yorkshire attack. Jardine proudly rode his luck after Arthur Wood had failed by a hairsbreadth to run him out. Jardine, cautiously playing forward, struck the ball on to his foot and momentarily lost his ground. Wood darted from behind the stumps to gather and scatter the bails and voiced a triumphant but unavailing appeal. Bob Wyatt, batting with a broken bone in his hand, was the heroic seventh-wicket partner in a stand with Jardine which yielded 128 runs.

With the match now out of Yorkshire's grasp, Jardine declared to allow Sutcliffe an hour to raise his season's aggregate to 3,000. He wanted 26 to reach the target, a task he approached with care. The milestone was duly reached with a drive for two runs, off a welcome full toss from Jupp. An on-drive for four by Sutcliffe then enabled him to beat his previous highest aggregate of 3,002, obtained in 1928. He thus headed the first-class averages for the second successive year and joined Ranjitsinhji, Tom Hayward, Mead and Hendren in twice scoring 3,000 runs in a season. His average of 96.96 in 42 innings exceeded the previous highest by an English player of 91.23 by Major R.M. Poore for Hampshire in 1899. Lord Hawke was among those who paid tribute to Sutcliffe's record in a rain-affected season. In the *Wisden* of 1932 Hawke reminisced about fifty years of Yorkshire cricket and dwelt upon the exemplary fitness of his colleague. 'Nobody I know trained, and trains, harder or more conscientiously than Sutcliffe. I ascribe much of his success to that fact.'

Sutcliffe's appetite for runs, often in circumstances which demanded vigilant technique, continued unabated in 1932. J.M. Kilburn wrote: 'Sutcliffe enjoyed a season that would have been remarkable once in a lifetime, but as it followed the magnificence of 1931 it approached the phenomenal.' In his thirty-eighth year Sutcliffe could have been excused for resting on his laurels. Instead, he remained the insatiable master in scoring 3,336 runs. The tally included fourteen centuries, five more than any other batsman in England; and his average of 74.13 gave him a lead of 15 runs over his nearest rival, Ernest Tyldesley in the national averages. Tyldesley, Ames and Hammond, all with notable aggregates, trailed him by more

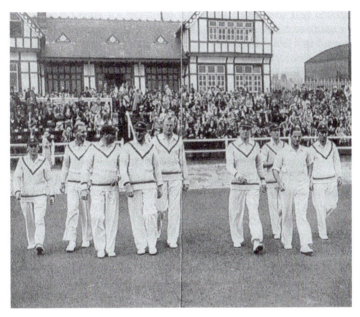

Jubilant Yorkshire: The Champions take the field at Park Avenue, Bradford. Pictured (left to right) are: Wilf Barber, Hedley Verity, Arthur Mitchell, Frank Smailes, Bill Bowes, Brian Sellers (captain), Leonard Hutton, Sutcliffe and Norman Yardley. (Herbert Witherington)

than 800 runs. In four innings in three consecutive matches Sutcliffe scored 777 runs.

Against Gloucestershire at Bradford he scored 132 to become the seventh batsmen to score 100 centuries in first-class cricket. The feat was acknowledged by the Yorkshire committee who granted him a sum of 100 guineas. They followed the example set by Surrey who made the same award to Jack Hobbs after he had reached this milestone.

Sutcliffe's 100th century, at Bradford, was one of the quickest and most dominating of his career. It was the centrepiece of a thrilling Yorkshire victory achieved in the final over of the match. In the first innings, Holmes and Sutcliffe had each scored over 80 in an opening stand of 161 and Mitchell was undefeated on 177 as Yorkshire totalled 472. Gloucestershire, with centuries by Sinfield and Hammond, were only 68 runs in arrears. Bev Lyon had before the start of the last day's play accurately prophesied the Yorkshire lead. He envisaged that the ball would begin to turn on a wearing wicket by mid-afternoon. He hoped that Yorkshire would have sufficient runs in hand to make a declaration and, as he put it, 'give us a chance of winning or losing the match'. Brian Sellers did make the declaration at three o'clock but neither he nor Lyon could have anticipated the fury of Sutcliffe's batting which made this possible, or that it would have led to such an extraordinary finale. The match, until the last fluctuating minutes, did appear to be dwindling to a draw.

'We felt that we had a chance of victory if we could get quick runs,' recalled Sutcliffe. 'But I know that when I started that second innings I never gave a thought to the likelihood of it producing my 100th hundred. Really, no one was more surprised than I was. I went for the bowling, found I could get runs, and simply went on scoring. I had expected to get out almost every over, but I had not cared about that because we were fighting to force a win.'

Sutcliffe reached his century out of 195 in an hour and three quarters. It included eight sixes and eight fours. He started with a couple of fours and two sixes off Hammond, following the fashion established by the Gloucestershire batsman in his rapacious century on the previous day. In the end his rate of scoring surpassed the belligerence of Hammond. Sutcliffe and Leyland, who was struggling with a leg injury, hit 107 in an hour. Leyland (58) was dismissed by Goddard at 164; but Sutcliffe did not slacken in his onslaught. There were four sixes off Parker, two before lunch and two afterwards and they included one into the adjacent football field to celebrate his century. 'Sutcliffe was hitting out as he had never done before,' reported the *Yorkshire Post*. 'He went on, gloriously sure of his power, to hit a ball from Sinfield into the terrace alongside the pavilion.' It was, said the report, probably the biggest and most exciting strike of a match of 19 sixes. With this tremendous blow Sutcliffe reached 132 out of a total of 240. A glorious running catch in the long field by Barnett off another towering hit ended Sutcliffe's superbly aggressive innings. 'He could not have completed his century of centuries in a more distinctive manner, and he could not have served his side better than he did,' added the *Yorkshire Post* correspondent.

Yorkshire's declaration followed Sutcliffe's dismissal. Macaulay, at his most antagonistic, then took up the challenge. Every ball he bowled from the football end expressed his belief that victory was possible. Macaulay took five wickets for 67 runs in 28 overs of unremitting effort. His grim resolution and skill changed the course of the game in a nerve-jangling twenty minutes. At a quarter to six there were still seven Gloucestershire wickets standing. The prospect of a finish seemed so remote that Bev Lyon, padded up for his innings, ran on to the field to suggest to Sellers that the match should be concluded. Sellers said: 'We will play on,' and Macaulay immediately bowled Dacre to end the stubborn fourth-wicket stand. At six o'clock Macaulay bowled Sinfield and Sellers claimed the extra half-hour. Lyon was lbw to Macaulay and the clock had moved on to five past six when Rogers was brilliantly caught by Sutcliffe, leaping high, at mid-off to accept the chance off Verity. Five minutes later Watkins played on to Verity's faster ball and, in the same over, Parker was defeated by his opposing left-hander. Five wickets had fallen in ten minutes and victory, unimagined half-an-hour before, was now tantalisingly within Yorkshire's reach.

Hammond was, however, still there, composed and assured. 'No longer was his bat an attacking weapon of the finest forging; it was the defensive shield which threatened to rob

Yorkshire of the triumph that the militant Macaulay's work had brought so near,' reported the *Yorkshire Post*. Goddard, encircled by an intimidatory ring of six close fieldsmen, now resisted Verity. Hammond was precise and certain against the predatory Macaulay. Over after over ticked by as did the big hand on the clock on the football stand. It moved nearer and nearer to 6.30. Then came Macaulay's last over of the day. Hammond desperately tried to obtain a single off the last ball; it was slung down fast on the legside and the batsman spun round to it, overbalanced and was almost stumped.

At twenty-seven minutes past six, Sellers won the match with a bold, inspired decision. He picked up the ball and strolled reflectively to the pavilion end and called for Bowes. As Bowes removed his sweater, Hammond walked up the pitch to talk urgently to Goddard. Bowes approached the crease in his casually deceptive style and released the perfect yorker. Goddard struck out feverishly but late, and the ball, swinging fractionally, just grazed the outside of the off-stump to topple the bails. Yorkshire had recorded a remarkable victory on the stroke of time. Hammond 71 not out, was combative until the end. He could only look on, pensively surveying the wreckage caused by bowlers who had triumphed against the odds. For Herbert Sutcliffe, so often cast in the role of the prudent helmsman, his whirlwind innings at Bradford was a daring tour-de-force. He was to show a cavalier spirit belying his veteran status on other occasions in this vintage season.

'The marvel of Sutcliffe grows,' wrote Kilburn, 'and at such a pace that those who keep their eyes on records, as well as the field of play, are left dumbfounded, wondering what this man, who is entitled to rank as the most perfect scoring machine the game has known, is going to do next.' The men of Essex, hapless against his might on a famous field at Leyton, would soon be able to give their own rueful answer to this question.

11

555 at Leyton

'By heck, Herbert, if it hadn't been for my bad back, we'd have brayed 'em.'

Percy Holmes

The record first-wicket stand against Derbyshire at Chesterfield was to last thirty-four years before it was overtaken by Percy Holmes and Herbert Sutcliffe. John Tunnicliffe, the upright and feted man of Pudsey, did not exactly revel in his run feast at Chesterfield. His was a stupendous display of endurance which would have driven all but the strongest of men to exhaustion. Tunnicliffe persevered on an empty stomach to achieve the distinction of his cricketing lifetime.

Before his magnificent stand with Jack Brown he had spent a sleepless night in what was described as a 'dirty inn' at Leeds, where he was reluctant to take his rest in a damp bed. Next morning he was in such a haste to catch his train that he left without partaking of breakfast. At lunch on this August day in 1898 he was more hungry for food than runs. He had had nothing to eat but a biscuit since the previous night. In

common with other Yorkshire professionals at the turn of the
century, he also had to make his own catering arrangements.
With remarkable forbearance, he confessed himself lucky to
grab a twopenny sandwich to ease his famine. The food stalls
had been besieged by supporters, seeking to appease their own
appetites before returning to their seats to witness the record
accomplishment at Chesterfield.

Tunnicliffe must have been amazingly fit to withstand the
faintness which afflicted him during his long innings. The
vigour of his batsmanship was, however, unchecked as he
and Brown unfurled their strokes. Weary as he was, and his
later recollections confirmed this as a fact, it was the severely
mauled Derbyshire attack which showed the greater distress.
A tea break was requested at five o'clock by the home captain,
S.H. Evershed. A.W Pullin, the Yorkshire historian, with a nice
irony, said the request was prompted by mutually humanitar-
ian motives. The match had so far diminished as a contest that
a pause was required for everyone to renew their energies.

Tunnicliffe described his feelings in an interview with
Pullin. 'I hardly knew how I kept my end up. Whether it was
the tea, or the stoppage, I don't know, but I felt that I should
like to be out as quickly as possible. But it so happened that I
was still in when play closed. We had scored about 500 and, of
course, the record had long been passed. I went to my hotel,
tired out, and, having half an hour to wait for tea, before I
knew anything I was as fast asleep as a tired man could be.'
A refreshed Tunnicliffe went out on the following morning,
armed with instructions from Lord Hawke, the Yorkshire captain, to 'hit and get out'. 'Jack and I followed the instructions
so literally,' said Tunnicliffe, 'that in a quarter of an hour we
added 51 runs, and then I was caught by Davidson.'

The record partnership of 554 by Tunnicliffe and Brown
at Chesterfield was achieved in a week of high scoring.
'The wildest imagination could scarcely have framed at the

beginning of the week anything so sensational as what actually happened,' commented a writer in the *Cricket* magazine. In ten matches nearly 7,000 runs were scored. Yorkshire and Surrey each topped 600 in an innings and Surrey and Middlesex also raised totals of 534 and 484. Tom Hayward and Bobby Abel were the leaders in the swarm of runs at the Oval against Lancashire and Kent. Hayward's 315 coincided with Brown's 300 for Yorkshire, and Abel and Tunnicliffe registered scores of 219 and 243. Hayward's triple century was the highest by a professional in first-class cricket; and Brown became the only player, apart from W.G. Grace, with three scores over 300, to twice exceed this figure. In this series of big innings the rate of scoring reflected the view of one commentator, who said when a match had to be won 'the quicker and more risky style of play is infinitely the better'. Brown, positively scampering along at 58 runs an hour, was closely followed by Tunnicliffe and Hayward (48 and 47). The trio all demonstrated the value of adventurous play.

Yorkshire's monumental achievement at Chesterfield had been preceded by a sharp rebuff for the champion county, administered by Middlesex at Leeds. Yorkshire were dismissed for 45 on a sticky wicket at Headingley. Tunnicliffe, with 31, was the only batsman able to resist the wiles of J.T. Hearne and Albert Trott. Middlesex were set a target of 60 runs and won by eight wickets.

Derbyshire, as Yorkshire's next opponents, were thus placed in an unenviable position. They had to contend with a team seeking to make amends after the rout at Leeds. One writer, in relating the events at Chesterfield, said Derbyshire had often been the 'sport of fortune' but had never undergone such an experience as that which befell them against Yorkshire. 'Never has a blow quite so crushing been struck against the most unfortunate of counties, as to be beaten by an innings and 387 runs, which might easily have been 800 had time allowed.'

In the previous season Tunnicliffe and Brown had shared a
first wicket partnership of 378 against Sussex at Sheffield. It
had been swiftly superseded by Abel and Brockwell for Surrey
against Hampshire at the Oval. At Chesterfield the Yorkshire
openers were resolved to build an unchallengeable total. By
half-past four on the first afternoon they had advanced past
the Surrey record. They continued to flay the Derbyshire
attack to reach 503 by close of play. The dimensions of the
tiny Chesterfield ground, with its invitingly short boundaries, were an incentive for sustained aggression. The stand
had, in the context of the innings, a relatively modest start.
'The two professionals played themselves in quietly,' said one
observer. The quiet progression resulted in 50 runs in the first
three-quarters of an hour in the morning. 'From this time the
bowling was quite collared and the runs came with alarm-
ing rapidity,' continued the correspondent. The first 100 was
obtained in an hour and fifteen minutes; the 200 was hoisted
after another hour; the 300 was passed in five minutes under
three hours; and the record 554 occupied only just over five
hours. Yorkshire actually scored at the rate of 109 runs an hour.

Brown, who knocked down his wicket as soon as he reached
300, was the more massive in his dominance, befitting a man
who had played in eight Tests against Australia. But Tunnicliffe,
if he did lag behind his partner, was, it should be remembered, heroically stifling the pangs of hunger. Derbyshire used
ten bowlers in a vain bid to stem the Yorkshire bombardment.
William Chatterton, excused the chore because of an injury, was
more able to find humour in his team's plight. He was reputed
to have sent a telegram to his family containing the wry message: 'We are confidently expecting a wicket any day now.'

John Tunnicliffe, in his retirement in Gloucestershire,
lived to see the dislocation of what had seemed an unassailable record. His was one of the first tributes to be received
by Holmes and Sutcliffe when the Yorkshire pair hoisted new

record figures against Essex at Leyton in June, 1932. Tunnicliffe did not forget his own association with Jack Brown. He also offered the blessings of his long departed partner.

The Yorkshire triumph, as in 1898, followed hard upon another assault on their dignity by Kent at Tonbridge. Yorkshire needed only 67 in their second innings to win, and, as Bill Bowes related: 'With our galaxy of batting talent, it seemed absurdly easy.' Rhodes, Wood, Macaulay, Verity and Bowes, the last five men in the order, had actually changed and were walking towards the exit when the debacle began. Sutcliffe was brilliantly caught by Chapman at silly mid-off off Freeman and six wickets went down for 32 runs. 'In one of the biggest cricket scrambles ever,' said Bowes, 'Arthur Wood and Rhodes, with their cricket shirts and trousers hastily pulled over their normal dress, were required to make the last 35 runs to give Yorkshire victory.' A chastened Yorkshire moved on to Leyton, where Essex might have expected a drubbing but not as devastating as proved to be the case.

The Essex bowlers were widely regarded in the 1930s as a band of cheerful stoics whose suffering often crossed reasonable bounds. They were infuriatingly unpredictable. After being hammered into oblivion, they did, without apparent reason, transform themselves into avenging spitfires to overwhelm their betters. One such occasion was against Yorkshire at Huddersfield in 1935. Morris Nichols and Douglas Read shared the wickets as Yorkshire were bowled out for 31. It was their lowest total for twenty-six years and the sensation of the season. Wood was top scorer with 13 and no one else reached double figures. Yorkshire's last six wickets fell for just nine runs. The young Leonard Hutton, batting at no.7, twice failed to score in the game. It must have been an unnerving county baptism for him. It was a commanding match for Nichols who hit 146 as well as taking 11 wickets for 54 runs. Yorkshire were dismissed for 99 when they followed on; and Essex won by an innings and 204 runs. The match was over by one o'clock on the second day. Doug Insole recalled that a high percentage of Yorkshire's first-innings runs were of the fortuitous, edged variety. Herbert Sutcliffe whose personal tally in the match was five runs, felt it might have been worse. In a cricket paradox, which needs no explanation, he said: 'If we'd played really well, we would have been lucky to have scored 20.'

In their jubilation at Huddersfield, Essex must have regarded the victory as just after the humiliation of three forlorn days in 1932. They were of such sorrow as to daunt even their resilient spirits. On a perfect wicket at the Oval before the Leyton record, they had been tormented by Jack Hobbs at his incomparable best. Hobbs scored a century, as did Gregory, and the Surrey pair compiled a partnership of 232 runs without being defeated. After this wearying experience, the Essex bowlers had earned a rest; but the toss was in Yorkshire's favour, and they set out again on what proved to be another hopeless quest. The thought of tackling Holmes and Sutcliffe on a fast-scoring wicket after a fruitless day in opposition to Hobbs was a fearful prospect. They had just one opportunity to break the stand. In the third over of the day Holmes offered a sharp but unaccepted chance to Sheffield behind the wicket off Nichols. There were no further lapses; and the resolution of the veteran Yorkshire openers, so assured in their understanding, directed them towards their last great conquest.

Holmes, then in his forty-fourth year, had to draw upon all his reserves of stamina; but his unfaltering feet still matched Sutcliffe stride for stride in their running between the wickets. As he was handicapped from the start by a severe attack of lumbago, each step towards the record was accompanied by stabbing pains. Holmes made light of his ordeal, as he did in later years, when racked by debilitating arthritis. Then he told Sutcliffe's son, Bill: 'I've got more pains than they have panes of glass at Buckingham Palace.' A lesser man might have

looked for sympathy after pounding between the wickets at
Leyton. But he could still find humour in his plight. 'By heck,
Herbert,' he said, 'if it hadn't been for my bad back, we'd have
brayed 'em.'

Sutcliffe remembered the pluck of his partner:

Holmes said he would be hard put to get going. I saw him
settle and stay, and I marvelled, for it was easy to tell that
many of his strokes were causing him acute pain. There was,
in fact, every excuse for Percy, when he had scored 50 or so
and given the side a lead, having a bang. But he stuck it out
until the end.

At the end of the first day the Leyton crowd were dazed by
the ease with which the Essex bowling had been trounced.
The Yorkshire total was 423 for 0, Holmes 180 and Sutcliffe
231. After tea 112 runs were scored in an hour, including 74
from the bat of Sutcliffe, who struck ten boundaries in one terrific spell of hitting. The Yorkshire pair's seventieth three-figure
stand was the highest and most memorable of them all, exceeding their previous best of 347 against Hampshire in 1920.

M.A. Tanfield, writing in *The Cricketer*, adopted a slightly
critical stance. He said the circumstances were completely
propitious for batsmen. 'The wicket was as true and easy as
it could possibly be, and Essex, truth to tell, have bowling
resources that are apt to be stretched by a long stand.' Tanfield
felt that Holmes and Sutcliffe displayed unnecessary caution in
the early stages of the partnership:

Smith, the slow leg-break bowler, was allowed to bowl for
over two hours without a man out straight; and it was not
until five o'clock that Sutcliffe first played the mashie-nib-
lick shot over the bowler's head. On such a perfect wicket
there was absolutely no risk in the stroke, and Smith, as

The scorecard of the Leyton match. (R.D. Wilkinson)

well as he bowled, overpitched many balls that asked to
be driven.

The ultimate triumph was, though, the sternest test ever faced
by Yorkshire's champions. By the next day a massive, expectant
crowd, including a film camera crew, had descended upon the
Leyton ground. 'We had to push our way through enthusiastic well-wishers, while in the dressing-room there was a huge
pile of letters and telegrams urging us, nay, insisting upon us,
breaking the record,' said Sutcliffe. One Hull man, after hear-
ing the overnight score, was impelled to travel south to watch
the historic feat. Sutcliffe considered this a wonderful tribute,
but he did not share the optimism of the Yorkshire traveller.
'A day's batting tells on the best-trained man. There is a stiff-
ness and a tired feeling for quite 48 hours afterwards.' Sutcliffe
said he would not have given twopence for their chances of
overtaking the record. Pelham Warner also acknowledged the
onerous demands placed upon the Yorkshire batsmen. 'Most
people hardly realise the strain, physical and mental, involved
in making a huge score. Apart from running some four miles
at top speed, encumbered with pads and bats, Holmes and
Sutcliffe had to exercise an unrelenting concentration of
which many great batsmen are incapable.'

Over the years, the hysteria over the missing run and the
convenient discovery of a no-ball has prompted the persistent and mischievous thought that the record was not actually
broken at Leyton. At ten minutes to one, when the score stood
at 547, Sutcliffe struck two fours off consecutive balls from
Eastman which seemed to have sealed the issue. 'The last quarter of an hour of the effort had been an overwhelming affair,'
wrote Sutcliffe. 'With the goal reached, I simply forgot everything to lash out in the best country style at the next ball. It
was pitched well outside my off-stump, but I managed to pull
it into my wicket and thereupon Sellers, our captain, declared.'

Wisden reported that Sutcliffe threw his wicket away with a 'rather casual stroke' and disapprovingly added that 'some of the circumstances surrounding the Leyton achievement were not quite desirable owing to the scorers being unable to see what was exhibited on the scoreboard'. One Yorkshire newspaper described it as a 'perturbing mishap' and another writer regretted that Sutcliffe had not put the matter beyond doubt with another four. He said the subsequent controversy about the total 'rather bore out the wisdom of such a measure'. Sutcliffe's rash stroke was, to be fair, an indication of his relaxed concentration and his joy at the apparent breaking of the record. He had faced Eastman in a final over which taxed his patience. Each ball, delivered well outside the off-stump, posed the question: 'fetch or leave 'em'. Sutcliffe stepped across to successive balls to pull them mightily to the square-leg boundary. He raised his bat with a sigh of satisfaction.

Before the target was reached both batsmen had glanced repeatedly and anxiously at the scoreboard. Sutcliffe had no reason to doubt the authenticity of the record figures, but his later response rather compounded his error in an admittedly nerve-racking situation. He should have anticipated the impending declaration. Yet surprisingly, for a normally precise man, he said that if he had realised that a declaration was to be made at the end of the over, he would have tried to carry his bat.

The scoreboard did deceive to Sutcliffe's anger; the total had reverted to '554' when he and Holmes came out to be greeted by a battery of photographers. The changed figures were roundly condemned as a falsehood by the *Yorkshire Post*:

> It was a piece of confusion, which set the stage for a tragic happening, almost beyond contemplation. Hundreds of spectators besieged the scorebox demanding to know whether the record had been broken or merely equalled.

The scorers checked their books and announced, after a considerable interval, that a no-ball from Daer had been overlooked and the total, after all, was a record-breaking one.

In the years of his retirement, Sutcliffe recalled his horror at the events and how the record had so nearly eluded him. Perhaps that was why Leonard Hutton received what he described as 'Herbert's famous black look', when he failed to support his senior in another attempt to convincingly break the record. The Leyton miscalculation still rankled in Sutcliffe's memory. Billy Ringrose, the Yorkshire scorer and a stickler for accuracy, was on duty in 1932. He was at first adamant that the score according to his book was 554 for 1. He would not accept the discovered no-ball until the fact had been checked with the umpire who had called it and the bowler who had bowled it. 'Tiger' Smith was the umpire who verified that the missing run was conceded in the first over of the match bowled by Daer to Holmes. He said that he received a signal of acknowledgement from Ringrose in the scorer's box. Tom Pearce, the former Essex captain, recalled that his county scorer, Charlie McGahey liked a drink and was known to absent himself from the box as a matter of urgency after partaking of liberal refreshments during play. So it is probable that McGahey was otherwise engaged, and Ringrose, in charge of two books, failed to record the vital run. The traces of the alterations in the Yorkshire scorebook are visible to this day. *Wisden* restrained its doubts about the achievement when it said: 'Whether the record was, or not beaten, there could be no question that the batsmen, had they not felt assured they had beaten it, could have put on heaps more runs.' The first-wicket stand was not the only record broken in the match. Sutcliffe's 313, including one six and 33 fours, was the highest of his career. Holmes had 19 fours in his score of 224. The Yorkshire partnership on the larger Leyton ground lasted seven hours and twenty-five minutes, more than two hours longer than the time taken by Tunnicliffe and Brown at Chesterfield.

Essex used eight bowlers during the record innings. Three of them, Nichols (105), Daer (106) and Peter Smith (138), conceded more than 100 runs. Their batsmen were also as ineffective against the Yorkshire bowlers as their bowlers had been against Holmes and Sutcliffe. They simply wilted under the weight of runs facing them. Hedley Verity, in another remarkable feat on a still perfect wicket, took five wickets for eight runs in seven overs. Essex were dismissed for 78 in a little over two hours. Nichols salvaged some pride with a brave half-century in the follow-on, but Yorkshire won by the towering margin of an innings and 313 runs. Holmes and Sutcliffe, the happiest of companions in their fourteenth season together, had scaled what seemed an impossibly high peak. They had defied logic in breaking a safe, almost sacrosanct record. The Yorkshire committee presented two of the balls hammered at Leyton to the two batsmen. They were circled with inscribed bands of silver, bearing the details of the feat, and mounted on sets of silver stumps. There were other mementoes to mark their great achievement. For Holmes there was a gold cigarette case, decorated with a white rose, and a gold watch for Sutcliffe. Bill Bowes remembered an amusing sequel to the record at Leyton. 'Almost as delighted with the score as the Yorkshire batsmen were a firm of cigarette manufacturers who made a brand of cigarettes corresponding in name to the Sutcliffe–Holmes total. They sent a whole crate of cigarettes to the Yorkshire dressing-room and the team smoked themselves silly.'

Herbert Sutcliffe was at his most magisterial in 1932, earning the accolade of the maestro in the Yorkshire ranks. He was also, as someone said, in the pink of condition. He could not have thrived so buoyantly had his strength and vitality deserted him. The power of his batting has rarely been equalled. Twice he scored 1,000 runs in a month, 1,193 in

Sutcliffe making the stroke off Eastman which established the new record.
(MCC)

June and 1,006 in August. After the marathon at Leyton he
scored 96 and 110 not out for the North against the South at
Old Trafford followed by 258 against Sussex at Leeds. In seven
days he brought his aggregate to 777 runs, and he was on
the field for all except forty minutes at Manchester. Between
June 15 and 22 Sutcliffe more than doubled his season's tally
to achieve an aggregate of 1,532 runs at an average of 102.13.
In making these scores, Sutcliffe surpassed the record of 758
runs by the Australian, Charles Macartney. Macartney, in
successive innings in 1921, hit 105 against Hampshire, 193
against Northamptonshire, 345 against Nottinghamshire, and
115 against England at Leeds. His triumph covered a period
of fifteen playing days.

Sutcliffe rejoiced in the sunshine at Scarborough in August to inflict yet more punishment on the sorely tried Essex. The match was played in a heatwave and one spectator remembered how the East coast holidaymakers, or at least those not intent on cricket, sought the sanctuary of shade beneath the trees in Peasholm Park. 'Sutcliffe made the innings into a glorious holiday, throwing aside with a wave of his bat the stern realities of championship cricket, and the spectators were happy with him,' reported the *Yorkshire Post*. Bill Bowes chose the match as the most memorable of his distinguished career:

> I never took ten wickets in any innings but on the first day I had nine for 121. One of the quirks was that O'Connor, the batsman who got away, was dropped off my bowling. Horace Fisher claimed him, caught by Herbert Sutcliffe.
>
> The wicket was in such magnificent shape that Essex scored 325 on the first day and Yorkshire were batting in the last half an hour. I bowled 40 overs in tremendous heat. There were times when I felt as though I was bowling on my hands and knees. That night I got cramp so often that I spent most of the time lying on a cold oilcloth on the floor of my room. I was sharing the room with Arthur Rhodes (another aspiring pace bowler). Arthur said: 'I had no idea this is what happened to fast bowlers. I would not have had your job today for £1,000.'

The *Yorkshire Post* said that Bowes bowled well enough to have dismissed two sides on a gruelling day. 'At the start he was beating the bat, and at the close, after his grilling in the sun, he must have welcomed the cooling breeze that came in the late afternoon of this glorious August day. Bowes was still beating the bat without having much luck.'

The writer said it was difficult to imagine how Yorkshire would have fared if Bowes, in that wonderful way of his, had not been able to whip himself up for one whole hearted effort after another. In an hour and a half after tea Bowes bowled unchanged from the Trafalgar Square end and took the last five wickets. He finished the innings by having Taylor, one of two Essex centurions, caught by Leyland at square-leg.

Essex, without a thought for the consequences, ended the day with a fierce bombardment of the Yorkshire batsmen. Mitchell and Verity, as the openers and later Fisher, grimly battled against a bumper onslaught by Farnes and Nichols. Sutclilfe, held in reserve for the following day, looked on from the pavilion, quietly contemplating his response.

Maurice Leyland was Sutcliffe's partner in the exhilarating counter-attack. He was remarkably overshadowed by the ferocity of Sutcliffe's hitting. The stand began sedately with 100 in five minutes over two hours. Sutcliffe then put Essex to the sword with a ruthlessness which reduced one of his hapless rivals, Ken Farnes, to tears. Of the 239 runs added by Yorkshire in the two hours between lunch and tea, Sutcliffe scored 156. In 40 minutes he hit 94 runs.

It was a salutary lesson for Farnes, the promising recruit in the earlier Test trial at Cardiff. There was a warning for him in the fact that 18 runs had been hit off Nichols when the Essex bowler took the new ball. Farnes was Nichols' replacement at the Trafalgar Square end. What followed was an astonishing annihilation. Twenty-one runs were taken off Farnes' first over, 19 off the second, 16 off the third, and ten off his fourth over. In six consecutive overs 102 runs were scored and Farnes conceded 75 of them. Sutcliffe hit three fours off successive balls and two sixes in another over from Farnes. Leyland, occupying an unusually subdued role for him, contributed only 45 in the whirlwind attack which put on 149 runs for the fourth wicket in fifty-five minutes. Ron Burnet recalled the monstrous power of Sutcliffe's hooking at Scarborough. 'Some feeling had built up and Sutcliffe and Leyland decided to go for Farnes, the upstart if you like, on that day.' Burnet later asked Leyland how many he had scored at the height of the rampage. Maurice replied: '16. I only had four balls – that's all Herbert left me – and I hooked each one of them for four.'

Sutcliffe himself recalled the barrage of short deliveries, waged on both sides, which precipitated his violent innings. One of the Essex players had told Bowes: 'Bounce 'em as much as you like, Bill; we've brought someone to bounce 'em too.' The jest – it could hardly have been a threat against Yorkshire – sadly misfired. Farnes and Nichols were the bowlers deputed to retaliate and find consolation after the havoc at Leyton. Sutcliffe, for whom the bouncing ball might have been invented, was in ominous mood. Sutcliffe said:

> Without saying a word to one another of our intentions, Maurice and I adopted the same tactics. We let go and it came off for us. We felt that our hooking and driving, some of which I have to admit was a little too daring, had been rewarded. Of course, it was a sheer 'blind'. On another day Farnes would have had our wickets before we got going. Reckless efforts such as these only come off once in fifty times.

Bob Wyatt was more inclined to savour Sutcliffe in a less dashing mode. 'Herbert's main shot when he was going for the runs was to hit the ball from outside the off-stump over mid-on,' he said.

Sutcliffe was missed twice, once by the rueful Farnes, before he opened his shoulders at Scarborough. These were crucial lapses; the later escapes came when he was hitting out off nearly every ball. Cutmore, on the square-leg boundary, ought to have taken a catch off Farnes when Sutcliffe was 115. The ball dropped out of the fieldsman's hands and went for four. Then, when Sutcliffe's score was 137, Nichols ran back from second slip and just failed to hold on to a skied catch. At 181, Cutmore, out at long-on, had yet another opportunity to check Sutcliffe's gallop but his nervous hands were unequal to the task. Sutcliffe, going for another six to complete his double century, was just short with another towering drive to long-on, and Pope gratefully took the catch. Sutcliffe's 194 (out of 292) in two and three-quarter hours, included three sixes and 20 fours. He had produced a cushion of runs for another innings victory and raised his total to 507 in two innings against Essex.

Bill Bowes provided an interesting postscript to the batting revel at Scarborough. He had words of counsel for Ken Farnes after the match:

> In the evening I met Ken on the Spa. He was in tears. He said: 'I shall never be any good as a fast bowler.' I cheered him as best I could by saying that he would not if he bowled bouncers at batsmen of the calibre of Sutcliffe and Leyland.

Bowes sternly advised his future England colleague to use them against other counties.

In June 1933, Sutcliffe enjoyed another heady day of six-hitting against Northamptonshire at Kettering. He delighted, as Gerald Brodribb neatly put it, in 'a parade of balls rocketing high into the blue sky.' It followed a rare deviation from the normal routine of retiring early before a match. During the previous winter Herbert and his wife, Emmie, had promised to attend a ball at Cambridge. 'Let's make a night of it for a change', suggested Emmie before the engagement. She pointed out that he had not been doing very well, even when he was going to bed early. Emmie emphatically declared that Herbert would make a hundred on the following day. It was an invigorating occasion. Sutcliffe stayed at the dance until it finished and then pleaded with his friends for release. He went to bed at four in the morning and awoke completely refreshed four hours later. The scene at Kettering dashed his high spirits. Rain had produced a sticky wicket which would pose problems even for a batsman who had had a proper night's rest. He was reprieved, at least for the next dramatic hour, by the decision of the Northamptonshire captain, W.C. Brown to bat first after winning the toss. He had, with the exception of Vallance Jupp, negligible bowling resources, nor the batting strength to withstand the spin of Verity and Macaulay. Sutcliffe was pleased with the decision because he felt that a 'preliminary canter in the field' would do him no harm after the previous night's festivities.

The morning exercise did not last long as Northamptonshire were dismissed for 27 in an hour and a quarter. It was the lowest total against Yorkshire since 1922 when Sussex were routed for 20 by Abe Waddington at Hull. A brilliant sun blazed down on the pitch and Macaulay and Verity prospered against batsmen who had little faith in themselves. 'The fame of the Yorkshire bowlers is such this season, in which almost every day has its own sensational piece of work, that sides are beaten before they take the field against them,' commented the *Yorkshire Post*. Macaulay conceded four runs and spent seven overs before taking a wicket. He then flung himself into a round-the-wicket attack and took seven wickets for nine runs in 14 overs. Verity bowled eight maidens in 13 overs and gathered the remaining three wickets.

Yorkshire's reply was not instantly commendable. They lost three wickets for 20 runs before lunch and it ought to have been four because Leyland was twice missed off Matthews. Sutcliffe did not linger in confusion. He announced his intentions on the resumption of play. He recalled:

> The wicket was getting no better and so I set out for a terrific bang. Every hit was from the best driving part of the bat. My century was reached in as many minutes and, when

it was all over, I found to my amazement that I had hit ten sixes. The stand on the low side of the ground was conveniently near, and somehow it seemed that I just had to lift the ball over it.

Sutcliffe did find the attractions of the short boundary on the legside irresistible. 'He decided that it was no use wasting time on fours when Jupp was bowling, and went for sixes. It was a procedure which justified the employment of a groundsman behind the side stand,' reported the *Yorkshire Post*. The innings had a special relish for Sutcliffe since the main victim of his big hitting was one of his former jinx bowlers, Vallance Jupp, the England off-spinner. Sutcliffe was reminded of his discomfort against Jupp who had tested him at the Oval during his pursuit of the second triple thousand of his career in 1931. 'I had to face him on a wicket that was responsive to spin. I never had to struggle so hard for runs in my life. I thought almost every ball that Jupp's off-break would account for me, and I believe that Jupp thought the same too.' The best part of the Kettering episode came at the end of the first day's play. Before he left the ground Sutcliffe received messages of congratulations from his friends at the Cambridge party. One of the first he opened was from his wife. Emmie wrote: 'Told you so – what a prophet!'

The record stand against Essex at Leyton in 1932 was the last of the major batting duets by Holmes and Sutcliffe. They had shared 74 century partnerships, including 69 for Yorkshire in an illustrious association. Holmes' overall tally of 67 centuries has only been exceeded by five other Yorkshiremen: Sutcliffe, Denton, Hutton, Leyland and Boycott. Towards the end of the 1932 season Holmes stood down with a knee injury which had become so painful that he had to retire during the match against Leicestershire. A subsequent operation failed to completely alleviate the problem. His form was still excellent until the time of his collapse. He scored 1,191 runs in 25 innings at an average of 47.64.

'The knee has concerned him throughout this season in which he has struggled with characteristic cheerfulness against the worst of luck,' reported the *Yorkshire Post* in 1933. 'At times there has been in his play the crispness, the sureness and the scoring readiness of the old Holmes, but always something has gone wrong to keep his footsteps off the path to recovery.' In his farewell season, Holmes played 50 innings, not one of which contained a century, and he scored only 929 runs.

In August, Yorkshire announced that they had decided not to re-engage Holmes after the end of the season. He was accorded a grant of £250 and the Yorkshire membership was asked to join the committee in wishing a great cricket servant many years of happiness and good health. Holmes felt that he had been prematurely discarded. He believed that after a winter's rest he would have been restored in fitness and able to hold his place in the Yorkshire team for a few more seasons. Sutcliffe also considered that the county committee had acted too hastily. A report in the Yorkshire yearbook for 1934 reflected the disbelief in the county ranks at the decline of Holmes. 'With much sorrow does one refer to the doings of Percy Holmes, who fell so far short of his high estate as clearly to suggest that in his forty-seventh year his powers had left him.' Holmes was undaunted by the parting of ways with Yorkshire. He placed a small advertisement in the *Yorkshire Post*. His jaunty message read: 'Percy Holmes, first wicket batsman for Yorkshire. Too fit and too young to retire. Engagements required for the coming season.'

Holmes did find employment as a cricket scout before taking up professional appointments at Ebbw Vale and Swansea. He later spent twelve years as a coach at Scarborough College until his retirement at the age of seventy. In 1969, he was belatedly elected an honorary life member of Yorkshire. As a player, who had flourished with untrammelled footwork, he was scathing of modern batsmen. 'How do they think they're going to make runs if they don't move into the right position,' he told one interviewer. He added:

> They don't seem to want to put bat to ball any more. They just prod at it as if they think it is going to come up and bite them. To me, the idea of the game was simple enough. A ball was something you tried to hit. A bat was something you were given to hit it with.

His old eyes sparkled as he recalled the duels of other years with Larwood and McDonald at Trent Bridge and Old Trafford. Percy never flinched against two of the most merciless of fast bowlers on the fiercest of wickets. He lifted one of his crutches in a demonstration of the old defiance. 'I'd give a bob each to those they duck away from now,' he said.

12

The Imperturbable Maestro

'There have been scores of better looking batsmen, but very few better players.'

Ian Peebles

His attitude was to live above the average and his self-possession in all circumstances was the keynote of his life. The ripples of doubt, which furrowed the brows of other great batsmen, were scorned by Herbert Sutcliffe. His peace of mind was rarely disturbed.

Sutcliffe's overriding asset as a cricketer was his indomitable temperament. He was so perfectly equipped as an opening batsman that he easily defeated all competition. Les Ames, remembering his own nervousness at the start of an innings, marvelled at the ease and deportment of his England colleague. 'Nothing worried Herbert. He never gave the impression that he was the slightest bit on edge.'

'His mind always seemed to rule his body,' wrote Sir Kenneth Parkinson, the former Yorkshire president. 'This enabled him to survive those difficult periods, where lesser men failed. That was the difference between him and other first-class cricketers; not that he could score runs but that he could do it in almost any conditions.'

Sutcliffe's career spanned the years between the wars, and he graced every one of those seasons with accomplishment. His records flowed lavishly like the bequests of a millionaire. He did not have a prolonged period of failure. In twenty-one years he scored 50,138 runs (average 51.95) and hit 149 centuries, including 112 for Yorkshire. Only six other batsmen (Hobbs, Woolley, Hendren, Mead, Grace and Hammond) have scored more runs. In Test cricket, in completed innings, his scoring rate gave him a hundred in each four and a half innings he played. Only Bradman was faster, with centuries every two and a half innings. In 1919, Sutcliffe scored 1,839, the highest aggregate by a batsman in his first season and he was the only player to register more than 1,000 runs in every season up to the Second World War. He passed 2,000 runs in 14 consecutive seasons. Three times, in 1928, 1931 and 1932, he scored more than 3,000 runs. Sutcliffe's county aggregate of 38,558 (50.20) is the highest for a Yorkshire player. His Test average is the highest for an Englishman. He is only surpassed by Don Bradman (99.94) Graeme Pollock (60.97) and George Headley (60.83). Sutcliffe scored 4,555 runs in 54 Tests and his average of 60.73 was eight runs above his overall first-class average. Significantly, he achieved an average of 66.85 against Australia, the true yardstick governing the mettle of international batsmen in his time.

Sutcliffe's monumental achievements would seem to automatically elevate him to cricket's peerage. Yet, by some quirk of contemporary judgement, he is often rated inferior to those who flamboyantly succeeded him in the England batting order. It has been said that he felt slighted by the criticism. He was not a batting plagiarist. He had a style all his own and was proud of it. His role was to dent the thrust of the new ball and enable others to profit from the legacy handed down to them. The responsibility he shouldered as an opening batsman has received less than full acknowledgement. The criticism levelled at him is that he was not 'box office' in the manner of Hammond, Woolley and Hendren. On the Test stage Sutcliffe was a severely practical performer. He had long since chained the extravagance which had excited supporters in his youth.

Bob Wyatt, one of the Yorkshireman's most fervent admirers, considered that Sutcliffe garnered his massive total of runs because he played within his ability. This view, though, neglects to take account of the burden carried by Sutcliffe as England's anchor man. Wyatt himself provided evidence to refute his qualification. He remembered a conversation with C.B. Fry, who said that he had as many as a dozen strokes during his time at Oxford. In Test cricket, said Fry, he limited himself to two of them, which went in different directions. 'That was why he [Fry] was so successful,' explained Wyatt. Sutcliffe was equally circumspect and this may have been the reason for the guarded praise of a consistently successful batsman.

Ian Peebles perhaps came closest to solving the puzzle of a player, who was idolised in Yorkshire but so often misprized in other quarters. 'There have been scores, maybe hundreds, of better looking batsmen than Sutcliffe; but there have been very few better players,' he said. Peebles believed that one of Sutcliffe's greatest attributes was an unerring assessment of line and length, which made him a hard man to beat in the air. This aspect of Sutcliffe's play was also admired by Cyril Walters, the elegant Worcestershire batsman, who opened with him for England after Hobbs' retirement. Walters said: 'Herbert was a superb judge of the ball outside the off-stump. He could gauge it to a margin of three or four inches.' Walters described this ability as a 'matter of geography':

He knew exactly where he was on the map. It was quite extraordinary. I used to think: 'What a nerve.' Herbert would lift his bat high in the air as if to say to the bowler: 'You don't really expect me to put a bat on that.' He was going to make runs and not be foolish. He was always in control on and off the field.

Sutcliffe, like Hutton after him, developed to a high degree the art of loosening the lower hand in order to reduce the risk of an edged ball carrying to the slips. Bob Wyatt described Sutcliffe as a 'great watcher of the ball off the wicket. He never played the pitch, as so many players do, especially on the forward stroke. He saw the ball right on to his bat.' Wyatt was also impressed by Sutcliffe's judgement of length, which he considered as the main art of a great batsman.

Stuart Surridge provided an example of Sutcliffe's composure in a match at the Oval. Alf Gover, the Surrey fast bowler, was the exasperated opponent in one championship duel with the Yorkshireman. Gover bowled one superb over of wicked outswingers at Sutcliffe. 'Herbert played at each one and didn't get a touch,' recalled Surridge. 'Alf said: "I've got you today, Herbert." Sutcliffe lifted his eyes and looked back at Gover. There was a mixture of disdain and merriment in his glance. "No, Alf, you've had your chance," he declared. "I'm here for a hundred now."' Surridge said Herbert was as good as his word; he did not falter again and moved inexorably on to another century. Another observer tellingly testified to Sutcliffe's unflappability. His observation ought to be incorporated in instruction manuals for young cricketers. 'Sutcliffe was fortunate enough to be blessed with a mental clarity, the realisation that, the previous ball cannot send you back to the pavilion.'

Bob Wyatt confirmed the assurance which so disconcerted Sutcliffe's opponents. 'If he was beaten, it did not have the slightest effect upon him. He was just as confident after a slice of luck as he was before it happened.' It was, though, in

Sutcliffe's case, a product of an amazing concentration. Players of lesser character might and did lose heart on those days of dark plots and when the bowling conspirators had devised a script of forbidding hazards. Wally Hammond said Sutcliffe was never a hostage of misfortune. 'He was one of those players who did not believe in luck. He made his own.' Arthur Mailey, a renowned Australian rival, said there was nothing apologetic about Sutcliffe's batting. 'Fieldsmen's mistakes were forgotten as quickly as borrowed umbrellas.'

Dudley Carew, in one affectionate essay, was attuned to the valour of an unruffled cricketer. 'There have always been those who find Sutcliffe antipathetic because of his bland refusal to be rattled and confused like any normal man would be when the ball was beating him, he was giving chances, and the wicket-keeper was wondering how the bails managed to stay on.'

Carew said this resulted from a suspicion that Sutcliffe was a very superior person:

> Swank was a quality in which Sutcliffe was entirely deficient. He had, however, what is the precise opposite of it, and that is a very exact idea of his own capacity, and a not unmischievous delight in staying at the wicket when by all laws of cricketing decency he should have been back in the pavilion. He was fallible but, and this is the point, his poise, his manner of playing, his air of superintending the whole game as though it were an amusement got up for his benefit, never betrayed the fact.
>
> Just as this imperturbability has led to an over-rating of Sutcliffe's own conceit of himself, so has it inclined people to under-estimate the essentially obstinate and combative side of his cricketing nature. His great value to a side lay in his cool, concentrated ability he brought to bear on any and every situation.

Ian Peebles supported the contentions that Sutcliffe often led a charmed life at the crease; but said that his good fortune was only what a very brave man deserved. There were, he said, many examples of a particularly benevolent guardian angel's bounty and, in every case, the one calm, unmoved figure of Sutcliffe as the recipient. Peebles recalled the sad spectacle of the Middlesex side on a gloomy day at Bradford in 1933. As they walked out to field, Patsy Hendren, indicating Herbert's immaculate figure, said: 'It's all right, he's out of luck this season – they don't drop him any more.' In Nigel Haig's first over Sutcliffe mistimed a hook and the ball spun gently through the hands of Jim Sims at mid-on and fell to the ground. Peebles was also ill-favoured when he took a turn with the ball. 'I straightaway bowled a very respectable leg-break. Herbert nicked the ball directly to Patsy at slip, and saw it fall like a stone from that usually unerring hand. Thereafter Patsy walked with a pensive tread as Herbert ran smoothly to his hundred.'

Sutcliffe did make the hearts of bowlers beat faster, either in disbelief or with frustration on those days when his bat had no edges. Bill Bowes regarded him as the chief soloist in Yorkshire's eminent ranks. He thought that had he wished, Sutcliffe could have mastered lions. Sutcliffe was psychologically looking forward to the next encounter, even when he could have no quarrel with his dismissal. Then, if it was a bowler who had courted his disapproval, he would not mask his condescension. Nigel Haig, the Middlesex amateur, was one bowler in this category. Relations between them had never been cordial. Haig once trapped Sutcliffe lbw in the first over at Lord's. It was an expertly pitched delivery, the definitive unplayable ball. Herbert refused to acknowledge that he had genuinely been beaten. It was, he said, caused by the distraction of a member moving in the pavilion. Passing the delighted bowler in a dignified stroll, Sutcliffe addressed his batting partner in a clear, suave voice: 'Sorry, Percy,' he said, 'that was a careless shot. I should have concentrated better.' As Peebles said, this was a beautifully calculated slight, and it did nothing to improve the rift between Sutcliffe and Haig.

One might hold reservations about this passage as unnecessarily fermenting discord. The story has the elements of Cardusian irony. In later years Sutcliffe would chide cricket's rhapsodist for falsely portraying him as some kind of genteel braggart. There was greater truth in the presentation of Sutcliffe's inimitable brand of courage. The Yorkshireman had few equals in terms of bravery. Les Ames said: 'There would never be any question of Herbert escaping to the other end. It was just the opposite. Herbert would say: "If you're not happy, I'll deal with him."' Sutcliffe was utterly fearless and adroit as a hooker of the fast bumping ball. He would not be panicked or hurried into making an injudicious stroke. The bumper represented for him a badge of fortitude, and he had little time for others who showed their fright. Bill Sutcliffe considered that his father might have been the exception to the rule that nobody likes fast bowling. 'If anyone bowled short, he would hook them out of sight. Herbert was the sort of player who could have dealt with and put a formidable West Indian pace attack of other years in its place.'

Ronald Mason put forward a fine image of Sutcliffe in full spate as an attacking batsman:

> When he hooked, he revealed his native quality as in no other of his masterful, forcing strokes. It expressed to perfection, as he went on to his right foot and slammed the bouncer contemptuously to the fence, the sudden emergence of a crude and overbearing power beneath his deceptive gentility.

The violence of his power-driven hook, said Mason, was of the nature of 'hard Pennine rock and the relentless strength which his native hills and his native people alike embody'.

Sutcliffe once hit the first three balls for six over fine leg in a Roses match at Park Avenue, Bradford. It was an impish exploit in such dour company. The six-hits were a lusty prelude to yet another century, one of eleven he obtained against Lancashire. One of his most formidable Red Rose rivals was the Australian fast bowler, Ted McDonald. Sutcliffe said he liked nothing better than for McDonald to bowl bouncers at him. 'Anyone who could make that particular proclamation and continue to live must have been of no ordinary timber,' reflected Ronald Mason. Sutcliffe did, however, have the highest regard for the Australian. He told Bill Bowes:

> He was one of the best bowlers I ever met. You never mastered him. Sometimes on a hot afternoon I have thought I had him, that he was losing his pace and bowling slower; and then, suddenly, he would hurl himself into the attack like a demon. The ball would hit your pad before you had picked up its flight, and you realised that previously he had been resting. Resting at me! You always wondered which ball would be his fast one. It made him dangerous even when he was resting.

Ron Burnet was taken by his father to watch his first Roses match at Old Trafford in 1927. Of McDonald, he had heard it said, that he left no footprints on wet ground because he was so light on his feet. Burnet looked on enthralled at the contest between Holmes and Sutcliffe and McDonald in which no quarter was given. 'It was a thrilling occasion for me because Herbert scored a century.' Burnet was to witness many other Roses battles and his abiding memory is of the ease with which the Yorkshire openers negotiated the perils of bouncers. 'They never looked in any danger as they swayed towards the offside. If they missed, the ball went over their left shoulder. It was a mistake if they got hit.' Sutcliffe regarded himself as culpable if he was struck by a bouncing ball. After one Roses match at Sheffield he visited the Turkish Baths in Glossop Road. The side of his body was covered by several large bruises suffered in a torrid duel with McDonald. When the other bathers commiserated with him, Sutcliffe was adamant that it was his own fault. 'I should have hit every single one of them for four,' he said.

Sutcliffe excelled in the intensely competitive Roses matches. A challenging enmity entered his cricket and the light of battle shone in his eyes. The combat, with no quarter given, was in sharp contrast to the atmosphere in other county games. 'I believe that we Yorkshiremen and Lancastrians, who have gained a reputation in international cricket as hard fighters, owe much to the training we receive in these battles,' said Sutcliffe. 'I think we are fortunate to have such games. They are ideal preparation for Test cricket.'

In 1937, at Sheffield, Sutcliffe chose Lancashire as his opponents to hoist his 100th century for Yorkshire. His customary serenity almost deserted him as he approached the milestone. On the brink of one of his proudest achievements there was just a flicker of tension. Cyril Washbrook, a feared adversary from the other side of the Pennines, remembered the growing excitement on the terraces as Sutcliffe's score moved into the nineties. 'What's going on?' asked Washbrook, who was fielding close to the bat. 'If I get this hundred, it will be my 100th for Yorkshire,' replied Sutcliffe. He added: 'There's no other team I would rather get it against, and no other ground on which I would want to do it.' A few minutes later the target was reached and it was greeted with tremendous cheers. Washbrook, recalling the salute to a great batsman in later years, said: 'It was the finest reception given to an English cricketer I have ever heard anywhere in the world.' Neville Cardus said Sutcliffe was given the ovation of a monarch and acknowledged it like a monarch.

Cardus, in earlier years, had cherished a 'conflict of mingled antagonism and grace' in the Roses duels between Sutcliffe and Ted McDonald. He was always captivated by the heroics of cricket. On one occasion at Old Trafford, Sutcliffe launched into a thrilling assault and hit 90 against McDonald in his most destroying vein. He scored 52 out of a total of 63 in just under an hour. There were 11 boundaries in this attack, including four in one over. 'The grandeur of McDonald's action was confronted by a young Yorkshireman whose movements were just as steeped in grandeur,' enthused Cardus. Sutcliffe said his innings at Old Trafford gave him more satisfaction than any he had played against Lancashire. 'McDonald was at his best. Right from the start, he tore away, dropping four or five bouncers an over. This was, of course, just to my liking, for he spoon-fed my favourite strokes – the hook or the pull.'

Sutcliffe's relish for the hook shot might have been expected to cost him dear, especially in the Test arena. Australia's Gregory and Wall used to try and snare him by posting a fieldsman at deep fine or square leg. Both Bob Wyatt and Les Ames felt that Sutcliffe lacked the technique of Bradman or Hendren as a hooker. They said that he was inclined to hit too much in the air against the big bouncers. The cause, according to Don Bradman, was Sutcliffe's adoption of a slightly open grip of the bat. But it is a fact that in twenty-seven Tests against Australia, Sutcliffe was only caught on the legside four times, once brilliantly by Ponsford at Brisbane.

Sutcliffe was, of course, dismissed cheaply because of his preference for the stroke. But he had calculated, in his shrewd Yorkshire way, that his boldness reaped sufficient rewards to outweigh the disadvantages. Wally Hammond and Peter May,

An intent Sutcliffe cuts a ball from Grimmett in the second Test against Australia at Lord's in 1934. The Australian wicketkeeper is Bert Oldfield. (W.H.H.S)

two players rooted in orthodoxy, would never commit themselves to the hook, at least not when the cricket was serious. They regarded it as the most spendthrift of strokes. Pelham Warner was of a similar mind. He thought the hook was a 'proceeding fraught with no little danger and ought only to be indulged in very occasionally'.

Herbert Sutcliffe did not regard the hook as an irresponsible stroke. He would certainly have applauded the audacity of Colin Milburn whose enforced retirement was a tragic blow and robbed the post-war game of an exciting cricketer and personality. Like Milburn, Sutcliffe was impelled in his service of the hook as a spectacularly inventive response to hostile bowling. Bill Bowes was once offered an explanation of this attacking gamble. Sutcliffe said:

> If a fast bowler bowls me a bouncer and he has a man fielding at fine leg and I think that I can hit him square, I will

have a go every time. I find that I can hit ten boundaries for every time out. It is the same if he has a fielder at square leg and nobody at fine leg. But if he has a man in both positions, I would not hit the ball in this direction until I've got 40 runs on the board. By that time I have so much confidence that I believe that I can miss both men.

He added: 'On average I succeed ten times to every failure. I reckon an average of 80 will do for me.'

After his early problems against Australia's Mailey and Grimmett in the 1920s, Sutcliffe was equally adept against spin. Bill O'Reilly, another superb leg-spinner, held the Yorkshireman in high esteem. It behoves one to listen to O'Reilly, a fiery and forbidding opponent and acknowledged as one of the greatest bowlers in the history of the game. In his eighty-fifth year, he looked back at the challengers who sought to quell him. He considered that Sutcliffe had the finest competitive spirit among all his rivals:

Herbie epitomised, for me, the long hard struggles which marked almost every Test contest between England and Australia in my time. I admired Herbie as a grand cricketer who fought every inch of the way through the toughest situation.

He was the very essence of combat, extraordinarily competitive, finely skilled and, generally speaking, highly delighted with himself, as he had every reason to be. His unbending attitude towards battling it out to the very last ditch was to me an inspiration, which drew forth the best I had to offer each time we shaped up to one another. I loved dishing it up to him and accepting it as sufficient compensation to get one through his defence. Herbie typified the English foe whose dismissal was my major programme for the day.

One of Sutcliffe's batting habits used to infuriate the Australian barrackers as well as the bowlers. An Australian observer wrote:

> He repeatedly went on little hikes along the pitch, tap-ping with his bat to flatten ridges and hillocks that nobody noticed. On his excursions Sutcliffe often discovered some microscopic scrap of grass and tossed it aside. After watch-ing him fossicking along the wicket at intervals for a few hours, a Melbourne spectator called out: 'Herbie, what are you looking for – gold?'

Freddie Brown, as a junior England colleague on the 1932/33 tour of Australia, remembered the tribute paid to him by Sutcliffe during the match between the Gentlemen and Players at Lord's in 1931. 'I got him out, caught by Duleepsinhji for eight, after making him play and miss quite often in the previous overs before his dismissal.' Brown treasured the com-pliment of a 'very great player', who had met and mastered many of the world's spin wizards. 'Herbert said it was the best leg-spin bowling he had ever faced.' The accolade, said Brown, was typical of a man who was always quick to praise young, aspiring cricketers.

Bob Wyatt judged Sutcliffe as an expert in 'reading' spin and, interestingly, revealed that Jack Hobbs triumphed without being able to spot the googly. According to Wyatt, Hobbs was not alone among the great players in being unable to fathom the direction of spin. Hobbs was still able to establish his command when opposed by the South African googly quartet of Faulkner, Schwartz, White and Vogler before the First World War. Hobbs was partnered by Wilfred Rhodes in one match against the South Africans. Rhodes told Wyatt that he was equal to the puz-zles set by the spinners. 'But,' said Wilfred, 'when the score had reached around 50 Jack had scored 47 and I, who could spot the googly, had only managed a handful of runs.' Wyatt said the reason for the apparent discrepancy was that Hobbs was either right forward, or away from the ball. 'Jack didn't have to know which way the ball was turning.' He added:

> The only real advantage in knowing is in playing the pull or the cut. If you are watching for the googly or the leg-break you have to check the hand and pick the ball up when it is much further forward in its flight. If you cannot see it you might just as well not bother because you are putting yourself at a disadvantage by looking for it.

Wyatt thought this was an opinion shared by Hobbs and other great batsmen of his time.

Bill Bowes, along with Bradman, Wyatt and Ames, accorded Sutcliffe the highest ranking in crisis. It was said of Sutcliffe that he visibly grew in stature in his determination to mount the obstacles set by difficult wickets. Ames said he would always want Sutcliffe in his side in such conditions and when runs were vitally needed. 'The whole thing about Herbert in important matches was that he was not going to give anything away,' recalled Wyatt. 'It didn't affect him if he was going slowly, and that is why he was such a great player on great occasions. He would score as quickly as possible but he was always playing for his side.'

John Langridge, another prolific batsman in Sussex, envied Sutcliffe's correctness in accumulating runs. Langridge sought to emulate the Yorkshireman's powers of concentration. As an ace slip fieldsman, he did not often allow Sutcliffe a second chance. More than once his safe hands brought about Sutcliffe's downfall. One of these dismissals was off the bowling of Bert Wensley at Hove in the late 1930s. 'You again, John!' said Sutcliffe, as he marched back to the pavilion.

Sutcliffe was unjustly accused of over-cautious batting tactics. One observer said that his critics did not realise that his progress was dictated by his captain. Upon his shoulders, as the automatically appointed helmsman, lay the responsibility of putting his team in a good position. 'Sutcliffe's ability to "play to orders" has been a great boon to all his captains... there are few players more effective than Herbert when the call comes for quick runs.' Sutcliffe once stopped a Yorkshire cricket correspondent in the street after Trevor Bailey had scored a dogged and painstaking century in Australia. 'They called me slow,' he said, 'but if you care to look up the books you will find that I averaged 25 to 30 (34 runs in all first-class cricket) an hour. You should also bear in mind that Jack Hobbs seldom left me more than two balls an over when he was going well.'

Sutcliffe's centuries usually occupied him for about three hours. Les Ames made an intriguing point when he said that the number of innings had to be taken into account when paying regard to the hundreds scored by individual players. 'Yorkshire would often need only one innings for victory and this restricted Herbert's chances. The opposite would be true of Hammond playing for a less dominant county. He would play many more innings for Gloucestershire and thus have more opportunities to increase his tally of centuries.'

There are differing views on the range of Sutcliffe's stroke-play. Jan Peebles remembered Sutcliffe's stiff, determined stance, with the bat facing mid-off, and his adequate but unspectacular repertoire of shots. His fluency as a batsman was said to lack the charm and flowing graces of Woolley or Hammond, but he could still match them in the runs ticking briskly along on the scoreboard. Bill Bowes remembered Sutcliffe as the master at easing the marginally short delivery past point or gully for safe singles, one or two nearly every over. Sutcliffe's off-drive, said Bowes, was of such controlled power and perfection as to earn an approving nod from the prince of offside stylists, Wally Hammond. Bob Wyatt also recalled the measured timing of Sutcliffe's cover drive and said that his England partner had another shot which was entirely one of his own. 'It was between a cut and a back stroke, played vertically down to third man. Herbert scored a lot of runs with this shot.'

The extreme concentration, which Sutcliffe exercised during a long innings, never left him trembling with nervousness. Bill Bowes said that many players suffered a reaction after making a century. Their hands shook so badly that they were unable to sign an autograph book:

> Herbert would return to the dressing-room as he left it, without a hair out of place. Having removed his pads in his chosen corner, he would put his gear away in its accustomed places, strip, hanging his clothes neatly to dry and, after a shower and a rub down, would dress methodically, and then produce a writing case and sit down to write several letters. He would concentrate on this job as intently as he had concentrated on his batting, undisturbed by the shouts and cheers or the coming and going of batsmen. After he had finished the task, he would look up and ask: 'How are we doing?'

Sutcliffe exuded polish, possessing, in the words of one writer, the sleekest hairdo in international cricket. His dark head gleamed in the sunshine. His appearance at the crease, from the elegant buckskin boots to the perfectly groomed and neatly parted hair, was as immaculate as his batting defence. He was an abstemious man in his playing days, who enjoyed a modest glass of champagne, or wine with a meal. He made a habit of not smoking before lunch and was able to embark on a regime of going without a drink or a cigarette for as long as a month. 'I like to keep a mastery of these things,' he said. He always prepared assiduously for an innings. One of his last tasks before going out to bat was to rinse his eyes in cold water to

Another brisk single: Sutcliffe pierces the field with another slide-rule shot past point. (The Hulton Picture Company)

clear the fug of the dressing-room. Doug Insole, a fellow Test selector in the post-war years, also recalled one of Sutcliffe's fitness gimmicks. Sutcliffe said that during his career he used to play a regular round of whist in the winter. He made a point of dealing with his left hand to keep his wrist in trim.

'There was something in his walk, his carriage, that compelled attention,' said Bill Bowes. 'Here was no ordinary man, but one who owned the terracing. Eyes turned on him automatically. One could hear the hurried, polite whispers: "It's Herbert Sutcliffe." Small boys ran and were ushered into a queue as he signed their books. Ripples of handclapping marked his progress.'

The last and most engaging impression of Sutcliffe was his unselfishness. Denis Smith, of Derbyshire, who opened with him in a representative match, thought Sutcliffe was the ideal batting ally. 'He is wonderful,' he once confided to friends. 'I reckon that if Herbert was my regular partner I'd average another 15 runs an innings.'

Bob Wyatt, who shared many of Sutcliffe's combative qualities, considered himself fortunate to open with the Yorkshireman. 'If you called him for a reasonable run, he would always come.' Wyatt remembered a match against Eastern Province on the MCC tour of South Africa in the winter of 1927. 'It was played on a fiery wicket, just matting laid on an ant heap.' In the provincial ranks was the fast bowler, Arthur Ochse. He took five wickets to humiliate the MCC, who were bowled out for 49 in their first innings. In the second innings, the tourists were set a target of 180 runs, a considerable task on a forbidding pitch. 'I was sent in first with Herbert and managed to get into the nineties,' recalled Wyatt. 'Herbert had then scored around 70. He came down the wicket and said: "Look here, you've a chance of a 100. I won't attempt any fours. I'll give you as much of the bowling as possible."' Wyatt did reach his century and Sutcliffe was undefeated and still in his seventies when the match was won by ten wickets.

Wyatt, as the junior partner, never forgot Sutcliffe's magnanimity. 'Many players of his stature would have preferred an equality in scores for reasons of their own glory. It was a very unselfish thing to do.'

13

The Snare of Bodyline

'If I had been the best batsman in the world, I could not have stood up to such an attack.'

Tommy Mitchell, the Derbyshire leg-spinnerand a member of the MCC party in Australia in 1932/33

The fiercest of cricketing critiques did not estrange Herbert Sutcliffe from his captain, Douglas Jardine. Sutcliffe's unwavering loyalty in the bodyline crusade was shared by his Yorkshire colleagues and fellow tourists, Bill Bowes and Hedley Verity during the 1932/33 series in Australia. Earning the approval of such men was a signal tribute from those who were not given to extravagance in lauding southern amateurs.

'They backed Jardine to the hilt,' said Bob Wyatt, England's vice-captain in a controversial campaign. 'Herbert never hesitated in his views about our bowling strategy. He did not see anything wrong about pursuing the tactics.' Les Ames also believed Sutcliffe favoured the mode of attack. 'The majority of the England team were against the method from a moral point of view. But Herbert's theory was: "The ball is there; it's

short; and you should hook it."' Ames thought that Sutcliffe,
even as a good hooker, would have been confounded by the
accuracy of Larwood had the position been reversed.

In later years Sutcliffe considered Jardine the best tactician
he had known as a captain. 'His method of studying the game
set every member of the team working on similar lines and his
fighting power was a wonderful source of inspiration to us all.'
Sutcliffe, in the view of one observer, was hard and superior by
nature, and probably similar in temperament to Jardine.

Many Australians, according to Bill O'Reilly, regarded
Sutcliffe as the strongest advocate of bodyline bowling. They
claimed that he was the unofficial captain, who often took
it upon himself to initiate the leg-theory method of attack.
In England, his close friend Sidney Hainsworth said that
Sutcliffe's dedication to the adopted cause was in keeping with
his status as England's senior professional on the tour. 'Herbert
was always behind authority; his standards of behaviour were
in tune with this stance. He did not like the animosity which
grew between the English and Australian players.' Hainsworth
maintained that Sutcliffe privately disliked the leg-theory
strategy although he did not admit this publicly. 'Herbert said
it turned good players into poor ones and the game became a
matter of survival.'

The question of loyalty to Jardine was also advanced by Bill
Sutcliffe. The younger Sutcliffe said that his father, who might
have been expected to let spill revelations within the privacy
of the family circle, severely restricted his comments on the
tour. There were suggestions of a mutinous attitude towards
Jardine, but Sutcliffe did not once single out any of his teammates for criticism.

Sutcliffe, in his autobiography published in 1935, placed the
emphasis on perfect wickets as the reason for the introduction
of leg-theory in Australia. 'There would never have been any
need for this method if perfect wickets had not been produced

to make good-length fast bowling innocuous,' he said. He added that batsmen had, for years, been given a great and not entirely fair advantage by the preparation of super wickets. Don Bradman, as the major target of bodyline bowling, agreed with Sutcliffe that it was a reaction against the dominance of bat over ball. He did, however, understandably regard it as the wrong remedy. 'Killing a patient is not the way to cure his disease,' he said.

The appeasement of the Australians, in the wake of the bodyline furore, checked a hostility which went beyond sporting outrage. There was the threat of a severance of friendly relations between the two countries. The rift was not completely healed until after the Second World War. Under the heading of 'Cricket Treason' a leader in the *Yorkshire Post* dwelt upon the dominating dissension of leg-theory. 'It seemed to loom up ludicrously like a constitutional affair, shaking the Empire, and its phases were watched wonderingly by half the civilised world.' The writer expressed his satisfaction that the Yorkshire tourists had steered clear of the temptation to take part in a 'lucrative but little honourable pursuit' of fermenting more discord. 'Those who are creating strife are assuredly traitors to the best interests of the game,' he added.

The disavowal by the MCC of the bodyline tactics was, however, a measure later regretted by Herbert Sutcliffe. He believed that the decision to outlaw fast leg-theory produced a slump in the fortunes of English cricket, which lasted until the Coronation renaissance and the recovery of the Ashes in 1953. 'The advantage for which we had worked so hard for many years, was handed to the Australians on a plate,' he said.

Bob Wyatt was first selected to bridge the impasse of enmity created by the bodyline series. Wyatt was, as the next England captain against Australia in 1934, the embattled legatee of the dissension. 'I was handed a "goodwill" series, with restrictions.'

Bound for Australia: Yorkshire's Test cricketers, Leyland, Sutcliffe, Bowes and Verity in London before the 1932/33 tour. (W.H.H.S)

Wyatt recalled his displeasure at the objections raised by the England selectors to legside field placings. Larwood and Voce, the architects of victory in Australia, had been withdrawn from the fray. One of the likeliest of the replacement candidates was Nobby Clark, the Northamptonshire left-arm fast bowler. His effectiveness was nullified by the MCC directive. 'Clark, with his line of attack, naturally required a legside field,' said Wyatt. 'It was an impossible handicap. I was very foolish not to have countered the objections and asked for someone else to captain the side.'

Sutcliffe, writing in 1951 about the repercussions of the bodyline tour, reflected on the elation of the Australians at the omission of Larwood. 'They were brimful of confidence in the knowledge that the only fast bowler they would have to face was Kenneth Farnes, whose action, whether bowling inswingers or outswingers, was easy to spot.' He felt the same reservation applied to Gubby Allen and added: 'Nobby Clark would have been our most devastating bowler but for the restrictions placed on fast bouncers.' In a telling aside on the 1934 series, Sutcliffe commented that if England's fast bowlers could have bowled as many bouncers as Lindwall and Miller did at Nottingham fourteen years later, the result of the series would have been reversed in England's favour.

The bodyline tour, for Douglas Jardine, was, in the words of one observer, 'a knightly quest'. One of his sayings carried an intimation that his mission of conquest would destroy him as a cricketer. 'One crowded hour of glorious life is worth an age without a name,' was a favourite quotation and rallying cry to his team. Bill O'Reilly regarded Jardine as a modern-day Hannibal, who could have escorted a troop of elephants across the Alps without great difficulties. 'He led his team like an army, demanding absolute obedience, and with rigid on-field discipline.'

O'Reilly said that Jardine knew that Australians right round the cricket concourse hated the sight of the 'lanky, red-faced, long-nosed man, with the cap of many colours'. Jardine was reciprocal in his hate, which probably emanated from the personal abuse he had suffered at the hands of Australian crowds on his previous tour to Australia, under Percy Chapman's leadership, in 1928/29. Jack Fingleton, another of his Australian rivals, said that Jardine was a 'barracking gift from the gods'. John Arlott believed that in his playing days Jardine associated all Australians with the barrackers. 'The Australian barrackers disgusted him,' said Arlott. Jardine did flaunt his colours as the aristocratic ruler and it was this posture, perhaps more than anything else, which resulted in his being reviled by the Australians for his tactics. The criticism only served to stiffen his resolve to bring back the Ashes. His personal popularity came second to that ambition.

Sutcliffe had thought Jardine was a 'queer devil' – 'he takes a lot of knowing' – when he toured with him in 1928/29, but he revised his opinion four years later:

> Then I learned that Jardine was one of the greatest men I have ever met. He was a stern master, as straight as they make 'em, and he had the courage of his convictions. It was unfortunate for him that they did not meet with general approval, but that did not alter his outlook. He planned for us, cared for us, and fought for us on that tour. He was so faithful in everything he did that we were prepared on our part to do everything we could for him.

At the height of the bodyline crisis in January 1933, the Australian Board of Control, in a cable to the MCC, condemned the English bowling methods as 'unsportsmanlike'. Tommy Mitchell recalled that but for the Board's subsequent apology and withdrawal of the charge, the tour would have been abandoned. Jardine called a meeting of the team to seek reassurance from them on his tactics. It was Sutcliffe, as the senior professional, who read out a statement pledging their unswerving support. There was an interesting sequel which clearly indicated the strong bond existing between Sutcliffe and Jardine. 'To Herbert for the Ashes. From a grateful skipper', were the words inscribed on an ashtray presented to Sutcliffe by Jardine after the tour.

Jardine was a man of strange contrasts. He did present himself as an austere, humourless autocrat, who, in Australian eyes at least, cared little about the feelings of others when pursuing an objective. In later years he astounded many people, including Bill O'Reilly and Les Ames, who had considered him 'cool and distant' as a player, in revealing a warmer, gracious side to his nature. His daughter, Mrs Fianach Lawry, believed that shyness was perhaps his most dominant personality trait. The 'iron side', she said, was essentially a shield to mask his shyness. O'Reilly, a good friend of his old rival after the war, said that he was surprised to find that Jardine was a pleasant host and a witty man, who could make and hold friends. These were attributes which he had never suspected in 1932 when he had but one expressive word in his vocabulary to describe Jardine. John Arlott remembered his apprehension before meeting Jardine, 'the ruthless Scot' of legend. 'But in his first sentences he made a few jokes and everything was all right. He had a dry sense of humour. He was very funny and could paralyse you with laughter.' Arlott's recollection can be coupled with another memory of Jardine as the practical joker. He sent Sutcliffe an umbrella on the first day of his benefit match.

Bob Wyatt also dwelt upon the contradictions of Jardine but said that his former captain 'actually had a very kind heart'. One example of Jardine's consideration for others off the field was related by Maurice Leyland, another Yorkshire member of the MCC party on the 1932/33 tour. 'To the old folks at home', was the greeting on Christmas cards which accompanied cases of Australian produce sent back to England. Leyland described as absolutely typical the action of Jardine in forwarding greetings and presents to every player's wife or mother during the tour.

Douglas Jardine was a 'powerful friend but a relentless enemy', in the words of Bill Bowes. Bowes said that Jardine had so much courage he would have tackled lions bare-handed. 'Players used to say: "If it ever comes to fighting for my life, I hope I have the skipper on my side."' Hedley Verity paid his captain the compliment of naming his second son after him. 'DRJ was a man any father could accept as a model for his son,' added Bowes.

Jardine's personal courage was acknowledged by even his strongest critics. Bob Wyatt illustrated his captain's pluck and resolution in recalling an incident in the fifth Test at Sydney. 'Australia had brought in Alexander (the Victorian fast bowler) to bowl 'bodyline' at us. He hit Douglas on the hip and the crowd roared its approval. Jardine started to rub his hip but stopped when the cheers started up. When we got back to the pavilion there was blood running down his leg.' Wyatt added: 'Douglas was full of guts.'

Herbert Sutcliffe recalled that Jardine, perhaps under orders, refrained from introducing leg-theory against the West Indies in England in 1933. 'It didn't stop the West Indians from bowling a really magnificent barrage of bouncers to a legside field, a thrilling attack with Constantine, Martindale and Griffith as the chief performers.' Wally Hammond, who deplored leg-theory, had his chin badly gashed by one of the many short-pitched rising balls. Sutcliffe was fervent in his praise of Jardine's response to the onslaught:

> What a really great innings Jardine played at Manchester. It was a classic and one of the best I have ever seen against such a magnificent attack which was sustained for an incredibly long time. There were scores of vicious bouncers, to which our skipper – as Stan McCabe had done at Sydney against Harold Larwood, when he scored 187 not out – found the right answer.

Sutcliffe said that when Jardine returned to the pavilion, after 127, the vast crowd rose to pay tribute to him. It did, said Sutcliffe, express their approbation of his captaincy in Australia in the previous winter.

Jardine was deeply moved by another ovation in the match between Surrey and Yorkshire at Sheffield in the same season. It was another demonstration of loyalty and admiration. 'If anyone needed confirmation of what Yorkshiremen thought about our tactics in Australia, they were made apparent on that day at Bramall Lane,' said Sutcliffe.

It is beyond question that no other England captain faced an assignment as formidable as subduing Don Bradman in the 1932/33 series. It was calculated that Bradman scored a century every second time he went to the wicket and that one in two of those centuries became a double century. Someone neatly described him as having a 'single-track mind with no sidings at the crease'. The magnitude of his task only served to quicken the pulses of the England captain. Jack Fingleton's obituary tribute, after Jardine's death at the age of fifty-seven in June, 1958, was an Australian's recognition that he had succeeded in his objective. 'He saw to it that Bradman was drubbed. Where I think Jardine made his mistake was in thinking the Australian team was made up of 11 Bradmans.'

Fingleton's assertion that Bradman was outmanoeuvred by Jardine requires some clarification. In the context of the enormity of his achievements, Bradman did display only fleeting glimpses of his genius in the series. He was, by his phenomenally high standards, a relative failure. The shackles of bodyline limited him to an average of 56.57 but it still surpassed those of Sutcliffe and Hammond, England's best batsmen, who played more innings. Bradman's average was higher than any other Australian batsman and ahead of any English batsman except Eddie Paynter, who played in only three Tests and was dismissed on only three occasions. Bradman reached 50 or more in one or other of the innings he played in four Tests in the series. Illness prevented him from playing in the first Test at Sydney. He made his runs at the rate of 4.5 for each six balls he received. His one century was an unbeaten 103 out of 191 in Australia's only victory in the second Test at Melbourne. The Australian umpire, George Hele, who officiated in the match, thought that this was

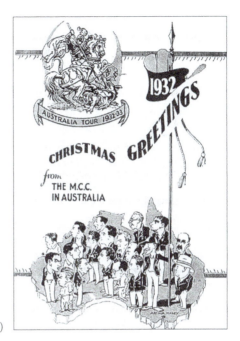

A Christmas card
designed by Australian
cricketer and cartoonist
Arthur Mailey. (W.H.H.S)

one of the finest innings he had ever watched. Even Jardine
admitted that Bradman, on this occasion, showed the mastery
which many people associated with his batting. Jack Hobbs,
in the role of cricket reporter, commented: 'I am satisfied that
only leg-theory can stop Bradman. The power he gets into his
shots, and their very wide range alike, are wonderful. He hits
freely where others would defend.'

The tactics employed by Bradman to counter the England
bowlers continue to puzzle many observers. A.G. Moyes, the
Australian writer, gave this explanation:

> He would walk away from the wicket and try to hit the
> ball through the offside field. If he succeeded, it would put
> the bowler off balance, and force him to weaken the leg-
> side field and strengthen the offside field. Then he could
> revert to normal batsmanship. His plan was, in effect, to

meet unorthodoxy with unorthodoxy. He was determined to make runs.

Bob Wyatt thought that Bradman would have fared better if he had taken guard outside the leg-stump. 'Don used to retreat against Larwood and slash the ball towards the offside, which meant that he had to be pretty quick. If he had stood outside the leg-stump to any ball regardless of length, he could have moved to the offside and let it go.' Wyatt added that Bradman, from the suggested guard, would have been sharp enough to play a straight ball in the correct manner. In addition, if the ball had risen above the normal height, he would have been in a perfect position to use the square-cut.

The rationale has merit in reflective contemplation but Wyatt, who employed the method against the less accurate bouncers of Bill Bowes, did concede that he might have discounted the idea against Larwood. 'But the Don could have done it. I often wonder why he did not adopt this batting policy in the bodyline series.'

There was, in truth, no certain counter against the accuracy and control of Harold Larwood. Tommy Mitchell, who twice dismissed the doughty Australian captain, Bill Woodfull, in his only Test at Brisbane, had no doubts about the command of Larwood. Mitchell, with a nod in the direction of Bradman, said: 'If I had been the best batsman in the world, I could not have stood up to such an attack.' The Derbyshire bowler gave his view of the development of the leg-theory plan, which remains a minefield of speculation. He maintained that the exploitation of bodyline was entirely Larwood's idea. They had discussed the plan on the voyage to Australia. 'Harold told me: "If we bowl just on the offside the Australians can play us from memory."'

Mitchell's remembrance is at variance with those of Bob Wyatt, Les Ames and Gubby Allen. Allen said:

It is my belief that Jardine never formed a positive plan before we arrived in Australia. The whole thing was really how we were going to keep Bradman quiet. We three will go to our graves saying that we never once heard it mentioned on the boat. I cannot believe that if this plot had really been hatched it could never have been once mentioned on the boat.

One of the most curious features of the first trial of Jardine's bodyline tactics is that it occurred when the England captain was not present. He had gone trout fishing and had left his deputy, Bob Wyatt, to lead the team. Wyatt set the leg-theory field against an Australian XI at Melbourne. 'It was a very fast wicket, greasy on top, and the ball was lifting,' said Wyatt. Wyatt, who was fielding at first slip, recalled his conversation with George Duckworth, the MCC wicketkeeper. 'Skipper,' said Duckworth, 'I'd like to go another ten yards further back. If I don't, I won't be able to reach them.'

Wyatt remembered that after Larwood had bowled a few overs with the new ball at Melbourne the shine had gone and the ball was not leaving the bat:

It tended to come in a bit and the Australians, as mainly bottom-handed batsmen, played the ball on the onside. There was little chance of catches in the slips, so I gradually moved the fielders over to the legside, not with a view to bowling bouncers, but simply to stop runs. Of course, every now and then the fast bowlers dropped one short. But this was a perfectly legitimate shock tactic.

Wyatt said he afterwards mentioned his use of leg-theory to Jardine. The England captain replied: 'That's interesting. We must pursue the matter.'

The effectiveness of the leg-theory tactics were, as Larwood himself said, utterly dependent on accuracy. It is beyond dispute that no other bowler could have deployed it with such success. 'It was only Harold's extreme pace and control that made it possible for us to pursue the plan,' said Wyatt. 'I don't think people realise just how accurate Larwood was. To bowl short either over the leg or off stumps requires tremendous skill. Harold didn't bowl so very short and most of the time the ball was rising by the time it reached the batsmen.'

Bob Wyatt and Les Ames both made reference to the problems of uneven bounce as a major source of concern for the Australian batsmen. Wyatt said:

> It was not necessarily the bouncer that posed the difficulty. The anxiety arose because you were not sure whether the ball was going to bounce or not. If you had known, you could have taken evasive action. The difficulty was in getting in line to play what might be a reasonable length ball and then finding it up around your armpits. You had to get out of the way or be hit.

Bill Bowes said that Larwood's bowling acquired what he described as a ricochet effect on Australian wickets. His deliveries did not seem to bounce so much as to skim off the pitch, like pebbles scudding off the water. Any ball, delivered by Larwood, was quite likely to take off towards the batsman's throat from only just short of a length. Another ball off roughly the same length might just as easily come through below bail height. Bowes attributed this effect to Larwood's tremendous speed, to the hard Australian wickets, and to his low trajectory.

Bob Wyatt has expressed his regret that the bodyline attack was mounted in Australia. His view was vigorously disputed by the Yorkshire contingent. It led to an interlude of banter between Wyatt and Bowes and Verity on the boat returning home from Australia. 'All the Yorkshiremen were arguing in favour of the England method of attack,' related Wyatt. 'They said that Jardine was absolutely right and that if a batsman had guts he could cope with it.' Wyatt was not convinced by this display of bravado. 'I think it was a pity that we adopted that form of attack,' he said. Bowes, with whom Wyatt had always enjoyed a fierce rivalry, took up the conversational cudgels. 'You're only saying that, Bob, because you're frightened of fast bowling.' Wyatt replied: 'Well, that may be, but how do you know? You can't bowl fast, you never have done.'

The decision was then taken to put the matter to a test. The Yorkshire bowlers teasingly told Wyatt that he would not get 50 against them in the following season. A five shilling stake on the contest was agreed. Bowes was absent from the match against Warwickshire at Birmingham and the bet, at Verity's instigation, was postponed until the return engagement at Leeds. 'When we went to Headingley they got us on a sticky wicket. Hedley bowled us out for 63,' said Wyatt. He was unbeaten with 33, having batted defiantly for ninety minutes. Warwickshire were forced to follow on. 'Verity and Bowes agreed that as I was not out I hadn't lost the wager and could count 25 towards my second innings score.' Wyatt was unimpressed by what he considered an extreme case of Yorkshire parsimony:

> That was not really fair, as my 33 not out on a bad wicket when my side had been dismissed cheaply was worth a good deal more. However, I agreed against my better judgement. In the second innings Hedley got me out for 24, so I lost my bet by one run.

In Australia in 1932/33, Herbert Sutcliffe was bereft of the wise counsel of Jack Hobbs. Douglas Jardine later wrote that it was clear the Yorkshireman had missed his old partner at the other end. The problem of finding a new partner for Sutcliffe was not resolved on the bodyline tour nor adequately during the rest of his Test career. In nineteen Tests in England between 1930, when Hobbs and Sutcliffe last opened an innings for England against Australia, and 1936, fifteen combinations were tried. Sutcliffe had seven different partners – Bakewell, Paynter, Holmes, Walters, Wyatt, Jardine and Leyland – at home and overseas during this period.

The permutations do serve to illustrate the weight of responsibility placed on Sutcliffe during his twilight years as an England opening batsman. Nowhere was this better demonstrated than in the first Test at Sydney in the 1932/33 series. Sutcliffe scored 194, his highest in Tests against Australia. He batted for seven and a quarter hours and was heavily criticised for his tardiness. His defiance even silenced the spectators on the hill. One man eventually raised his voice in protest at the Australians' impotence against Sutcliffe. 'Wanted at the members' gates – two bowlers, please!' he called out. The course of his innings, as Sutcliffe related, was dictated by his captain. 'I longed to have a go after lunch on the third day, and I suggested to Jardine that I might see what I could do.' Jardine replied: 'No, we are on top now; we will consolidate and stay there.'

Sutcliffe, his powers of concentration severely intact, shared three century partnerships with Wyatt, Hammond and Pataudi. Bob Wyatt, who opened with Sutcliffe at Sydney, defended the caution of his partner. Sutcliffe's obduracy paved the way for Larwood, and England's victory by ten wickets. 'At one stage in our partnership I was well ahead of Herbert,' said Wyatt. 'The difference was that I scored only 38 and he collected 194.'

At Sydney, Sutcliffe was opposed for the first time by Bill O'Reilly. He survived three justifiable appeals for lbw by the Australian leg-spinner. In a letter to the author O'Reilly remembered his irritation at the Yorkshireman's defensive tactics. It spilled over into a truculent verbal exchange. 'Herbie adopted the policy of raising his bat shoulder high while he "smothered up" comprehensively with his pads each time

I bowled my wrong 'un to him.' O'Reilly was so incensed by the tactic that he turned to the umpire, George Hele, to make, as he put it, the 'occasional enquiry'. Sutcliffe, with equal indignation, suggested that his opponent should limit his appeals. 'Break it down a bit,' he tartly remarked. At lunch, Sutcliffe intercepted O'Reilly, as the Australian, accompanied by his teammate, Vic Richardson, marched off the field. He tendered an apology. 'I'm sorry, Bill, for what I said to you. Sometimes I do and say things for which I realise later that I need a good kick up the backside.' O'Reilly had no time to respond to the overture. Vic Richardson looked across at Sutcliffe and said: 'My bloody oath you do, Herbie, I often feel like applying my foot to your posterior myself.'

It was during the Sydney innings that Sutcliffe had his incredible escape against O'Reilly. When he was 43 he played a googly from the Australian bowler on to the inside of his left thigh. The ball then rebounded to his right thigh, dropped down on to his heel and rolled against the stumps, but did not disturb the bails. Sutcliffe always denied that his wickets were in danger and said it would have been a 'miracle' had the bails fallen. His recollection conflicted with those of Wyatt and Les Ames. Wyatt recalled that the ball ricocheted almost as far as the popping crease. 'The bails wobbled and started to fall off and then settled back into their grooves as if to say: "No, this batsman is Herbert Sutcliffe."' Ames said that Sutcliffe, in attempting a run to third man, chopped the ball hard on to his stumps. 'Herbert got a very thick under-edge. I should think the ball bounced a couple of feet and hit the wicket. Everyone was running to check if the bails were out. Herbert was quite unflustered by the incident. He just wanted to get on with the game.'

England required one run to win in their second innings at Sydney. The following anecdote told by Bob Wyatt refutes allegations that Jardine's authority was ever usurped by

Sutcliffe on the tour. 'Herbert said: "I don't suppose, skipper, you will want me to go in now." Douglas drew himself up to his full height and replied: "Sutcliffe, when I want to alter the batting order, I will inform you."'

Sutcliffe scored four other centuries in his first six innings on the Australian tour. He had, in addition, six scores over 50, and was associated in ten century stands. In the opening match against Western Australia at Perth he began with 54 and then hit 169 against a Combined Australian XI. In this match he shared a stand of 283 for the second wicket with Pataudi, which was then a record for the ground. Sutcliffe followed this feat with 154 against South Australia at Adelaide. He was partnered by Leyland in an opening stand of 223. 'Sutcliffe's effort was just the kind of innings for a Test,' reported one observer. 'He showed that he could be every bit as stolid as Woodfull, and successfully followed the latter's policy of wearing down the bowling.' Sutcliffe batted faultlessly for just over four hours. After reaching his century he moved on to the offensive to score his last 54 runs in thirty-nine minutes. Sutcliffe's marvellous start to the tour continued with 182 against New South Wales at Sydney. He drove handsomely to reach another 100 against Tasmania at Launceston.

In the Tests, Sutcliffe thrice scored over 50 – 52 at Melbourne, 86 at Brisbane, and 56 in the final match at Sydney. He shared second place behind Paynter in the averages with Hammond. Their figures were identical, both playing nine innings, four more than Paynter, who played in only three Tests, and each scoring 440 runs and averaging 55.00 per innings. Sutcliffe was the only England batsman to score more than 1,000 runs in all first-class matches on the tour. He achieved an aggregate of 1,318 runs at an average of 73.22.

Sutcliffe, with yet another opening partner, Cyril Walters, was relatively unsuccessful against Australia in England in 1934. This was a series of batting plunder by Bradman, Ponsford and

McCabe, relieved only by Hedley Verity's masterly performance in taking 15 wickets in the solitary victory over Australia at Lord's. Sutcliffe had a modest tally of 304 runs in four Tests, with a highest score of 69 not out in the third Test at Manchester. He still averaged 50.66 and this was the sixth successive series in which his average had exceeded 50. The fifth Test at the Oval was to prove his final appearance against Australia. Only Hobbs, with 3,636 runs, Gower with 3,269, Boycott with 2,945, and Hammond, with 2,852, have scored more runs against the old enemy. Hobbs and Boycott each played 71 innings, and Hammond 58 innings, compared to Sutcliffe's 46. Sutcliffe totalled 2,741 runs at an average of 66.85 and far exceeded the averages of Hobbs (54.26), Hammond (51.85) and Boycott (47.50). In fact, Sutcliffe's average against Australia is 16 more runs per innings than it was in county cricket, a clear indication of his mettle against the major Test opposition of his time. After Hobbs' retirement from international cricket, Sutcliffe played in nine Tests against Australia, and made only one century against them. It was signal proof that he missed the sage and reassuring presence of his friend of many summers.

The sad decline of Gubby Allen's team, after winning the first two Tests in the 1936/37 series in Australia, adds substance to the view that Sutcliffe's experience might have tipped the scales in a fluctuating series. England chose only two recognised opening batsmen – Charles Barnett and Arthur Fagg – for the tour. Fagg contracted rheumatic fever and had to return home. Bob Wyatt, as the proven campaigner and likeliest replacement, broke a bone in his left wrist in a one-day game and missed the first three Tests. Stan Worthington, of Derbyshire, was given three opportunities, failing on each occasion. Hedley Verity was deputed to open with Barnett in the fourth Test at Adelaide, and it is one of the curiosities of the series that Barnett and Verity, with partnerships of 53 and 45, achieved the highest opening stands set up by either side.

Verity, until the demands of bowling caused him to assess his priorities, had considerable potential as an all-rounder. Bob Wyatt considered that the batting mannerisms of Verity pointed to the fact that he had modelled himself on Sutcliffe. R.C. Robertson-Glasgow said that, in common with Sutcliffe, Verity could make his dismissal from the wicket seem due to a regrettable lapse on the part of Providence. He whimsically noted that a casual observer might easily have mistaken Verity for Sutcliffe a little out of form, for he appeared to have something of the master's style and gesture.

The master himself, neglected by England, had undertaken a lecture tour at home in which he doubtless expounded on how he had honed his batting technique. His stature as a teacher might have been more profitably placed at the disposal of the fledgling cricketers in Australia. Sutcliffe's Test career had closed after playing in two Tests against the victorious South Africans in 1935. *Wisden*, at this time, considered that the decision to omit him was prompted by a desire to experiment with younger players. 'There seemed no grounds for believing that Sutcliffe's abilities as an opening batsman are not on par with those of any other player in the country. At all events, he remains a prolific run-scorer for Yorkshire.'

In 1936, Sutcliffe, then in his forty-second year, failed to reach 2,000 runs for the first time since 1921. Yet he still scored over 1,500 runs and his claims for a place on the forthcoming Australian tour might have been enhanced had he not dropped, at his own request, to lower in the Yorkshire batting order. He had briefly relinquished his opening place to aid the establishment of Arthur Mitchell and Leonard Hutton. Sutcliffe's fitness, as a deterrent to his selection, could not have been counted against him. At Scarborough, against Middlesex, he scored a double century to demonstrate his unflagging stamina. His 202, out of the Yorkshire total of 469, occupied him for six hours and ten minutes. 'It was an innings in which there was definitely a reminder to the England selectors,' reported the *Yorkshire Evening Post*.

One Leeds correspondent commented: 'There is a strong and growing feeling among serious students of the game that we cannot leave out Herbert Sutcliffe. In spite of his lack of form in the early part of the season – and every cricketer has his lapses – his skill and experience of Australian wickets make him indispensable. The steadying influence of Sutcliffe among the younger batsmen would be invaluable, and no other batsman in Test cricket has ever been so consistent.' Another writer endorsed the views of many Australians who said that no England side could be complete without Sutcliffe in it. 'He is still a great first wicket player. Indeed, it is doubtful if there is a better one in the country.'

A feud between Sutcliffe and the England captain, Gubby Allen, possibly stemming from a division of views on the previous tour, has been cited as the reason why Sutcliffe did not make his fourth tour of Australia in 1936/37. Bob Wyatt was a late replacement for Errol Holmes on the tour. Wyatt, as a close friend, has disclosed that Allen did not want Sutcliffe in the MCC party. He was unable to provide an explanation for the exclusion of a knowledgeable and loyal veteran. Wyatt believed that it was a mistake not to select Sutcliffe. 'Herbert should have gone instead of Fagg. We hadn't any experienced opening batsmen in the party and the only real success among the new players was Charles Barnett. Too many of the team lacked class.'

Les Ames also considered that, with hindsight, the selectors' decision to leave out Sutcliffe was misguided. 'Herbert's fielding might have been a factor, but he was still a very good player and his experience might have helped because we were not all that strong in batting.' Two other Yorkshiremen, Maurice Leyland and Hedley Verity, gained Gubby Allen's approval as respected and intelligent advisers on the Australian tour. Their choices indicated that there was no bias against Yorkshire, and it is beyond question that Allen would have wanted to field the strongest possible team. Yet he unaccountably ignored Sutcliffe, who was acknowledged as one of the finest senior professionals of the period. Ames said: 'Gubby was a little unkind in his attitude towards Herbert. There was no one more self-opinionated than Gubby and this probably produced a clash of personalities between the two players.'

Ames, like Wyatt, would have chosen the twenty-year-old Leonard Hutton, newly capped by Yorkshire, and Denis Compton and Bill Edrich, for the tour. They were all considered too young; but as Wyatt pointed out, their talents and not their ages would have been the criteria for selection had they been born Australians.

Herbert Sutcliffe expressed his own deep disappointment in a letter to his devoted friend and supporter, John Witherington. 'The selectors are evidently most ungrateful,' he said. 'They probably know best, but I would like to have been out there.'

As events were to prove, Sutcliffe's batting powers gained a new momentum in the years leading up to the war. The impetus was provided by his blossoming association with Leonard Hutton. Sutcliffe was able to nurture and foster the gifts of his Pudsey townsman. Alongside the veteran, Hutton, young, diligent apprentice, assumed his own majestic command in a riot of runs before the curtain fell on a golden era.

14

Sutcliffe and Hutton

'Herbert was a formidable presence. I was very nervous batting with him for Yorkshire. I never ran him out, thank goodness.'

Sir Leonard Hutton

The poise of the seventeen-year-old Leonard Hutton held abundant promise to whet the appetite on a June day at Bradford in 1935. He gave a brisk tug at the coat-tails of his veteran partner, Herbert Sutcliffe. The lineage of this master craftsman was re-emphasised in one of the greatest innings of his career against Kent. Hutton's self-confessed bashfulness in the presence of his senior did not prevent him from going boldly for his shots. The sparkle of his play was abruptly dimmed when he struck his own wicket, attempting a forcing back stroke off Freeman.

This delightful batting miniature was remembered by Les Ames, one of his Kent opponents. 'Len was being built up as one to watch for the future,' said Ames. 'His 42 probably took him an hour and a half; but he played beautifully. Even at that age he was a stylist and I was very impressed by the way he played off the back foot.'

Sutcliffe would soon be raising his own voice in praise of a gifted young cricketer. At Bradford, Hutton was the beginner, announcing his pedigree. He stood absorbed at the other end, rapt in admiration as he watched yet another display of controlled determination. Sutcliffe was in impervious mood. His unruffled composure and unerring judgement carried Yorkshire through a crisis to victory by two wickets. This was a match which was also graced by the enduring talents of Frank Woolley and, greatly to Yorkshire's unease, the wizardry of Tich Freeman.

Yorkshire were set a target of 192 to win after an overnight thunderstorm. 'The temperature was in the eighties and it was a fearful sticky wicket,' remembered Ron Burnet, the former Yorkshire captain. 'Tich Freeman had mesmerised our batsmen in the first innings. Nobody thought Yorkshire had a chance but Herbert got his hundred. The duel between him and Freeman was one of the most memorable struggles I have ever seen.'

On the first day, Kent gained a lead of 51 on the first innings. Sutcliffe and Hutton actually scored 70 for the first wicket in their reply. The procession of woefully perplexed batsmen after tea mocked the resolution of the Yorkshire opening batsmen. Yorkshire collapsed to 131 all out. Freeman's full return was six wickets for 47 runs; but when he changed to the football end he conceded only 26 runs in 17 overs and took six wickets. Batting against the Kent leg-spinner, said one observer, was a matter of supreme good luck or superb skill. ''It em, 'Erbert,'was the plea of one despairing supporter in the forlorn period after tea, when the Yorkshire batsmen were shackled in strokelessness. 'Nay,' said his friend, 'it is all very well shouting 'it 'em; if Sutty can't do it, there's nobody in England can.' Sutcliffe could do no more than grimly defend his wicket. Scoring runs was out of the question. 'Chapman blocked every ball at mid-off with hands as big as bath mats,' reported the *Yorkshire Post*. 'During one over the order of play was Freeman to Sutcliffe, to Chapman, and back to Freeman – a three-cornered contest, with all the other players looking on.' At last Sutcliffe obtained a single and ironical applause greeted the feat. The applause was drowned in laughter when Sutcliffe held out his bat at arm's length, in a gesture which indicated plainer than any words: 'If any of you think you can do better, come in and try.'

Eighteen wickets fell on a thrilling second day in which Sutcliffe reached his match-winning century. The runs flowing from his unhesitant bat were considered, by the Kent players, more than seemed likely to have been compiled by the entire Yorkshire team. Early in the day Yorkshire appeared to be slipping towards defeat. Woolley, with a masterly 73, and Ashdown increased Kent's advantage with a stand of 107 runs in 65 minutes. 'Woolley has never charmed more magical runs from unwilling opponents than he did in the first unforgettable hour of the morning,' related J.M. Kilburn. 'Woolley's innings ended on a golden note; he hit Macaulay for six to long-on, and was bowled next ball. He returned to the pavilion to honest cheers that made cricketers of us all.'

Woolley struck a six and 11 fours in a feast of hitting during which Smailes bowled two maidens to perhaps his own and certainly the crowd's relief. The extent of Woolley's greatness can be judged from Kent's subsequent decline. Within fifty minutes they were all out, adding just 33 runs. After Woolley's dismissal, Macaulay and Verity changed instantly from the innocuous to the unplayable. They each took five wickets; Verity twice had two wickets in two balls; and the next biggest stand was 12 between Todd and Ashdown for the fourth wicket.

Yorkshire required 192 to win. It was a monumental task in the circumstances. Sutcliffe and Leyland, who was promoted as Woolley had been to gain vital runs, gamely adopted an

aggressive policy. They scored 38 in half an hour before Leyland
was magnificently caught by Chapman off a full-blooded
pull. 'There was never a moment's peace of mind throughout that dramatic afternoon,' wrote Kilburn. 'No sooner were
Yorkshire inclining to believe that a match-winning partnership had been established than another wicket fell and Kent
were hopeful again.' Yorkshire lost six wickets for 120 runs by
quarter-past four. 'There were those who said the match was
gone – not in any defeatist spirit, but as people acknowledging harsh realities,' related one observer. With the match at a
delicate stage, Kent sought the respite of a tea interval. Sutcliffe
insisted that the proposed break was fifteen minutes too early
according to the card; and the umpires agreed with him. The
minutes were precious to Yorkshire; Sellers came in to hit two
fours and a six; and the deficit was reduced to 51.

Shortly after five o'clock, Sutcliffe arrived at his hundred
with a legside boundary off Wright. It was acclaimed in near
frenzy by the Yorkshire crowd; their hoarse voices, rasping
with tension, spilled over into pandemonium. Les Ames, in
our last conversation, remembered the stature of Sutcliffe's
innings at Bradford. 'It was a very fine knock. Had we succeeded in removing him, we should no doubt have won the
game.' Kilburn, with partisan fervour, enthused about one of
the 'truly great innings'. 'It was a display of unbroken concentration, swift hooking, masterly defence and uncanny
judgement.' Seven runs from victory Sutcliffe was out, lbw to
Freeman, and Verity was bowled first ball. Macaulay came to
the wicket amid whispers of torment. He pushed forward a
defensive bat with his chin almost touching the top of the
handle. For two more overs the result was in doubt, and then
Sellers swept Freeman to the boundary to settle the issue.

Leonard Hutton had made his debut for Yorkshire against
Cambridge University at Fenners in May 1934. He was the
youngest player to represent Yorkshire in first-class cricket

since George Hirst in 1889. Hutton's debut was marked by the dispiriting statistic of a duck, a fate which also awaited him in his first England appearance against New Zealand at Lord's in 1937. These lapses did not diminish the glowing testimonies to his burgeoning talents. In 1936 he was capped by Yorkshire and, as already related, pronounced good enough to have won England recognition against Australia in the following winter. The *Yorkshire Post* commented: 'His advance this season has been most marked. In his early days with the team, when he went out to bat with either Sutcliffe or Mitchell, he was very much the apprentice. Now, as a capped player, Hutton stands out as a junior partner whose knowledge of the business is rapidly increasing and whose experience is growing. His defence is as sound as a rock and his attack contains more fascinating shots than is generally realised.'

The verdict of Herbert Sutcliffe on Hutton was that the Pudsey boy was 'a marvel – the discovery of a generation' and unquestionably destined to become England's opening batsman. Sutcliffe said that Hutton at the age of fourteen was equipped to play for most county sides. 'He has as many shots as a Bradman or a Hammond. His technique is that of a master, he has a great amount of patience, and he is a fighter. In temperament, he might be the brother of Wilfred Rhodes.'

Lord Hawke, as the Yorkshire president, was more cautious in his judgement. He tried to persuade Sutcliffe to withdraw, or at least temper the tribute. Hutton himself found the extravagant attention, however well-meaning, a heavy burden. He is generally regarded as Sutcliffe's protégé; but, in conversation, he tended to play down the influence of his senior. 'You do learn a lot from watching a player of Herbert's class. It was an enriching and invaluable experience to bat with him. But it was really George Hirst who started me on the road to fame.' Sir Leonard added:

As a young player in 1934, I joined a team of class and I found other seniors, such as Bill Bowes and Hedley Verity, to whom I could turn for help. It would be wrong to say that Herbert made me. He was, in fact, very kind during our association; but I was only seventeen and shy and I had hero-worshipped him for years. The gulf in our ages was another handicap. I did not find it easy to talk to him.

One of Hutton's recollections of Sutcliffe amusingly concerned their tastes in tea. 'Herbert drank the strongest tea of any cricketer I have ever known. In my early days I would hand him a cup of tea and he would turn up his nose in disgust at its weakness. I often had to wait for my cup until the pot was almost empty.'

Sutcliffe's disdain at the tea table was more than compensated for by his compliments on Hutton's cricket ability. He was not prone to praise when it was unwarranted. His eulogy could not, therefore, be considered an aberration, even if it did represent almost a command to an aspiring youngster. It was founded not only on their Yorkshire alliance, but also on Sutcliffe's observations as Hutton practised in the nets at his Woodlands home. It was in the nature of an act of faith, expressing the wish that the sporting glory of Pudsey would gain renewed distinction through the exploits of Hutton. Other cricket celebrities would endorse Sutcliffe's commendation. George Hirst, watching Hutton as a sixteen-year-old for the first time in the Yorkshire nets, simply told the boy: 'Keep on wi' that.' A few weeks later he took another look at his charge and said: 'Booger off, lad, there's nowt we can teach thee.' Hirst knew that he was viewing a great player in embryo. In later years there were others who became Hutton's disciples. Colin Cowdrey considered the Yorkshireman to be the most complete batsman he had ever seen. The opinion was shared by Brian Close, Ray Illingworth and Johnny Wardle.

Fred Trueman described Hutton as 'a batsman whose bat had no edges'.

In 1936, Leonard Hutton was still marshalling his resources in tandem with Sutcliffe. They were associated in an opening partnership of 230 for Yorkshire against Surrey at Headingley. It was one of 15 century stands, including two over 300, during the precious and formative years of Hutton's career. 'Sutcliffe was at all times the senior partner,' wrote Kilburn in his report of the match at Leeds. 'Hutton spent nearly an hour before he found the opportunity for his first boundary and the whole morning brought him only 34 runs. He made all the shots recognised in the orthodox range and he made them all well in turn, but he would only abandon his severe defence when he could do so with safety.' By his caution, Hutton was obeying the cardinal principles of an opening batsman. For some less discerning critics, in these early years, it bordered on the excessive. He was accused of holding his strokes in check. The discipline was, though, a means of forging a defensive technique without which his career would have foundered. Hutton never forgot the advice of another great Yorkshireman, Bobby Peel. 'Wait for the loose ball,' said Peel. 'Once you think about getting quick runs you are finished.'

The blueprint of security, first drawn up by Sutcliffe and then emulated by Hutton, received endorsement from Kilburn in the match against Derbyshire at Bramall Lane in the following season. 'The batsmanship of Sutcliffe and Hutton had always assurance, maturity and polish. There were no rough edges, no feverish strivings for big hits or frantic speeds. Long hops were hooked or square-cut; half-volleys were driven with unfailing deliberation. Sutcliffe and Hutton were artists preserving always a true sense of perspective.'

Against Surrey at Bradford, in Arthur Mitchell's benefit match, Sutcliffe scored 138, his ninety-ninth century for Yorkshire. Kilburn reported:

Sutcliffe and Hutton are in such wonderful form just now that for them the beginnings of one day seem merely the continuation of yesterday's success; to them all the bowling seems but fuel for their fires; and the first over is as good as any for the production of courageous and creative strokes.

In 1937, Hutton's stride lengthened to place him in the forefront of England's new batting guard. It was matched, happily, with Sutcliffe returning to his best form. He scored four centuries and, like Hutton, recorded over 2,000 runs in all matches. Hutton finished third in the first-class averages with 2,888 runs (56.62). Sutcliffe obtained an aggregate of 2,054 runs at average of 43.70. *Wisden* reported: 'The occasion may conceivably arise when this pair of Pudsey batsmen will open for England, for judging from his achievements Sutcliffe must be regarded as a long way from the stage where retirement is indicated.'

The fluctuating selections, the subject of a later testy exchange between Sutcliffe and Lord Hawke, did indeed give more than a hint that Sutcliffe, even at 42, and Hutton would have produced the required steel as England's openers. The closest contender was Charles Barnett, who shared two century partnerships with Hutton against New Zealand and Australia, and was then curiously discarded. Hutton did not enjoy the comfort of a permanent partner until he was joined by Cyril Washbrook after the war. Jim Parks, a prolific scorer for Sussex in 1937, was given one Test against New Zealand; and Gimblett, Fagg, Edrich and Keeton all failed to capitalise on their promotion.

Sutcliffe did not return to the England fold. His influence, as on the 1936/37 tour of Australia, might have afforded a breathing space until the emergence of a younger player with the right credentials. It is a matter for conjecture whether Hutton would have governed so masterfully with Sutcliffe as an England partner. The selectors did provide a precedent

The veteran master and his Yorkshire and England successor, Leonard Hutton, described by Sutcliffe as 'a marvel – the discovery of a generation'. Sutcliffe and Hutton were associated in 15 century stands, including two over 300, in a fruitful alliance. (W.H.H.S)

when they recalled another Yorkshire veteran, Maurice Leyland, for the Oval Test against Australia in 1938. Leyland was a key figure, warmly reassuring in helping to shepherd Hutton to his record score. Hutton was less certain about an extension of his Yorkshire alliance with Sutcliffe. He said that he was sometimes glad to get away from him. 'I was terrified of him. He was a formidable influence. I was very nervous batting with Herbert for Yorkshire. I never ran him out, thank goodness.'

Hutton's anxiety was unfounded judging from the profits which accrued from the county association. He celebrated his twenty-first birthday in June 1937 by joining Sutcliffe in an opening stand of 315 in four and a quarter hours against Leicestershire at Hull. Hutton's share was 153 and it was his third century in successive innings in which he had scored 560 runs. It was the seventh stand of over 300 for the first wicket in Yorkshire's history, and Sutcliffe had figured in five of them.

'All the elements of a schoolboy epic were set before us today,' reported the *Yorkshire Post*. 'The young hero goes to the wicket for his county on his 21st birthday accompanied by a fellow townsman of worldwide fame, and together these two achieve an enormous partnership chancelessly, easefully and majestically, all beneath the blue skies of a midsummer's day.' Fifty runs came in the first fifty minutes; 104 were on the board at lunchtime; 60 were added in the first forty-five minutes of the afternoon, and the master and pupil reached the summit of 315 by the tea interval. Sutcliffe reached his hundred by twenty past three; Hutton arrived at his three figures twenty minutes later; and though Hutton gained in momentum in the latter stages there was only the difference of one run between them when the partnership was broken. 'All cricket's shots were shown by one player or the other,' reported the *Yorkshire Post*. 'Hutton late cut, drove through the covers and placed to leg, while Sutcliffe square-cut and hooked. All the beauty of his great years shone from his cricket.'

The biggest surprise of a day of inexorable command was the downfall of Hutton. Smith's first ball after tea bowled Hutton, who played forward rather casually and seemed startled by the rattle of the stumps behind him.

The reason for the fright, if not the dismissal, was probably the suggestion of Sutcliffe at tea that they might 'go for 556'. This would have overtaken the record partnership of 555 achieved by Holmes and Sutcliffe in 1932. The confusion over the missing run at Leyton had long been a source of irritation for Sutcliffe. He quite clearly recognised an opportunity to resolve the matter beyond doubt. Unfortunately, Hutton was unable to comply with the request. He remembered Sutcliffe's wrath and the dreaded 'black look' boring into his back as he returned to the pavilion.

A greater slight for Sutcliffe was the introduction of the new lbw law in 1935, which was aimed to discourage the over-use of pads as a second line of defence. It enabled batsmen to be given out to a ball pitched on the offside. 'Batsmen will be driven to take risks, for playing "doggo" will be fraught with danger and, in the end, disaster,' wrote Sutcliffe. He was able to overcome his misgivings and did, in fact, move up to second position in the first-class averages, an advance of fifteen places on the previous season. His gloomy forecast that the new rule would reduce his effectiveness was not borne out by his aggregates of runs in the following seasons. Sutcliffe did, though, believe that the alteration swung the pendulum too far and gave the bowler an unfair advantage. He was concerned at the effect it would have on a batsman's technique.

One Yorkshire observer, Ron Burnet, thought the ruling might have been explicitly brought in to counter Sutcliffe, as the master of pad play. 'Of all the players in the 1930s,' said Burnet, 'nobody knew as accurately as Herbert where his off-stump was. He had the ability to pad up to a ball marginally outside his off-stump.' Burnet said the new rule did 'throw' Sutcliffe for a while, because hitherto, if he did not want to play the ball, he padded up. One correspondent recalled Sutcliffe being given out lbw under the new rule while batting against Larwood in a match against Nottinghamshire at Leeds:

> I wish I could describe to you the incredulous look Sutcliffe gave the umpire. The decision was indicated to the scorers by a Nazi-style signal, which must have haunted him long before the war started. In this game he did not move for some time and, just for a second, I thought he was going to refuse to go.

Both Sutcliffe and Bob Wyatt vigorously opposed the lbw rule which, they said, greatly encouraged in-swing and off-break bowling and was responsible for slow and negative cricket. Gubby Allen, initially an advocate of the change, later regretted that he had not opposed the alteration. Allen then thought that the alteration had made a fundamental change for the worse in the technique of batsmanship, pandering to defensive forward play and militating against the back-foot exponent. Wyatt, one of the shrewdest of cricket observers, considered the move counter-productive and to the detriment of the game. He declared that it put the premium on a type of bowling which had thrown the game mainly to the onside. Wyatt also said that the law was entirely illogical:

> A batsman may play forward defensively to a ball short of a length, which would have hit the wicket but was pitching outside the line of the stumps, and in so doing intercept the ball with his front leg outside the line of the wickets – and by law he is 'not out'. Yet, if he attempts to play a correct forcing back-stroke to the self-same ball, and misses, he is out when he intercepts the ball with his back leg. This must be morally wrong.

Advance and retreat are the cardinal principles of the art of batsmanship, and, in Wyatt's thesis, forward and back play were complementary to each other:

> A good back player compels the bowler to pitch the ball up and, therefore, gives him more opportunities of play-ing forward and driving through the covers. Conversely, a good forward player makes the bowler drop the ball a little shorter, which provides him with more chances of forcing the ball off the back foot.

Wyatt believed that most critics would agree that it was just as much a transgression of batsmanship to play forward defensively to balls short of a length as it was to play back to half-volleys. It cost the batsman the initiative and made him unable to dictate to bowlers. 'Yet the law encourages this and thereby increases the amount of defensive cricket.' Wyatt, like Sutcliffe, thought the answer was a reversion to the old law and a widening of the wickets by two or three inches to compensate bowlers. By this means the purpose of the new law would be achieved as would the spirit of entertainment. Their lament was the loss of the glories of offside play.

Ron Burnet has dwelt upon the influence exercised by Sutcliffe on Hutton during the early years of their Yorkshire partnership:

> Len did learn an awful lot from 1934 onwards, while batting with Herbert. Herbert was the dominant partner up to 1938, when, in their century stands, he would be around 60 to Len's 40. After Len's record score at the Oval, which increased his confidence, the ratio was reversed to 70:30 in his favour. Len was tearing attacks apart in 1939 and Herbert was by then playing second fiddle.

'The essence of the side was its virility,' commented J.M. Kilburn, as Yorkshire moved unshakably to their twelfth pre-war championship in 1939. Sutcliffe, at the age of forty-four, was still the proud maestro, a ruler with the strength to match this disarming image. He might well have had figures to compare with Hutton, who scored 2,883 runs, including 12 centuries, but for an injury which kept him out of the side for a long period. It was a recurrence of a shoulder injury, sustained on an Australian tour, and it caused him considerable pain and anxiety. Despite the absences, Sutcliffe scored over 1,400 runs and was sixth in the national averages behind Hammond, Hutton, Compton and Hardstaff. 'Time has dealt lightly with this great batsman, whose career has been an example to players the world over,' commented a writer in *The Cricketer*. Sutcliffe completed his 1,000 runs by mid-June and in four consecutive innings he scored 165, 116, 234 not out and 175. No other player of his age had ever accomplished this feat. Eight years had elapsed since he had thrilled his admirers with an identical sequence of centuries in 1931. Sutcliffe reached a career milestone of 50,000 runs against Sussex at Scarborough in July. 'What a batsman he still is,' reported one observer, after Sutcliffe's century against Middlesex at Lord's. 'His bat looked broader than ever, and as he came back to the pavilion after his great innings, the crowd rose to him. If we had to select an England XI to play in a match on which the fate of the country depended, he would still be our no.1 choice.'

On Whit Monday, Sutcliffe played his last Roses innings at Old Trafford. It was another day of unceasing toil for Lancashire, who had to concede defeat in four consecutive matches before the outbreak of war. Sutcliffe hit his eleventh century, his ninth for Yorkshire against Lancashire. 'For 20 years he has been tormenting the Lancashire bowlers, and he is still doing it,' reported the *Sheffield Telegraph and Independent*. 'There were two superb off-drives against Nutter and one of his old swirling hooks, which revived memories of his duels with McDonald, but the lasting memory of the innings is that the Yorkshire veteran was as strong and safe as ever against the old foe.'

Sutcliffe and Mitchell were associated in a defiant Roses alliance. They added 288 runs for the second wicket in the Yorkshire total of 528. There was wit as well as pleasure in Kilburn's account of the partnership in the *Yorkshire Post*. 'Sutcliffe began today's part of his innings in apparent anxiety, encouraging the bowlers to believe him fallible and thereby adding to their hopelessness upon discovery of their error.' Sutcliffe, at the start of his extraordinary sequence of centuries in his farewell season, batted for five hours and forty minutes. His 165 included 16 fours. 'It might have been a much bigger score if the Lancashire bowlers had wilted in the heat, or had he managed to miss the fielders more often with his strong offside strokes,' commented the *Sheffield Telegraph*. 'Sutcliffe had it all worked out, as he usually has. Over after over, hour after hour, he was working to a timetable. He knew exactly what Yorkshire had to do to put themselves into a winning position, and he played with that object in view.'

Another observer remembered the sparkle of Sutcliffe in his last championship season. The Yorkshireman was still unmistakably the batting emperor. He prospered like an artist with a palette of many colours, anxious to add the final brush strokes to his own gleaming portrait. 'He sent for his cap with the air of a king demanding his sceptre, made his strokes with grandiloquent gestures, and pursued his calm, familiar way to yet another century.'

The Sheffield reporter, watching another great innings in the holiday sunshine at Old Trafford, seemed to have anticipated that this was to be Sutcliffe's swansong against his old rivals. 'Lancashire matches have always brought out all that is finest in Sutcliffe's cricket make-up and he was the Sutcliffe we will all want to remember after he has laid away his bat for the last time.'

Leonard Hutton's superb match-winning century against Lancashire at Leeds, ranked by him as perhaps the finest of his career, was the dramatic highlight of Yorkshire's last season before the war. This had the iron-clad qualities for a Roses occasion, unlike the feast of runs against Hampshire at Sheffield in June, which had the colour and zest of a carnival. Sutcliffe and Hutton exactly duplicated their previous triple-century partnership against Leicestershire in hoisting 315 for the first wicket in four and a half hours. Sutcliffe hit 116 before being bowled by Heath, and Hutton was unbeaten on 280 when Yorkshire declared at 493 without losing another wicket. It was Hutton's highest innings for Yorkshire, only 84 behind his record score for England. It was achieved in six and a quarter hours, seven hours less than the Oval marathon.

It is interesting to reflect upon the changed order of authority in the partnership. Sutcliffe and Hutton built upon their overnight score to add 153 together in the morning. Hutton reached his 100 at quarter-past twelve and Sutcliffe did not reach his century until a few minutes before lunch. 'There was a considerable disparity here but in actual fact Sutcliffe's opportunities were distinctly limited, for he had curiously little of the bowling,' reported the *Yorkshire Post*. It could not have happened a few years earlier. The baton had now passed between the two batsmen. Hutton had now assumed the role of the master. Sutcliffe readily acknowledged that another great Yorkshireman was knocking loudly on his door.

Herbert Sutcliffe and Leonard Hutton both embodied the finest ideals of Yorkshire cricket; they were plucked, like lustrous fruits, from the same Pudsey tree. Sutcliffe is remembered as a legendary mainstay in cricket folklore. He was the epitome of security in an all-conquering Yorkshire team. Hutton, his genius forged in a competitive environment, was coaxed to maturity in equally favourable circumstances. The talents of Sutcliffe and Hutton thrived because of the spur they received from other seasoned campaigners.

Geoffrey Boycott, the third of the Yorkshire centurions, was denied the assurance of an integrated team and the disciplines imposed by rigorous leadership. Boycott, self-fulfilled as a record breaker and a superb technician, was cast adrift among less accomplished peers. He did not enjoy the privileges and advantages of his predecessors. It was, and is, a dilemma only dimly perceived by the factions who either admire or dislike him. Hutton described Boycott as a 'prisoner of circumstances'. 'At another time he would have been only one of several titans, each enjoying a share of the public adulation,' he said. Sir Leonard recalled that there were occasions during his own career when he experienced the fervour surrounding

Boycott. 'I was highly embarrassed, and had it been with me all the time I would have been deeply worried.'

Ted Lester, the former Yorkshire batsman and county scorer, believed that much of the distrust of Boycott stemmed from jealousy among his contemporaries. 'Boycs was not an angel – he did many stupid things – but he was not as bad as many people made him out to be.' The wounds of the Yorkshire conflict – and the decline following the championship years in the 1960s – deeply angered Sutcliffe in his old age. The dissension would not have been allowed to engulf the club if the clock could have been turned back to allow Brian Sellers to assert his authority. He would have stamped his foot firmly down on the disorder. Sellers encapsulated the general feeling of more neutral observers about Boycott when he said: 'He is an awkward so-and-so; but, by crikey, he can laik.'

Lester disputed the widely held view that Boycott was a selfish player and only interested in his own average:

> During the years when Geoffrey was captain he carried a great responsibility. If he did not get runs, there was a very fair chance that Yorkshire would be bowled out cheaply. He wanted the side to do well. I think that he genuinely felt he had to stay there and this built up the selfish image.

Lester's exonerating verdict does need the qualification that such an approach was hardly likely to bolster the confidence of young players struggling to gain a foothold on the Yorkshire ladder. However, in a Yorkshire starved of success the subject has become so emotive that it will always be difficult to achieve a rational analysis of the situation.

The merits of Sutcliffe and Hutton, who prospered in an age unsullied by personality cults, allow an easier assessment. According to Bill Bowes, Sutcliffe was the first to admit that he did not possess the same ability as Hobbs, Hammond or

Hutton. What Sutcliffe did have, in overflowing measure, was the concentration and the will to harness his resources and become England's most successful batsman. Tommy Mitchell, the Derbyshire and England bowler, who played against both Sutcliffe and Hutton, thought the younger man was a more naturally gifted player. 'Herbert would play safe where Leonard would score runs,' he said. Hutton himself put the emphasis on opposing methods which separated him from his senior. 'I could not hold the bat as Herbert did. At the wicket his weight was on the left foot, which enabled him to play his hook shot so well. My weight was on the right foot.' It was the means by which Hutton developed his lovely forward style and his quick elegant footwork. A vivid recollection is of the slide-rule certainty of his strokes which constantly pierced a three-ring cover field against South Africa at Headingley in 1951.

Bill Sutcliffe considered that there was only a narrow divide between his father and Hutton. He accepted the view that Hutton could call on greater skills. 'Herbert was not quite so flowing as Len although he still notched up his runs pretty quickly. He was probably better in a crisis. When the pressure was on, you would look to Herbert more than any other cricketer.'

A grim dominance and purpose pressed Hutton, almost unwittingly, to his record 364 against Australia at the Oval in 1938. He batted for thirteen hours and twenty minutes. Bob Wyatt described the innings as 'one of the most astonishing feats of endurance and prolonged concentration in the history of the game'. The record innings catapulted Hutton to overnight fame; but, as with Bradman, it was a near insufferable millstone for a twenty-two-year-old. From then on there was an air of expectancy every time he went in to bat. Hutton rarely disappointed his admirers; but it was a tribute to his unswerving dedication that he was able to conquer the anxieties which beset him.

Of the Oval achievement, Les Ames said: 'It was a brilliant effort and Len had to fight hard; but he would never have had a better chance of breaking the record than on that wicket.' Australia went in to the field without a fast bowler. Their opening attack consisted of two unstartling medium pace bowlers, McCabe and Waite. Bill O'Reilly, as one of the greatest of leg-spin bowlers, posed the only real threat, and the power of his spin was nullified by a somnolent pitch. His accuracy had to be carefully husbanded. At the other end was the occasionally mesmeric left-handed wrist spinner, Fleetwood-Smith, whose erratic length made him an unreliable ally. O'Reilly and Fleetwood-Smith between them bowled 172 overs as England reeled off the runs, 903 in all. O'Reilly's figures of three wickets for 178 in 85 overs illustrated his mean and grudging length. By contrast, Fleetwood-Smith bowled two more overs and conceded 298 runs. Les Ames said: 'With Fleetwood-Smith, if you stayed there, there was always a four off every other over, if not each over. Len had the ability and patience to pick up the runs. He just went on and on.'

Ted Lester shared the commonly held view that Hutton had more natural talent than Sutcliffe. 'Len played in an era of spin and he was a superb player against slow bowling, a wonderful cover driver. He would not have fared quite so well against the quicks.' Lester's views on Hutton against fast bowling give pause for doubt, bearing in mind that his fellow Yorkshireman was sorely handicapped by a shortened left arm, the legacy of a wartime accident. It led to reduced power in his grip and forced Hutton to eliminate the hook shot, which he had employed so profitably before the war.

The alleged frailty of Hutton against nerve-quivering speed requires statistical proof as well as an appreciation of the task he shouldered as the bulwark of England's batting in the immediate post-war years. The instances of his dauntless authority in those embattled years place him in cricket's regard for all time.

In these circumstances, he would have been less than human if he had not chosen to stand aside and take a respite from the bruises from time to time. There is one story of Hutton batting in a post-war Test match with a promising Lancastrian, Jack Ikin. One Australian player watched Ikin courageously withstand the bumpers of Lindwall and Miller. He was impressed by the manner in which Ikin had coped with an unpleasant attack. Hutton, with an inscrutable smile, listened to the praise of his partner. 'Aye,' he said, 'but, you know, if he had been a better player he would have stayed at the other end.' Bob Wyatt, in telling the story, said that he would never have accused Hutton of lacking courage. 'But I don't think Herbert Sutcliffe would have made the same remark.'

Hutton always maintained that he did not fear fast bowling. In one speech in Yorkshire he wryly recalled that Bill Hudson, the terror of his Pudsey schooldays, had caused him greater concern than Lindwall and Miller. His words prompted a *Yorkshire Post* feature writer to interview Hudson. Hudson was a coal merchant, standing 6ft 3ins tall and weighing 16st 10lbs. He was a chilling sight, even without a cricket ball in his hand. Reminiscing about Hutton, Bill said:

He were t'only one I could bowl to. T'others wouldn't stand up to me – not even t'big 'uns. Mind you, I could chuck 'em down a bit in them days. I could throw the ball across the St Lawrence ground and twenty-four yards into the next field. And I'm not saying I couldn't lay 'em out. There were often a couple lying dead in't pavilion when I'd been on.

The young Hutton was unperturbed by this formidable rival. He stood at the crease without flinching. 'Think on, he were nobbut a lad of thirteen,' said Bill. 'A wonder, he was. He would hook the ball into t'tennis ground off his chin.

The gardener would come next morning with half a dozen of them.' Hudson, with pardonable exaggeration, thought that Hutton's 115 against Bradford in a Priestley Cup game was far better than his 364 at the Oval. 'Think of it,' he said, 'fifteen years old and playing against veterans!'

Sir Donald Bradman, in a more lofty sphere, has coupled the mature Hutton with Hobbs as the possessor of the finest technique of any batsman in his experience. 'They had no weaknesses,' said Bradman, 'but they both lacked the aggression and attacking power of players such as Weekes and Sobers.' Bradman was convinced that, in Hutton's case, it was a mental attitude. 'I did see him play a couple of superb cameo aggressive innings, but they were rare. His normal mood was a little defensive.' A lack of flamboyance, such as paraded by Denis Compton, might have been a better description of Hutton's cricket. As Sir Leonard himself pointed out, he must have displayed a measure of aggression in scoring 12 centuries for Yorkshire in the last pre-war season in 1939. Bradman did concede that the constant demands of professional cricket might have taken the edge off Hutton's enthusiasm. 'It is extremely difficult to maintain a light-hearted aggressive spirit of batsmanship for years on end and when playing cricket every day. This pressure is increased when the fierce spotlight demands runs in addition to style.'

Herbert Sutcliffe, like Hutton, was moulded in the furnace of North-country cricket. Each of the Yorkshiremen was subject to fierce scrutiny before they reached their promised land. Ames and Bradman saluted them for their prowess and vigilance in the most critical of situations. Despite Hutton's technical superiority, they were unanimous in placing Sutcliffe ahead on the grounds of temperament. 'Herbert would go first into my side before Len, mainly because of his unruffled approach and tremendous belief in himself,' said Ames.

Sutcliffe would never admit to nervousness, even when going out to bat in a Test match. 'I was anxious to do well, of course, but not nervous,' he said. 'You have this apprehensive-ness, but as soon as I left the shade of the pavilion and stepped on to the ground, it all disappeared and I wasn't excited.' His doctor said that he had the lowest blood pressure in Pudsey. 'I think that may have played an important part in my tempera-ment,' conceded Sutcliffe. His remarkable coolness prompted the doctor to exclaim: 'If you have a thrombosis, it will be a miracle.'

15

Fanfares in Retirement

'He was to me, as to every Yorkshire boy of my generation, a boyhood hero. His technique was as immaculate as his appearance.'

Lord Wilson of Rievaulx

The shared accomplishments of a great cricket partnership ought to have ensured a division of favours in the Queen's Birthday Honours list of 1953. Jack Hobbs became the first professional to receive a knighthood. The delight in sporting circles at this deserved accolade was tinged with regret that Herbert Sutcliffe, his boon companion of many illustrious summers, was not similarly rewarded.

The newly knighted Hobbs showed his awareness of Sutcliffe's contribution in a letter in which he said that he would rather have had his friend's congratulations than any other person he had known. Writing to Sutcliffe from his retirement home in Sussex, Sir Jack, with typical modesty, communicated his unease at the high honour accorded to him. 'I am easier in my mind now, for I realise that it is a compliment not only to myself, but to cricket in general and the professional in particular. As I told you at Leeds last week, you have done your part in bringing this about.' In a postscript to the letter, Hobbs said that his wife, Ada was also thrilled to receive Sutcliffe's congratulations. 'It was the first one to be addressed to Lady Hobbs. A charming thought – and she will thank you one day.'

Herbert Sutcliffe will always be coupled with Jack Hobbs in cricket lore; he cherished being given pride of place in his partner's esteem, and yet he was also angry at the lack of official recognition. He was 'Sir Herbert' to his legions of admirers, and the title was fairly his due. Along with Hobbs – and Wally Hammond, before the latter's criticised reversion to amateur status in 1938 – he had worked long and hard to advance the cause of the professional cricketer. 'Our profession, as a respected one, started with Jack and Herbert. They gave us a new status,' commented Stuart Surridge, a close business associate and friend of the Sutcliffe family.

A telegram from the War Office during Yorkshire's triumphant southern tour in 1939 had first lowered the curtain on a distinguished playing career. Sutcliffe, as a reservist, was the first of the Yorkshire players to be called up for military service with the Royal Army Ordnance Corps. His last championship innings was played against Hampshire at Bournemouth. The bowling of Hedley Verity, in the dying fall of another magnificent sporting life, held its customary terrors at Bournemouth. Sutcliffe's batting was measured in support of the rampant Verity. His half-century helped pave the way for an innings victory over outclassed opponents.

Sutcliffe played in three one-day Red Cross charity matches at Leeds, Sheffield and Bradford in 1940. Watched by a crowd of 7,000, he made the last century of his career for a Yorkshire XI against the Bradford League at Park Avenue. The League XI included Lancashire's Eddie Paynter and the formidable

West Indian bowling duo of Constantine and Martindale. Constantine was in irrepressible mood as a batsman. He struck three sixes and 14 fours in reaching a 100 (out of 141) in an hour. Sutcliffe's 127 took longer in execution, occupying an hour and fifty minutes; but it lost nothing in comparison with Constantine's innings. It included a six and 16 fours. Sutcliffe and Paul Gibb added 100 in only thirty-five minutes in the biggest stand and fastest scoring of the match. 'Sutcliffe treated the crowd to a dashing innings,' wrote one observer. If he was in the 'sere and yellow' now, there was ample evidence that Sutcliffe retained his zeal for conquest. Constantine's batting flourish was matched by an adventurous response.

The correspondence between Sutcliffe and his devoted supporter, John Witherington, which had started before the war, marked a great cricketer as a warm and generous man. Sutcliffe presented Witherington with the bat (now in the Headingley cricket museum) he had used in the 1938 season. It was inscribed with his scores and centuries recorded during that summer. The tone of their letters indicated an affectionate bond. The strength of their friendship was shown by Sutcliffe's concern when Witherington, as a Royal Air Force bomber pilot, moved in to action. Witherington's death, as he attempted to land his badly damaged aircraft in Lincolnshire, deeply shocked Sutcliffe. 'You have chosen a very dangerous yet thrilling section of the war,' Sutcliffe had written earlier. 'That you will come through unscathed is, I can assure, my sincere wish.' 'We had a grand match at Park Avenue,' related Sutcliffe, in reference to his century for Yorkshire. 'I just loved being able to go in and have a crack. Constantine's innings was a real gem, and he batted far better than ever I've seen him.' Later, in the same letter, Sutcliffe told the story of another match at Darlington and a run-out mishap. 'I had the most awful luck to be run out for ten. It was my call but the young cadet at the other end allowed me to get halfway down the

Yorkshire goes to war: Pictured in this cricket assembly are, from left to right: Hedley Verity, Frank Smailes, Sutcliffe, Maurice Leyland and Leonard Hutton. (Alan Hill)

wicket before saying "No".' It was obviously a familiar run-stealing situation for Sutcliffe. His embarrassed young partner must have wished for the ground to open up and remove him from Sutcliffe's gaze. 'I did feel annoyed but said nothing,' said Sutcliffe. 'There was a big crowd there, too,' he added. He was sorry that he had cheated the spectators.

In his letters, Sutcliffe allowed John Witherington to eavesdrop upon his family affairs. Into the picture comes another John, born in 1939, and described by Sutcliffe as a 'real treasure'. 'My wife and young John, plus Nanny and the maid are coming to join me (at his Richmond depot) this week. It will be grand to have them but I fear they are leaving a town, which is reasonably safe, for a military objective.' During this grim period in 1940, Sutcliffe wrote: 'We are in for a gruelling time and a long one, too. It is disorganising almost every family circle. It is most annoying to think that in this glorious summer we are taking part in a terrible war.'

Sutcliffe gained a respite from the trials of war in his cricket interludes, one of which caused him immense amusement. In

a charity match at Baildon he scored 83 and one of his opponents was the Yorkshire wicketkeeper Arthur Wood. Wood had
discarded his pads to chance his arm as a bowler against his old
county colleague. Astonishment at the move probably caused
Sutcliffe to relax his concentration. 'I was caught out on the
boundary off Arthur's first ball. He was very, very delighted,'
recalled Sutcliffe.

In May 1941, Sutcliffe was reunited with old friends
at Pudsey Britannia. He scored 41 in a local cup-tie. It was
his first game of the season. 'How stiff I felt on Sunday and
Monday,' he admitted in a letter to Witherington. Later in the
season he represented the Army in a one-day match against an
RAF XI at Harrogate. The Army XI included nine Test players. Sutcliffe, Hutton and Frank Smailes were three of the six
Yorkshiremen in the team. The RAF XI were dismissed for
144 before Major Sutcliffe and Sergeant Hutton paraded their
skills in putting on 78 for the first wicket. Sutcliffe starred as
a batsman and bowler in another match at West Hartlepool.
His batting contribution was 82 not out (in a total of 124) and
he was clearly pleased at reviving his side's fortunes. 'We lost
two wickets in the first over without a run on the board,' he
reported. Four other wickets went down as the total advanced
to 26. 'When the last man came in to join me, we had scored
only 70, so our final stand of 54 was a very useful one.' It
proved conclusive, as the opposition was dismissed for 74. 'You
will realise how terrible their batsmen were when I tell you
that I took three wickets for 12 runs.'

In another note, Sutcliffe, aghast at his expanding waistline,
commented: 'I have really put on too much weight to play in
first-class cricket.' Away from cricket he also had to acknowledge
that the passing years had taken the edge off his mental agility. After a strenuous crammer course, lasting six weeks instead
of two years in normal times, he said: 'My poor old brain was
very seriously taxed. I was rather disappointed with the result.

I thought I had done better than the 62 percentage allowed. At 46, though, it is very difficult to imbibe every lecture.'

The progress of Sutcliffe's eldest son, Bill, while a pupil at Rydal School in North Wales, was also charted in the correspondence with Witherington. One note contained parental praise and a reprimand. 'I am so very pleased with young Billy's form at cricket. Would that he paid as much attention to his school work! Then I should feel much more satisfied.' The quality of Bill Sutcliffe's cricket earned further commendation from his father:

> He has done very well at school, this last term, from a cricket point of view. He was very consistent and got his 1st team colours. Billy has an average of 32 for the first team, which, for a boy of 14, is quite good. The other lads are aged between 16 and 17.

Young Bill, at sixteen, played for H. Sutcliffe's XI against a Northern Command XI at Headingley in August 1943. The Yorkshire report said that he 'bowled his leg-breaks confidently without reward and in the brief period his father's side were batting, earned further praise for a watchful defence.' After three wickets had fallen for 14, the younger Sutcliffe helped Vic Wilson, later to captain Yorkshire, to add 54 before being bowled by Maurice Leyland.

His father must have found pleasure in these exploits and even more pride watching Bill play for the Rest against the Lord's Schools. Bill took two wickets for 28 runs and then opened the Rest's first innings and scored 41. He obtained three more wickets for 45 and scored another ten before blotting the family escutcheon by being run out. At Rydal School he hit two centuries during the season 'and gave further proof of the class inherited from his famous father'.

Herbert Sutcliffe's war ended in November 1942. Early in the year, he underwent two operations, one on his nose for sinus trouble, a recurrence of a complaint which had first affected him on the 1932/33 tour of Australia, and the other to deal with a shoulder injury. At the age of forty-eight, he was discharged from the army on medical grounds. Sutcliffe was thus able to channel his energies into fund-raising activities on the cricket field.

In 1944, he played in four matches, including one as captain of a North Wales XI against an Empire XI at Colwyn Bay. The match realised £4,000 for the Red Cross Prisoner of War fund. Sutcliffe won the toss and, going in at no.4, hit 47 in what was termed his 'best style'. His teammates were less assured against the bowling of Martindale and Parkin, and the Empire XI won by seven wickets. Sutcliffe also captained the North of England against a Royal Australian Air Force XI at Old Trafford.

He was, interestingly, partnered by Cyril Washbrook, who was to achieve distinction in his England alliance with Leonard Hutton in the post-war years.

There was a poignant cricket occasion at Roundhay Park, Leeds in September. A crowd of 10,000 gathered on the slopes leading down to an arena upon which merry big-hitting had cheered the cricket folk of Leeds during the war. They had assembled to pay tribute to Hedley Verity, who had died of wounds sustained in action in Sicily in the previous year. The memorial game was between Sutcliffe's Yorkshire XI and a team assembled by charity match organiser, Jack Appleyard and captained by Wally Hammond. The celebrities in the teams wore black armbands and before the match began two minutes' silence was observed in memory of a great Yorkshire and England cricketer. Sutcliffe and Leonard Hutton paid their respects to a much lamented colleague with a brisk

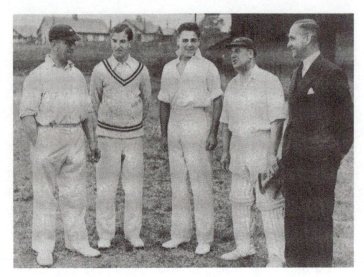

Bill Sutcliffe, a future Yorkshire captain (third from right), as a sixteen-year-old, was a representative in his father's XI which played the Northern Command at Headingley in 1943. Others picture are, from left to right: Maurice Leyland, Geoffrey Keighley, Arthur Wood (captain) and Herbert Sutcliffe. (W.H.H.S)

partnership of 62, and the match raised £1,000 to endow a bed in Leeds Infirmary.

Early in March, 1945, a Reuter message from Wellington, New Zealand, where Sutcliffe was on a business assignment, reported him as saying that he did not intend to play any more serious cricket when hostilities ceased. 'I have had a long innings and a most enjoyable one,' he said. 'I will now be quite happy to sit back and watch the younger generation.' Sutcliffe did, in fact, make one more appearance, his last for Yorkshire, when the Scarborough Festival was resumed in August. He captained a Yorkshire XI against the Royal Air Force. Batting at no.5, he was associated in a partnership of 50 runs with Hutton. His only other traceable match in top company was in 1946 for an Old England XI against Surrey. The match was staged to celebrate the centenary of Surrey and the Oval ground. The umpires were Hobbs and Strudwick. Sutcliffe was unhappily lbw to Watts for one, but Hendren, at the age of fifty-seven, batted two and three-quarter hours for 94; and Jardine, pugnacious to the last, scored 54.

In the same season, Sutcliffe accepted the captaincy of the Leeds Cricket Club. Before the end of the 1943 season he had taken a club XI to Mexborough to play in the first of the annual fixtures in aid of the Montagu Hospital in the South Yorkshire town. He scored 85 in the first match and 42 in the following year. He returned in 1947, when he was fifty-three, and very nearly matched his own age in hitting 51, off an attack which included fellow Yorkshiremen, Bill Bowes and Alec Coxon.

Sutcliffe was later invited to stand for Parliament, first as a Liberal and then as a Conservative, but declined because of business commitments. His active involvement with the long-established sports retailers in Leeds ended after the war. Bill Sutcliffe took over the management of the shop after his demobilisation from the Coldstream Guards in 1948. His father became the Northern Area representative and later a director of the paper manufacturers, Thomas Owen, the fore-runner of the Wiggins Teape company. The firm employed a number of distinguished cricketers. Douglas Jardine was the company secretary, and other representatives included Maurice Leyland, Bill Edrich and Len Hutton.

Bill Sutcliffe remembered his father's meticulous attention to business affairs and care in dealings with the company's clients. Typewritten dossiers were drawn up on each of the customers with the object of maintaining smooth and friendly relations. 'If you wanted any work done, there was only one cricketer to do it – and that was Herbert,' recalled Stuart Surridge. Sutcliffe also conscientiously upheld what Surridge described as a 'gentleman's agreement' with his family's sports goods manufacturers. During his career, Sutcliffe had used

Playing for Old England: Sutcliffe was a member of the celebrity XI which played Surrey at the Oval in 1946. Back row, from left to right: Jack Hobbs (umpire), E.R.T. Holmes, Maurice Allom, Maurice Tate, Ted Brooks, Andrew Sandham, Herbert Strudwick (umpire). Middle row: Patsy Hendren, Douglas Jardine, Percy Fender, Sutcliffe, Frank Woolley. Front row: Donald Knight, Alf ('Tich') Freeman. (W.H.H.S)

Surridge equipment – bats and pads – which were annually serviced by the London company. It was a mutually rewarding association, with the benefit to Sutcliffe of a flow of royalties from the sales of bats bearing his name at home and overseas continuing long after his retirement from the game.

Sutcliffe was accorded honorary membership of the MCC in 1949, joining a select company of English professionals, among whom were his county colleagues, George Hirst and Wilfred Rhodes, and his former England partner, Jack Hobbs. In 1951, Sutcliffe was also appointed a member of the Royal Commission on Betting and Gambling and wryly told one newspaper that he had been a pools fan for many years but had never won a penny. He also, voluntarily, gave his services as a broadcaster, providing commentaries on Yorkshire county games for patients in Bradford hospitals.

In March 1959, Sutcliffe became a Test selector, an honour
which produced a characteristic comment: 'Australia plays to
win and this is the only way to play the game. We must select
players with the guts to fight, and especially two opening
batsmen. This job of opening needs specialists.' Sutcliffe had
three terms as a selector, all under the chairmanship of Gubby
Allen, for the home series against India, South Africa and
Australia. Peter May, the England captain during that period,
paid tribute to Sutcliffe's expertise and said that he made a fine
contribution to the success of the team. Wilf Wooller was a
fellow member of the selection committee. 'Herbert had the
acumen to recognise technical ability at Test level which made
him a valuable selector,' said Wooller. 'He did not contribute
on bowlers or fieldsmen but he assessed batsmen accurately
and without fuss. He was always quiet and moderate in
speech.' Wooller, in his own career with Glamorgan, had been
fascinated by the numerous discussions, analysing and dissect-
ing the various aspects of cricket. One particularly intriguing
source of inquiry was questioning the difference in performance of the prolific run-scorer in championship cricket and
the same player batting in a Test match. 'Very few critics, even
among selectors, can detect that often tiny flaw in technique,
which, apart from temperament, separates success and failure.
Herbert had this gift of assessment and I could appreciate his
value as a selector, even if it was not always recognised by dear
old Gubby.'

Doug Insole, as another selector colleague, first met
Sutcliffe at the Scarborough Festival. Insole said that his initial
impression was of a rather forbidding figure. 'Herbert took a
bit of getting to know, but once the ice was broken he was
very good company.' He remembered partnering Sutcliffe in
a golf foursome at Ganton on a Sunday during the festival.
Insole said, as a then non-golfer who had been 'dragooned
into action', he was extremely nervous at the prospect of this

sporting excursion. 'I became even more apprehensive when, just before going in for dinner at the Grand Hotel about nine o'clock on the Saturday evening, I bumped into Herbert walking his dog.' Sutcliffe told Insole that he was just about to go to bed to prepare himself for the game. Insole had other plans for the evening; he did not expect to retire until around 2a.m. The course of the action on the following day exceeded Insole's worst fears:

> Herbert played off a crafty 15 and hit the ball very straight. At the first hole, playing alternative shots, I transferred our ball first from the fairway into the gorse and then from the fairway to a deep bunker, while our opponents were on the green in two.
>
> I expected a blast of some sort but the old boy was quite superb. 'It can only get better,' he said. 'Our day will come.' And, amazingly, it did; but principally because he should have been playing off about eight.

Insole recalled that Sutcliffe was a 'peculiar mixture as a judge of a player' in their selection debates. 'He liked batsmen who played the hook shot and seemed to look upon it as a badge of courage. Herbert was a very staunch Yorkshire supporter and always conscious of what the reactions to individual selections might be.' After one long discussion about the respective merits of Brian Close and Ray Illingworth, Sutcliffe cast his vote in favour of Close. It was a narrow decision and he had some misgivings about the popular opinion back home in Yorkshire. 'They'll be amazed in Yorkshire that we haven't chosen Illingworth, who is in great form at the moment.'

At another Sunday morning selection meeting, Sutcliffe abruptly concluded his part in the talk at midday. He excused himself on the grounds that he had to catch a train. The meeting was held at Gubby Allen's flat in London. The selectors still had three players to pick when Sutcliffe made his departure. An astonished Allen was for once almost rendered speechless by the desertion of his colleague, with the business of the day not yet completed. Sutcliffe, with quite breathtaking aplomb, declared: 'I have complete confidence in my colleagues to do the right thing.'

Sutcliffe served on the Yorkshire committee for twenty-one years before being elected a vice-president. He is remembered with respect and affection for his efforts in promoting the welfare of the club. His pursuit of perfection did place him in opposition to those who fell below the highest standards. Ron Burnet said: 'You always felt that Herbert took what was the right line in committee. He was never prejudiced but if he thought anyone was wrong he would say so and stand alone, if necessary.' Even Brian Sellers, his old county captain, who expected to govern in the 1960s as he had done in the 1930s, was not exempt from criticism. Sellers and Sutcliffe, two of Yorkshire's most powerful and influential personalities, voiced their opinions without much restraint in the privacy of the committee room. The strident exchanges were, though, between two men who were both passionately devoted to Yorkshire cricket. Raymond Clegg, a long standing Bradford representative, said that Sellers and Sutcliffe were by no means alone in the committee tussles. 'They both did their utmost to further our great cause.'

Michael Crawford, a colleague for twenty years, said that the tenacity which Sutcliffe displayed in his batting was also evident in his committee work. 'If he had a fault,' said Crawford, 'it was that he tended to show an impish delight in disagreeing with what was otherwise a unanimous view on a particular matter.' Crawford believed that this eccentricity was a reflection of Sutcliffe's relish of fighting against the odds as a cricketer. 'It seemed that he had to show his independence in the committee room.'

Capt. J. D. W. Bailey, as a Lancastrian and the only non-York-shireman on the committee, served with Sutcliffe for ten years. Bailey described himself as 'highly privileged to have known Herbert as a friend. He was a great, kindly and humble man'. Sutcliffe, in Bailey's view, was the reverse of the egotist and completely without side in his relations with people. 'In committee he respected another man's view and what he had to say was in keeping with the time and to the point at that time. Herbert was a great encourager of young cricketers, and especially those who were prepared to listen to his advice.'

There have been many testimonies to Sutcliffe's kindness and courtesy. Capt. Bailey provided another instance of these qualities. The occasion was a shopping expedition to Leeds, when he and his son, then an eight-year-old waiting to go to preparatory school, visited the Sutcliffe shop to buy a new set of cricket gear. 'This great and famous man came down from his fourth-floor sanctum to personally serve my little boy.' Soon afterwards Sutcliffe sent one of his coaching booklets to Bailey minor.

The courtesy was not just extended to the scions of Yorkshire. A.H. ('Podge') Brodhurst recalled a wartime meeting with Sutcliffe. Brodhurst was the Cambridge batsman who had taken a hundred off the vaunted Yorkshire attack before the war. In 1940, he was posted to the Yorkshire L.A.A. Regiment. As a raw second lieutenant, Brodhurst was immensely reassured by the genial presence of Maurice Leyland, his troop sergeant. During the summer Brodhurst was one of three young officers who played in a charity match at Sheffield. The teams were captained by Leyland and Brian Sellers. The umpires were George Hirst and Wilfred Rhodes. 'We felt very honoured to be in such exalted company,' said Brodhurst. 'When it was our turn to bat, Maurice turned to me and said: "Right, lad, you'd better open." I did what I was told, borrowed some pads and asked Maurice for the loan of an old bat.' Sutcliffe, who was listening to the conversation, came to the aid of the young officer. 'Here you are, young man: take this' – and promptly held out a bat of pristine quality. Brodhurst politely demurred but Sutcliffe insisted. 'I always used a new bat, if I had one. Do take it,' he said. Brodhurst, with considerable alarm, did accept the offer. 'I went out with this wonderful new blade. I managed to collect a dozen or so runs, and hope that I did have too many on the edge.' Brodhurst never forgot Sutcliffe's spontaneous gesture and the manner in which he befriended him. One of his happiest memories was of a marvellous Yorkshire team and the store of knowledge he accrued in his association with an esteemed assembly.

Yorkshire acknowledged Sutcliffe's long and distinguished service when they appointed him a life member of the club in February 1963. Two years later, in July 1965, Sutcliffe was the proud recipient of a permanent tribute. Sir William Worsley, the county president, opened the Sutcliffe Gates in the St Michael's Lane approach to the Headingley ground. They had been suggested by Sutcliffe's lifelong friend, Sidney Hainsworth. As chairman and managing director of Fenner's, the power transmission engineers, Hainsworth was a keen supporter of cricket causes. He organised annual matches featuring celebrity players at his company's ground at Marfleet. The proceeds of one of these games were donated towards the erection of the handsome black and gold painted gates at Headingley. The gates are a near replica of those designed by Louis de Soissons for Jack Hobbs at the Oval. They carry the inscription: 'In honour of a great Yorkshire and England cricketer.'

Among the many messages of congratulations was one from Harold Wilson, the Prime Minister. It read: 'He was to me, as to every Yorkshire boy of my generation, a boyhood hero. His technique was as immaculate as his appearance. His contribution to his county and his country and, above all, to the game of cricket is something which far transcended even the brilliant records and statistics which filled the pages of *Wisden* for so many years.' At the opening ceremony at Headingley Sir William Worsley said of Sutcliffe: 'To him the success and good name of the side were much more important than his own individual achievement. He always accepted his success with great modesty and worked continuously for the good of the game.'

The last years of Herbert Sutcliffe's life brought tragedy and the increasing disability of arthritis. In April 1974, his wife Emmie died in distressing circumstances. She was aged seventy-five. Emmie, a heavy smoker for many years, was severely burned in an accident at their home at Ilkley. She had dozed off in bed and her cigarette had set light to her nightdress. Her daughter, Barbara, a former deputy headteacher at a local primary school, recalled the family's intense grief. Emmie Sutcliffe was first admitted to the Airedale General Hospital for treatment. She spent two weeks there before being transferred to Pindersfields Hospital at Wakefield. Barbara was told that there was a slight chance of recovery. 'It depended upon how much she wanted to hold on to life. Mother did not want to live at all.'

David Frith, then employed in liaison work at Benson and Hedges cricket matches, recalled that Sutcliffe was the Gold Award adjudicator at a game at Old Trafford, only a few days after his wife's death:

> We sat in comfort for a long period during the afternoon, and I listened, enchanted to a stream of reminiscence, delivered in his soft and carefully enunciated voice. All the while he was fortifying himself with gin and tonic. Suddenly, as if relating another tale from a Test match of the 1920s, he told me that his wife had just died. His voice wavered and his eyes moistened as he spoke of the harrowing accident.

As they chatted on, Frith realised that the time was fast approaching when Sutcliffe would have to make his adjudication. He was also aware that his celebrity guest would have difficulty in reaching the pavilion steps to make the award. 'Not only had he taken in a fair amount of top-class gin, but his arthritic knees (he now used walking sticks) rendered the journey through the throng of members and down the steps very hazardous indeed.'

Frith said he then embarked on a campaign of trying to persuade Sutcliffe to make his award speech on a trailing microphone from the committee room. 'With unmistakable firmness he refused. "I shall carry out my duties as they were described to me," he said. "I must earn my fee."' The terrifying prospect of Sutcliffe having to fight his way, even with help, through an impatient crowd and down a flight of perilous steps to deliver his speech, mercifully vanished when rain intervened and play was suspended for the day.

Bill Sutcliffe always firmly denied that his father abandoned the temperate habits of his playing days to become a heavy drinker in his retirement. 'Herbert was never a toper,' said his son. 'He liked a glass of champagne or a gin and french. In his seventies he would drink a little more to conquer the pain induced by severe arthritis.' One family friend remembered a courteous man, who might, to the uninitiated, appear to have taken a drop too much. He rejected, as unpardonable, any suggestion of excessive drinking. 'Herbert did enjoy a dry martini and a gin and tonic as a mix; but he was far from being an alcoholic.' Sutcliffe's physical condition could, he believed, have led to uncharitable conclusions in some quarters. This observer recalled carrying Sutcliffe, with the aid of his wife, to bed on a chair. 'His knees literally creaked when he tried to bend them. At first we thought the noise was coming from the stairs; but we soon realised that he was in considerable pain from some extreme form of arthritis.'

As a palliative to the unceasing pain, Sutcliffe did find comfort in drink, and he even found humour in his fortitude. Len Creed, the former Somerset chairman, recalled a joke which was thoroughly enjoyed by Sutcliffe at Old Trafford. Sutcliffe was the match adjudicator in a NatWest tie between Lancashire and Somerset. 'Mr Herbert,' said Creed, 'expressed a wish to sample Somerset cider.' By good fortune, one of the visiting committee men had a stone flagon of cider in his car. He collected the receptacle; a pint was poured and duly offered to Sutcliffe. He was solemnly assured that it was much better laced with gin. Creed nodded in affirmation and agreed that it was indeed the perfect mix. Having drunk the potion, Sutcliffe exclaimed: 'My, that was delicious', and promptly called for another draught. The effect of the drink was to send him off into a quiet, refreshing sleep. An hour and a half elapsed and Creed, conscious that Sutcliffe had a duty to perform, gently tapped him on the shoulder. Sutcliffe awoke from his reverie and said: 'Who's the man of the match?' Creed, who had been watching the tumble of Lancashire wickets, instantly replied: 'Mr Herbert, I think you will agree that it must be Ken Palmer.'

Sutcliffe regarded Scarborough, agreeably situated just up the coast from the family holiday home at Filey, as one of his favourite cricket venues. He felt especially honoured to be elected as the president of the Scarborough Festival in succession to Lord Harewood in 1967. At Scarborough, Sutcliffe, invariably accompanied by his boxer dogs, displayed the same efficiency and took his duties as seriously as he had done as a cricketer. He retained his debonair appearance, and was particularly charming when there were any young ladies around. All his guests revelled in his company.

One of the admiring disciples at Scarborough was the violinist and musical director Max Jaffa. Jaffa was the Surrey supporter who became an honorary Yorkshireman

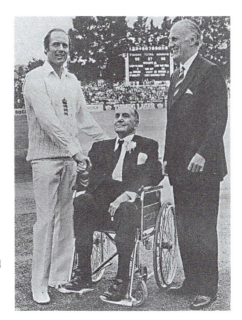

Yorkshire's centurions:
Geoffrey Boycott,
Sutcliffe and Sir Leonard
Hutton pictured at
Headingley in 1977.
(Ken Kelly)

in his twenty-seven years as an entertainer on the Spa at
Scarborough. For his services he was elected a freeman of
the town. He remembered the 'tremendous respect and love'
extended towards Sutcliffe by everybody who met him, cricketers and non-cricketers alike. 'Had Herbert been eight feet
tall, rather than a dapper man of medium height, the admiration could not have been more unstinting.' Jaffa cherished his
friendship with Sutcliffe during their summer meetings. 'We
did become conversationally close. I probably knew a little
more about cricket than he did about music. It enabled me
to talk to him about the game and it was a privilege to be
allowed to do so.' As a musician, Jaffa took particular note of
Sutcliffe's hands. 'When I looked at them, I thought: "Thank
goodness, he doesn't play the fiddle." They were so gnarled and
knocked about.'

Jaffa jocularly recalled his sole claim to cricket fame and
how the news of his exploit had reached Sutcliffe's ears. As a

Above: Courageous and gallant in old age. (W.H.H.S)

Left: The Sutcliffe gates at Headingley. (John Featherstone)

young student at the Guildhall School of Music, Jaffa, the last man in, had once scored seven not out and the winning run in a match against the Royal Academy of Music. The distinction assumed the proportions of an epic feat at one social gathering in Scarborough. The guests included Leonard Hutton. To Jaffa's surprise and pleasure, Sutcliffe turned to Hutton and said: 'You see Max, here, he could play cricket a bit.' Sutcliffe proceeded to regale the suitably impressed Hutton and the rest of the company with a highly decorative account of Jaffa's cricket triumph. 'I don't think that if some great violinist had complimented me on my skill as a musician, I would have experienced the same thrill as I did when Herbert told Len about my batting,' said Jaffa.

Sutcliffe stoically battled against the crippling arthritis in his declining years; he found pleasure in the excursions to Filey, often alone with his dogs, and he enjoyed a daily swim until his late seventies. When he celebrated his eightieth birthday he was bedridden with double pneumonia, and the Harrogate hospital was inundated with cards and congratulations from cricket lovers all over the world. He overcame this illness and his strength, despite his physical travail, seemed inexhaustible. Even in his last days in a nursing home, he retained some of the ardour of his youth. His dalliance with one elderly female patient really demanded a celebration rather than the indignation of the appalled staff. It was only with extreme reluctance that he finally accepted a wheelchair. Friends remembered his unfailing cheerfulness as they escorted him on outings to local hostelries. Sutcliffe reminisced about his great cricket years with customers and signed autographs. On one of his last visits to Headingley in August 1977, only a few months before his death, he was photographed with the two other Yorkshire centurions, Sir Leonard Hutton and Geoffrey Boycott.

In his eighties, as Don Mosey recalled, Sutcliffe's mind was 'razor-sharp and his tongue could have a cutting edge, too'. Before he at last settled in more amenable company in a Keighley nursing home, there were quarrels with medical staff, including one overbearing matron who strictly rationed his gin intake. One doctor friend of the family was more sympathetic.

He thought that the gin would be good for Sutcliffe's circulation. The verdict was endorsed by another medical consultant when Sutcliffe visited the Airedale Hospital for a hernia operation. 'Certainly, he must have some gin,' he said.

Don Mosey related his unavailing attempt to evade the vigilance of the nursing staff at one home:

> Mr Sutcliffe was fond of a gin and mixed (Vermouth), which was not in liberal supply at the nursing home. It became necessary to use orange juice as a mix. Then the staff began to insist that, for one reason or another, a glass or two of Gordon's was not good for him. It then became necessary to smuggle the stuff past a Praetorian guard of nurses, sisters and matrons, who became as expert at spotting the gin-smugglers as customs officers are at detecting those with more than their allowance of duty-frees.

On one occasion Mosey called at the home with a bottle hidden in a holdall and covered by a tape recorder:

> The staff headed me off before I could start up the stairs to his room, searched out the gin and confiscated it. In the utmost dread I tapped on his door, went in and met the peremptory demand I knew awaited me: 'Have you brought the gin?' Silently, I looked at the carpet; there was nothing to say. Mr Sutcliffe sat bolt upright in his chair. 'You've let those bloody awful creatures take it, haven't you?'

Sutcliffe, who had always been a fighter against the odds, roared with anger. He was appalled at the incompetence of his accomplice.

The poignant story of Sutcliffe's last canine friend was told by his daughter, Barbara. It was a labrador called Billy and it was given this name because Sutcliffe had had a row with his son. He thought that the gesture would effect a reconciliation. It did, however, have the opposite effect. 'Fancy naming a dog after me,' retorted the younger Sutcliffe. Billy was discovered through an advertisement in the local newspaper. 'The boxer dogs had become too boisterous for Herbert,' said Barbara. 'But he was desperate for a dog and Billy was the answer.' She always took Billy with her on visits to her father at the Keighley nursing home. Sutcliffe's last words were to the dog. 'Herbert had fallen into a coma and they couldn't wake him up,' said Barbara. 'It must have been the dog licking his hands that brought him round.' Sutcliffe opened his eyes and smiled in response to Billy's caresses. 'Hello darling,' he said.

The image of Herbert Sutcliffe as an incorrigible dandy has been perpetuated in many chronicles. Bob Wyatt, one of his cricket contemporaries, believed that he was not as cultivated as he appeared to be. Sutcliffe was, though, a sophisticate by inclination, and he acquired a polish which furthered his quest to rise above his humble origins. In his old age he self-mockingly and occasionally withdrew into the Yorkshire vernacular to tease and shock friends. It revealed the impish side of his nature as a counter to the lordly disdain which had become his trademark as a cricketer. The attributes of distinction prompted one observer to say that he was playing on the wrong side in the annual Gentlemen versus Players matches. Yet, in an era of a strong amateur-professional divide, he could not have achieved his eminence as a cricketer and a businessman if his standards had not been consistent with respect for authority and good behaviour. He fulfilled his ambition, a unique accomplishment, to gain parity with the amateur and at the same time to march steadfastly in league with his fellow professionals.

Herbert Sutcliffe died at the age of eighty-three on 22 January 1978. At the funeral service held at the Otley Congregational Church, the Revd Geoffrey Tillison described

Sutcliffe as a prince of honour who would be remembered as one of Yorkshire's greatest men. Bill Bowes, in his obituary tribute, said: 'Never once did I know or hear of him doing a shabby or underhand act. On and off the field, seldom with a hair or word out of place, he left a memory to be cherished and never obliterated from the record books.'

Statistical Appendix

Herbert Sutcliffe in First-Class Cricket 1919-1945

Born: Summerbridge
Nr Harrogate
24 November 1894

Died: Cross Hills
Keighley
22 January 1978

Compiled by Roy D. Wilkinson

Debut for Yorkshire: *v.* Gloucestershire at Gloucester
26 May 1919

Last Match for Yorkshire: *v.* Royal Air Force at Scarborough
29 August 1945

Debut for England: *v.* South Africa at Birmingham
14 June 1924

Last Match for England: *v.* South Africa at Lord's
29 June 1935

Note: Some statisticians have recently suggested that the matches in which
Herbert Sutcliffe and Jack Hobbs appeared for the Maharaja of Vizianagram's
XI in India and Ceylon in 1930/31 should be classified as first-class. The
present compiler prefers to accept the generally held view that these
matches cannot be regarded as first-class. Indeed, both Herbert Sutcliffe and
Jack Hobbs regarded these games as exhibition matches arranged only for
the entertainment of the Maharaja.

BATTING AND FIELDING

Season	M	I	No	Runs	Hs	Avge	100s	50s	Cent P'ships	C
1919	31	45	4	1839	174	44.85	5	8	9	22
1920	30	45	3	1393	131	33.16	4	7	7	15
1921	29	43	2	1235	97	30.12	–	8	6	17
1922	34	48	5	2020	232	46.97	4	12	11	20
1923	38	60	8	2220	139	41.11	3	15	11	24
1924	36	52	8	2142	255★	48.68	6	9	9	20
1924/25 (A)	12	18	0	1250	188	69.44	5	4	8	6
1925	36	51	8	2308	235	53.67	7	10	10	36
1926	35	47	9	2528	200	66.52	8	13	17	33
1927	35	49	6	2414	227	56.13	6	12	12	25
1927/28 (SA)	14	23	3	1030	102	51.50	2	9	8	4
1928	34	44	5	3002	228	76.97	13	13	23	15
1928/29 (A)	11	16	0	852	135	53.25	2	5	6	4
1929	31	46	4	2189	150	52.11	9	8	11	17
1930	29	44	8	2312	173	64.22	6	14	12	21
1931	34	42	11	3006	230	96.96	13	9	18	21
1932	35	52	7	3336	313	74.13	14	9	22	26
1932/33 (A)	13	19	1	1318	194	73.22	5	6	10	4
1932/33 (NZ)	3	3	0	27	24	9.00	–	–	–	–
1933	35	52	5	2211	205	47.04	7	6	9	35
1934	31	44	3	2023	203	49.34	4	12	11	22
1935	36	54	3	2494	212	48.90	8	11	9	19
1935/36 (J)	3	4	0	81	42	20.25	–	–	–	2
1936	35	53	7	1532	202	33.30	3	6	7	21
1937	33	54	5	2162	189	44.12	4	11	15	22
1938	32	50	7	1790	142	41.62	5	8	8	12
1939	21	29	3	1416	234★	54.46	6	2	6	7
1945	1	1	0	8	8	8.00	–	–	–	–
Totals	747	1088	123	50138	313	51.95	149	227	275	470

OVERSEAS TOURS

1924/25	MCC to Australia
1927/28	MCC to South Africa
1928/29	MCC to Australia
1932/33	MCC to Australia and New Zealand
1935/36	Yorkshire to Jamaica

FIRST–CLASS MATCHES FOR YORKSHIRE

Season	M	I	No	Runs	Hs	Avge	100s	50s	Cent P'ships	C
1919	31	45	4	1839	174	44.85	5	8	9	22
1920	30	45	3	1393	131	33.16	4	7	7	15
1921	29	43	2	1235	97	30.12	-	8	6	17
1922	33	47	5	1909	232	45.45	3	12	10	20
1923	32	48	3	1773	139	39.40	2	12	10	20
1924	28	42	6	1720	255★	47.77	5	7	7	17
1925	34	48	8	2236	235	55.90	7	9	9	33
1926	26	33	5	1672	200	59.71	5	9	12	25
1927	28	40	4	1814	176	50.38	4	9	8	23
1928	27	35	5	2418	228	80.60	11	9	18	12
1929	22	30	3	1485	150	55.00	5	6	7	15
1930	20	31	6	1636	173	65.44	5	9	9	16
1931	28	33	8	2351	230	94.04	9	8	13	18
1932	29	41	5	2883	313	80.08	12	8	21	25
1933	30	45	4	1986	205	48.43	6	6	8	31
1934	23	30	2	1511	203	53.96	4	8	7	17
1935	32	47	3	2183	212	49.61	8	8	7	17
1935/36 (J)	3	4	0	81	42	20.25	-	-	-	2
1936	33	49	7	1295	202	30.83	2	5	6	19
1937	32	52	5	2054	189	43.70	4	10	14	20
1938	30	46	5	1660	142	40.48	5	7	8	10
1939	21	29	3	1416	234★	54.46	6	2	6	7
1945	1	1	0	8	8	8.00	-	-	-	-
Totals	602	864	96	38558	313	50.20	112	167	202	401

COUNTY CHAMPIONSHIP MATCHES

Season	M	I	No	Runs	Hs	Avge	100s	50s	Cent P'ships	C
1919	26	36	3	1601	174	48.51	5	6	9	19
1920	28	41	3	1301	131	34.23	4	6	7	13
1921	25	36	2	1119	97	32.91	-	8	6	15
1922	30	41	3	1674	232	44.05	2	11	9	17
1923	29	42	2	1453	139	36.32	1	9	7	19
1924	23	33	4	1342	255★	46.27	3	6	7	11
1925	30	40	5	1787	235	51.05	5	8	8	26
1926	23	29	4	1424	200	56.96	3	9	10	25
1927	25	35	4	1625	176	52.41	4	8	7	19
1928	23	29	4	2137	228	85.48	11	7	17	9

1929	20	28	3	1361	150	54.44	4	6	6	14
1930	13	19	3	980	150★	61.25	3	5	5	12
1931	23	27	6	2049	230	97.57	8	8	13	16
1932	24	35	5	2624	313	87.46	12	6	19	20
1933	27	40	3	1636	205	44.21	4	5	6	29
1934	18	23	2	1089	203	51.85	3	4	6	10
1935	26	36	3	1966	212	59.57	8	6	7	14
1936	29	43	6	1143	202	30.89	2	5	5	14
1937	27	45	5	1822	189	45.55	4	9	13	18
1938	25	37	2	1451	142	41.45	5	6	7	8
1939	19	26	2	1230	234★	51.25	5	2	5	7
Totals	513	721	74	32814	313	50.71	96	140	179	335

TEST MATCHES

Season	M	I	No	Runs	Hs	Avge	100s	50s	Cent P'ships	C
1924 (SA)	5	5	1	303	122	75.75	1	2	2	2
1924/25 (A)	5	9	0	734	176	81.55	4	2	5	2
1926 (A)	5	7	1	472	161	78.66	1	3	3	8
1927/28 (SA)	5	10	1	418	102	46.44	1	2	3	-
1928 (WI)	3	3	0	165	63	55.00	-	2	2	2
1928/29 (A)	4	7	0	355	135	50.71	1	2	3	-
1929 (SA)	5	9	1	513	114	64.12	4	-	2	2
1930 (A)	4	7	2	436	161	87.20	1	3	3	2
1931 (NZ)	2	2	1	226	117	226.00	2	-	2	-
1932 (I)	1	2	0	22	19	11.00	-	-	-	-
1932/33 (A)	5	9	1	440	194	55.00	1	3	5	1
1932/33 (NZ)	2	2	0	24	24	12.00	-	-	-	-
1933 (WI)	2	2	0	41	21	20.50	-	-	-	2
1934 (A)	4	7	1	304	69	50.66	-	3	2	2
1935 (SA)	2	3	0	102	61	34.00	-	1	1	-
Totals	54	84	9	4555	194	60.73	16	23	33	23

OPPONENTS COUNTY CHAMPIONSHIP

Yorkshire versus	M	I	No	Runs	Hs	Avge	100s	50s	Cent P'ships	C
Derbyshire	35	49	2	1702	182	36.21	3	8	5	34
Essex	34	46	8	2747	313	72.28	9	9	15	24
Glamorgan	26	33	6	1239	147★	45.88	5	2	5	21
Gloucestershire	33	49	5	1790	134★	40.68	4	11	9	27

Hampshire	35	48	6	2078	131	49.47	6	13	11	22
Kent	32	45	3	1691	230	40.26	3	6	8	18
Lancashire	41	61	4	3006	195	52.73	9	14	14	22
Leicestershire	33	42	5	2761	234★	74.62	10	10	18	15
Middlesex	32	48	4	2343	235	53.25	7	8	16	17
Northamptonshire	34	42	3	1447	150	37.10	5	6	7	26
Nottinghamshire	33	52	7	2122	169	45.14	6	12	11	24
Somerset	13	15	2	900	213	69.23	4	-	5	7
Surrey	36	58	8	2824	232	56.48	9	14	16	22
Sussex	36	58	6	2265	270	43.55	4	11	11	19
Warwickshire	35	48	3	2614	206	58.08	8	12	21	19
Worcestershire	25	27	2	1285	200★	51.40	4	4	7	28
Totals	513	721	74	32814	313	50.71	96	140	179	335

OTHER MATCHES FOR YORKSHIRE

Yorkshire versus	M	I	No	Runs	Hs	Avge	100s	50s	Cent P'ships	C
Australians	6	7	1	221	69	36.83	-	1	-	2
Indians	1	1	0	31	31	31.00	-	-	-	-
New Zealanders	1	1	0	42	42	42.00	-	-	-	-
South Africans	5	8	1	266	113	38.00	1	1	1	3
West Indians	3	5	0	237	98	47.40	-	2	1	2
Aust. Imp. Forces	1	2	0	13	13	6.50	-	-	-	1
Cambridge University	17	26	7	1294	173★	68.10	4	6	5	10
MCC	29	52	7	2005	171	44.55	7	8	10	26
Middlesex	1	1	0	39	39	39.00	-	-	-	-
Oxford University	9	13	3	466	125★	46.60	1	3	2	8
Rest of England	9	17	3	771	124	55.07	2	5	3	8
Royal Air Force	1	1	0	8	8	8.00	-	-	-	-
Scotland	1	1	0	4	4	4.00	-	-	-	-
Sussex	2	4	0	266	173	66.50	1	1	1	1
Jamaica	3	4	0	81	42	20.25	-	-	-	2
Totals	89	143	22	5744	173★	47.47	16	27	23	66

TEST MATCHES

England versus	M	I	No	Runs	Hs	Avge	100s	50s	Cent P'ships	C
Australia	27	46	5	2741	194	66.85	8	16	21	15
India	1	2	0	22	19	11.00	-	-	-	-
New Zealand	4	4	1	250	117	83.33	2	-	2	-

South Africa	17	27	3	1336	122	55.66	6	5	8	4
West Indies	5	5	0	206	63	41.20	–	2	2	4
Totals	54	84	9	4555	194	60.73	16	23	33	23

OTHER MATCHES – IN UK

	M	I	No	Runs	Hs	Avge	100s	50s	Cent P'ships	C
Eng *v.* The Rest	9	13	0	759	227	58.38	2	4	4	1
Lord Hawke's XI *v.* MCC SA XI	1	1	0	35	35	35.00	–	–	–	1
H.D.G. Leveson Gower's XI *v.*										
Australians	3	6	1	176	45	35.20	–	–	–	–
Indians	2	4	1	278	106	92.66	1	1	1	1
MCC Aust. XI	2	4	0	213	102	53.25	1	1	2	4
MCC WI XI	1	2	0	97	96	48.50	–	1	–	1
New Zealanders	1	2	1	149	126	149.00	1	–	1	–
South Africans	1	2	0	112	96	56.00	–	1	1	1
West Indians	2	4	0	106	64	26.50	–	1	–	1
MCC Australian XI *v.*										
Lord Hawke's XI	1	1	0	16	16	16.00	–	–	–	–
H.D.G. Leveson Gower's XI	2	4	1	178	119*	59.33	1	–	1	–
CI Thornton's XI	2	4	0	100	52	25.00	–	1	–	2
MCC South African XI *v.* C.I. Thornton's XI	1	2	1	69	61*	69.00	–	1	1	1
North *v.* South	3	5	2	390	131*	130.00	2	2	1	–
North of England *v.* Australians	1	1	1	35	35*	–	–	–	–	–
Players *v.* Gentlemen	18	29	5	1113	120	46.37	2	8	8	14
Rest of England *v.* Lord Cowdray's XI	1	2	1	121	119	121.00	1	–	–	2
Lancashire	4	5	0	337	139	67.40	2	1	3	1
C.I. Thornton's XI *v.* Australians	1	2	1	50	42*	50.00	–	–	–	–
MCC South African XI	1	1	0	111	111	111.00	1	–	1	–
South Africans	1	2	0	12	7	6.00	–	–	–	–

	M	I	No	Runs	Hs	Avge	100s	50s	Cent	C
Uncapped *v.* Capped	1	2	1	62	35	62.00	–	–	–	1
Totals	59	98	16	4519	227	55.10	14	22	24	31

OTHER MATCHES — IN AUSTRALIA

MCC *v.*	M	I	No	Runs	Hs	Avge	100s	50s	Cent P'ships	C
Australian XI	3	5	0	189	87	37.80	–	1	–	2
Combined XI	1	1	0	169	169	169.00	1	–	1	1
New South Wales	4	4	0	311	182	77.75	1	1	3	2
Queensland	3	3	0	93	35	31.00	–	–	–	–
South Australia	4	7	0	548	154	78.28	2	3	4	3
Tasmania	2	2	0	289	188	144.50	2	–	3	1
Victoria	2	3	0	174	88	58.00	–	2	–	1
Western Australia	3	3	0	118	54	39.33	–	1	–	1
Totals	22	28	0	1891	188	67.53	6	8	11	11

OTHER MATCH — IN NEW ZEALAND

MCC *v.*	M	I	No	Runs	Hs	Avge	100s	50s	Cent P'ships	C
Wellington	1	1	0	3	3	3.00	–	–	–	–

OTHER MATCHES — IN SOUTH AFRICA

MCC *v.*	M	I	No	Runs	Hs	Avge	100s	50s	Cent P'ships	C
Eastern Province	1	2	1	85	79★	85.00	–	1	1	–
Griqualand West	1	1	0	100	100	100.00	1	–	1	–
Natal	2	2	0	93	93	46.50	–	1	2	1
Orange Free State	1	1	0	73	73	73.00	–	1	1	1
Transvaal	2	4	0	190	59	47.50	–	3	–	–
Western Province	2	3	1	71	62	35.50	–	1	–	2
Totals	9	13	2	612	100	55.63	1	7	5	4

GROUNDS IN YORKSHIRE

Ground	M	I	No	Runs	Hs	Avge	100s	50s	Cent P'ships	C
Bradford	62	88	8	3528	187★	44.10	11	13	15	56
Dewsbury	14	19	3	1453	213	90.81	5	5	8	13
Harrogate	15	19	2	592	86	34.82	–	4	3	9

Huddersfield	14	21	4	920	147★	54.11	2	6	5	13
Hull	28	33	4	1560	234	53.79	7	4	11	20
Leeds	61	90	11	4038	270	51.11	9	20	24	40
Scarborough	57	97	13	4276	202	50.90	14	16	24	42
Sheffield	72	104	14	4783	200★	53.14	12	28	26	43
Totals	323	471	59	21150	270	51.33	60	96	116	236

OTHERS IN UK

Ground	M	I	No	Runs	Hs	Avge	100s	50s	Cent P'ships	C
Bath	3	3	1	84	43	42.00	–	–	–	1
Birmingham	22	29	1	1618	205	57.78	7	4	11	5
Blackheath	1	1	0	23	23	23.00	–	–	–	–
Bournemouth	7	11	2	393	112	43.66	1	2	1	5
Bristol (County Ground)	8	12	1	638	227	58.00	1	4	4	10
Bristol (Greenbank)	2	3	0	43	24	14.33	–	–	–	4
Cambridge	17	26	7	1294	173★	68.10	4	6	5	10
Cardiff	9	12	1	250	51★	22.72	–	1	–	6
Chesterfield	12	18	0	514	91	28.55	–	3	–	9
Derby	4	5	0	205	111	41.00	1	1	1	1
Dover	4	6	0	254	174	42.33	1	–	2	2
Dudley	1	1	0	33	33	33.00	–	–	–	1
Eastbourne	2	2	0	229	228	114.50	1	–	2	1
Folkestone	1	1	0	230	230	230.00	1	–	1	–
Gloucester (Spa Ground)	3	4	0	122	88	30.50	–	1	1	–
Gloucester (Wagon Works Ground)	5	9	1	361	134	45.12	2	–	1	–
Gravesend	1	1	0	10	10	10.00	–	–	–	2
Hastings	2	4	2	183	119	91.50	1	–	–	3
Hove	18	33	4	1144	173	39.44	2	6	3	8
Ilford	3	5	0	182	61	36.40	–	2	1	1
Ilkeston	1	2	0	66	35	33.00	–	–	–	2
Kettering	2	2	0	113	113	56.50	1	–	1	1
Leicester	19	24	1	1630	212	70.86	6	6	10	9
Leyton	12	13	3	744	313	74.40	3	1	3	9
Lord's	52	81	8	3266	175	44.73	7	20	20	35
Maidstone	3	6	0	262	92	43.66	–	2	1	1
Manchester	31	42	5	2038	165	55.08	5	13	10	15
Neath	1	2	1	164	135★	164.00	1	–	–	–
Northampton	13	15	2	631	150	48.53	3	1	3	9

Nottingham	21	31	4	1355	111	50.18	4	9	9	6
The Oval	42	67	8	3822	232	64.77	15	17	24	19
Oxford	9	13	3	466	125★	46.60	1	3	2	8
Peterborough	1	1	0	104	104	104.00	1	-	1	1
Portsmouth	6	7	1	398	131	66.33	2	2	3	6
Southampton	4	5	0	97	47	19.40	-	-	-	5
Southend-on-Sea	2	3	2	402	255★	402.00	2	-	2	1
Stourbridge	2	3	0	51	29	17.00	-	-	-	1
Swansea	4	6	1	78	22	15.60	-	-	-	4
Taunton	3	5	1	88	26	22.00	-	-	-	1
Tonbridge	3	5	0	166	70	33.20	-	1	1	2
Tunbridge Wells	1	2	0	56	33	28.00	-	-	-	2
Westcliff-on-Sea	1	2	0	88	48	44.00	-	-	-	-
Worcester	10	11	0	535	138	48.63	2	2	4	7
Totals	368	534	60	24430	313	51.54	75	107	127	214

IN AUSTRALIA

Ground	M	I	No	Runs	Hs	Avge	100s	50s	Cent P'ships	C
Adelaide	7	13	0	737	154	56.69	2	5	5	4
Brisbane	6	8	0	70	86	33.75	-	1	1	1
Hobart	1	1	0	188	188	188.00	1	-	2	1
Launceston	1	1	0	101	101	101.00	1	-	1	-
Melbourne	7	12	0	995	176	82.91	4	5	5	3
Perth	4	4	0	287	169	71.75	1	1	1	2
Sydney	10	14	1	842	194	64.76	3	3	9	3
Totals	36	53	1	3420	194	65.76	12	15	24	14

IN NEW ZEALAND

Ground	M	I	No	Runs	Hs	Avge	100s	50s	Cent P'ships	C
Auckland	1	1	0	24	24	24.00	-	-	-	-
Christchurch	1	1	0	0	0	0.00	-	-	-	-
Wellington	1	1	0	3	3	3.00	-	-	-	-
Totals	3	3	0	27	24	9.00	-	-	-	-

IN SOUTH AFRICA

Grounds	M	I	No	Runs	Hs	Avge	100s	50s	Cent P'ships	C
Bloemfontein	1	1	0	73	73	73.00	–	1	1	1
Cape Town	3	5	1	199	99	49.75	–	2	1	2
Durban	3	5	0	200	93	40.00	–	2	3	1
Johannesburg	3	6	1	299	102	59.80	1	2	1	–
Kimberley	1	1	0	100	100	100.00	1	–	1	–
Pietermaritzburg	1	1	0	0	0	0.00	–	–	–	–
Port Elizabeth	1	2	1	85	79★	85.00	–	1	1	–
Pretoria	1	2	0	74	57	37.00	–	1	–	–
Totals	14	23	3	1030	102	51.50	2	9	8	4

IN WEST INDIES

Grounds	M	I	No	Runs	Hs	Avge	100s	50s	Cent P'ships	C
Kingston (Melbourne Park)	2	2	0	45	42	22.50	–	–	–	1
Kingston (Sabina Park)	1	2	0	36	32	18.00	–	–	–	1
Totals	3	4	0	81	42	20.25	–	–	–	2

GROUNDS — SUMMARY

Grounds	M	I	No	Runs	Hs	Avge	100s	50s	Cent P'ships	C
In Yorkshire	323	471	59	21150	270	51.33	60	96	116	236
Others in UK	368	534	60	24430	313	51.54	75	107	127	214
Totals in UK	691	1005	119	45580	313	51.44	135	203	243	450
In Australia	36	53	1	3420	194	65.76	12	15	24	14
In New Zealand	3	3	0	27	24	9.00	–	–	–	–
In South Africa	14	23	3	1030	102	51.50	2	9	8	4
In West Indies	3	4	0	81	42	20.25	–	–	–	2
Totals	747	1088	123	50138	313	51.95	149	227	275	470

HOW OUT

Caught	514	53.26%
Bowled	255	26.42%
Lbw	140	14.50%

Stumped	25	2.59%
Run out	28	2.90%
Hit wkt	3	0.31%
Totals	965	100%

CENTURIES

1919

145	Yorkshire	v. Northamptonshire	Northampton
118	Yorkshire	v. Gloucestershire	Leeds
132	Yorkshire	v. Lancashire	Sheffield
103	Yorkshire	v. Middlesex	Lord's
174	Yorkshire	v. Kent	Dover

1920

112	Yorkshire	v. Worcestershire	Worcester
107	Yorkshire	v. Nottinghamshire	Nottingham
125★	Yorkshire	v. Essex	Southend-on-Sea
131	Yorkshire	v. Hampshire	Portsmouth

1922

114	Yorkshire	v. Surrey	Bradford
232	Yorkshire	v. Surrey	The Oval
101★	Yorkshire	v. MCC	Scarborough
111	C.I. Thornton's XI	v. MCC South African XI	Scarborough

1923

105★	Yorkshire	v. Cambridge University	Cambridge
139	Yorkshire	v. Somerset	Hull
119	Rest of England	v. Lord Cowdray's XI	Hastings

1924

108★	Yorkshire	v. Cambridge University	Cambridge
213	Yorkshire	v. Somerset	Dewsbury
160	Yorkshire	v. Sussex	Sheffield
122	England	v. South Africa	Lord's
255★	Yorkshire	v. Essex	Southend-on-Sea
108	Yorkshire	v. MCC	Scarborough

1924/25

115	England	v. Australia	Sydney
176	England	v. Australia	Melbourne
127	England	v. Australia	Melbourne
188	MCC	v. Tasmania	Hobart
143	England	v. Australia	Melbourne

1925

130	Yorkshire	v. Warwickshire	Birmingham
121	Yorkshire	v. Glamorgan	Huddersfield
129	Yorkshire	v. Leicestershire	Hull
235	Yorkshire	v. Middlesex	Leeds
206	Yorkshire	v. Warwickshire	Dewsbury
171	Yorkshire	v. MCC	Scarborough
124	Yorkshire	v. Rest of England	The Oval

1926

102	Yorkshire	v. Warwickshire	Birmingham
107	Players	v. Gentlemen	Lord's
200	Yorkshire	v. Leicestershire	Leicester
161	England	v. Australia	The Oval
131★	Yorkshire	v. Surrey	The Oval
107	Yorkshire	v. MCC	Scarborough
109★	Yorkshire	v. MCC	Scarborough
136	Rest of England	v. Lancashire	The Oval

1927

134	Yorkshire	v. Gloucestershire	Wagon Works Ground, Gloucester
176	Yorkshire	v. Surrey	Leeds
131★	North	v. South	Sheffield
169	Yorkshire	v. Nottinghamshire	Bradford
277	England	v. The Rest	County Ground, Bristol
135	Yorkshire	v. Lancashire	Leeds

1927/28

| 100 | MCC | v. Griqualand West | Kimberley |
| 102 | England | v. South Africa | Johannesburg |

1928

129	Yorkshire	v. Essex	Leyton
140	Yorkshire	v. Lancashire	Sheffield
101	England	v. The Rest	Lord's
147★	Yorkshire	v. Glamorgan	Huddersfield
111	Yorkshire	v. Derbyshire	Derby
111	Yorkshire	v. Nottinghamshire	Nottingham
100★	Yorkshire	v. Nottinghamshire	Nottingham
104	Yorkshire	v. Middlesex	Leeds
126	Yorkshire	v. Lancashire	Manchester
119	Yorkshire	v. Leicestershire	Leicester

} †

138	Yorkshire	v. Derbyshire	Dewsbury
228	Yorkshire	v. Sussex	Eastbourne
139	Rest of England	v. Lancashire	The Oval

1928/29

| 135 | England | v. Australia | Melbourne |
| 122 | MCC | v. South Australia | Adelaide |

1929

113	Yorkshire	v. South Africans	Sheffield
114	England	v. South Africa	Birmingham
150	Yorkshire	v. Northamptonshire	Northampton
100	England	v. South Africa	Lord's
133★	Yorkshire	v. Essex	Bradford
106	Yorkshire	v. Lancashire	Bradford
104	England	v. South Africa	The Oval
109★	England	v. South Africa	The Oval
123★	Yorkshire	v. Surrey	The Oval

1930

108★	Yorkshire	v. Essex	Leyton
150★	Yorkshire	v. Essex	Dewsbury
132★	Yorkshire	v. Glamorgan	Sheffield
161	England	v. Australia	The Oval
173	Yorkshire	v. Sussex (Non Champ.)	Hove
102★	Yorkshire	v. MCC	Scarborough

1931

173★	Yorkshire	v. Cambridge University	Cambridge
129	Yorkshire	v. Warwickshire	Birmingham
120	Players	v. Gentlemen	The Oval
120★	Yorkshire	v. Middlesex	Lord's
107	Yorkshire	v. Hampshire	Portsmouth
230	Yorkshire	v. Kent	Folkestone
183	Yorkshire	v. Somerset	Dewsbury
117	England	v. New Zealand	The Oval
195	Yorkshire	v. Lancashire	Sheffield
187	Yorkshire	v. Leicestershire	Leicester
109★	England	v. New Zealand	Manchester
101★	Yorkshire	v. Surrey	The Oval
126	H.D.G. Leveson Gower's XI	v. New Zealanders	Scarborough

1932

| 109 | Yorkshire | v. Warwickshire | Birmingham |
| 104★ | Yorkshire | v. Hampshire | Leeds |

153★	Yorkshire	*v.* Warwickshire	Hull
313	Yorkshire	*v.* Essex	Leyton
110★	North	*v.* South	Manchester
270	Yorkshire	*v.* Sussex	Leeds
132	Yorkshire	*v.* Gloucestershire	Bradford
135	Yorkshire	*v.* Lancashire	Manchester
182	Yorkshire	*v.* Derbyshire	Leeds
194	Yorkshire	*v.* Essex	Scarborough
136	Yorkshire	*v.* Somerset	Sheffield
112	Yorkshire	*v.* Hampshire	Bournemouth
122★	Yorkshire	*v.* Sussex	Hove
106	H.D.G. Leveson Gower's XI	*v.* Indians	Scarborough

1932/33

169	MCC	*v.* Combined XI	Perth
154	MCC	*v.* South Australia	Adelaide
182	MCC	*v.* New South Wales	Sydney
194	England	*v.* Australia	Sydney
101	MCC	*v.* Tasmania	Launceston

1933

205	Yorkshire	*v.* Warwickshire	Birmingham
113	Yorkshire	*v.* Northamptonshire	Kettering
177	Yorkshire	*v.* Middlesex	Bradford
174	Yorkshire	*v.* Leicestershire	Leicester
107	Yorkshire	*v.* MCC	Scarborough
119★	MCC Australian XI	*v.* H.D.G. Leveson Gower's XI	Scarborough
114★	Yorkshire	*v.* Rest of England	The Oval

1934

152	Yorkshire	*v.* Cambridge University	Cambridge
166	Yorkshire	*v.* Essex	Hull
203	Yorkshire	*v.* Surrey	The Oval
187★	Yorkshire	*v.* Worcestershire	Bradford

1935

135★	Yorkshire	*v.* Glamorgan	Neath
200★	Yorkshire	*v.* Worcestershire	Sheffield
110	Yorkshire	*v.* Kent	Bradford
100	Yorkshire	*v.* Hampshire	Hull
121	Yorkshire	*v.* Glamorgan	Bradford
135	Yorkshire	*v.* Nottinghamshire	Sheffield
212	Yorkshire	*v.* Leicestershire	Leicester
138	Yorkshire	*v.* Worcestershire	Worcester

1936			
129	Yorkshire	*v.* Surrey	Leeds
202	Yorkshire	*v.* Middlesex	Scarborough
102	H.D.G. Leveson Gower's XI	*v.* MCC Australian XI	Scarborough

1937			
189	Yorkshire	*v.* Leicestershire	Hull
138	Yorkshire	*v.* Surrey	Bradford
122	Yorkshire	*v.* Lancashire	Sheffield
109	Yorkshire	*v.* Leicestershire	Leicester

1939			
125★	Yorkshire	*v.* Oxford University	Oxford
165	Yorkshire	*v.* Lancashire	Manchester
116	Yorkshire	*v.* Hampshire	Sheffield
234★	Yorkshire	*v.* Leicestershire	Hull
175	Yorkshire	*v.* Middlesex	Lord's
107★	Yorkshire	*v.* Northamptonshire	Northampton

} †

† Consecutive Innings

CENTURY PARTNERSHIPS

With P. Holmes – for Yorkshire

1st Wicket

1919	
279	*v.* Northamptonshire at Northampton (HS 145, PH 133)
253	*v.* Lancashire at Sheffield (HS 132, PH 123)
197	*v.* Leicestershire at Leicester (HS 88, PH 140)
106	*v.* Warwickshire at Bradford (HS 36, PH 84)
159	*v.* Middlesex at Lord's (HS 78, PH 133)

1920	
126	*v.* Worcestershire at Worcester (HS 112, PH 75)
191	*v.* Middlesex at Lord's (HS 70, PH 149)
101★	*v.* Gloucestershire at Huddersfield (HS 50 , PH 48★)
347	*v.* Hampshire at Portsmouth (HS 131, PH 302★)

1921	
118	*v.* Warwickshire at Sheffield (HS 97, PH 48)
100	*v.* Nottinghamshire at Nottingham (HS 87, PH 43)
107	*v.* Essex at Bradford (HS 62, PH 57)

1922

100	*v.* Middlesex at Lord's (HS 46, PH 129)
145	*v.* Warwickshire at Huddersfield (HS 61, PH 220★)
143	*v.* Kent at Maidstone (HS 92, PH 107)
123	*v.* MCC at Scarborough (HS 101★, PH 26)

1923

127	*v.* Middlesex at Bradford (HS 72, PH 50)
238★	*v.* Cambridge University at Cambridge (HS 105★, PH 126★)
119	*v.* Middlesex at Lord's (HS 76, PH 89)
104	*v.* Kent at Tonbridge (HS 70, PH 46)
131	*v.* Sussex at Leeds (HS 59, PH 95)
110	*v.* Warwickshire at Hull (HS 55, PH 51)
274	*v.* Somerset at Hull (HS 139, PH 199)
120	*v.* MCC at Scarborough (HS 62, PH 60)
180	*v.* Rest of England at The Oval (HS 74, PH 99)

1924

110	*v.* Warwickshire at Birmingham (HS 64, PH 44)
195	*v.* Sussex at Sheffield (HS 160, PH 83)
107	*v.* Glamorgan at Bradford (HS 55, PH 118★)

1925

118	*v.* Worcestershire at Worcester (HS 55, PH 71)
199	*v.* Warwickshire at Birmingham (HS 130, PH 79)
140★	*v.* Middlesex at Lord's (HS 58, PH 315★)
221	*v.* Glamorgan at Huddersfield (HS 121, PH 130)
272	*v.* Leicestershire at Hull (HS 129, PH 194)

1926

102	*v.* Essex at Harrogate (HS 48, PH 86)
199	*v.* Lancashire at Manchester (HS 89, PH 143)
105	*v.* Surrey at The Oval (HS 71, PH 51) (ist Innings)
265★	*v.* Surrey at The Oval (HS 131★, PH 127★) (2nd Innings)
133	*v.* MCC at Scarborough (HS 109★, PH 72)

1927

274	*v.* Gloucestershire at Gloucester (HS 134, PH 180)
141	*v.* Sussex at Sheffield (HS 64, PH 70)
143	*v.* Surrey at The Oval (HS 64, PH 73★)

1928

268	*v.* Essex at Leyton (HS 129, PH 136)
142	*v.* Lancashire at Sheffield (HS 140, PH 79)
166	*v.* Warwickshire at Birmingham (HS 81, PH 91)

158	*v.* Middlesex at Lord's (HS 73, PH 105)
125	*v.* Derbyshire at Derby (HS 111, PH 67)
184	*v.* Nottinghamshire at Nottingham (HS 111, PH 83) (1st Innings)
210★	*v.* Nottinghamshire at Nottingham (HS 100★, PH 101★) (2nd Innings)
290	*v.* Middlesex at Leeds (HS 104, PH 179★)
134	*v.* Lancashire at Manchester (HS 126, PH 54)
227	*v.* Leicestershire at Leicester (HS 119, PH 110)
141	*v.* Sussex at Eastbourne (HS 228, PH 63)

1929

106	*v.* Warwickshire at Harrogate (HS 31, PH 91)
241	*v.* Surrey at The Oval (HS 123★, PH 142)

1930

200★	*v.* Oxford University at Oxford (HS 80★, PH 107★)
131	*v.* Essex at Dewsbury (HS 76, PH 63)
235	*v.* Glamorgan at Sheffield (HS 132★, PH 130)
105	*v.* Surrey at The Oval (HS 59, PH 54)

1931

120	*v.* Warwickshire at Leeds (HS 67, PH 58)
309	*v.* Warwickshire at Birmingham (HS 129, PH 250)
140	*v.* Leicestershire at Sheffield (HS 75, PH 63)
130	*v.* Somerset at Dewsbury (HS 183, PH 59)
323	*v.* Lancashire at Sheffield (HS 195, PH 125)
112	*v.* Leicestershire at Leicester (HS 187, PH 43)

1932

555	*v.* Essex at Leyton (HS 313, PH 224★)
161	*v.* Gloucestershire at Bradford (HS 83, PH 81)
139★	*v.* Nottinghamshire at Leeds (HS 54★, PH 77★)
161	*v.* Northamptonshire at Huddersfield (HS 89, PH 69)

1933

141	*v.* Nottinghamshire at Bradford (HS 96, PH 65)

3rd Wicket

1925	135	*v.* Middlesex at Leeds (HS 235, PH 50)
1926	114	*v.* Kent at Sheffield (HS 68, PH 56)
1930	131	*v.* MCC at Scarborough (HS 102★, PH 86)

FOR OTHER TEAMS

1st Wicket

1927

269★	North *v.* South at Sheffield (HS 131★, PH 127★)
107	Players *v.* Gentlemen at Lord's (HS 64, PH 50)

1927/28
203   MCC *v.* Orange Free State at Bloemfontein (HS 73, PH 279★)
103   MCC *v.* Natal at Durban (HS 93, PH 42)
140   England *v.* South Africa at Cape Town (HS 99, PH 88)

WITH J.B. HOBBS — FOR ENGLAND

1st Wicket
1924
136   *v.* South Africa at Birmingham (HS 64, JBH 76)
268   *v.* South Africa at Lord's (HS 122, JBH 211)

1924/25
157   *v.* Australia at Sydney (HS 59, JBH 115)
110   *v.* Australia at Sydney (HS 115, JBH 57)
283   *v.* Australia at Melbourne (HS 176, JBH 154)
126   *v.* Australia at Melbourne (HS 143, JBH 66)

1926
182   *v.* Australia at Lord's (HS 82, JBH 119)
156   *v.* Australia at Leeds (HS 94, JBH 88)
172   *v.* Australia at The Oval (HS 161, JBH 100)

1928
119   *v.* West Indies at Manchester (HS 54, JBH 53)
155   *v.* West Indies at The Oval (HS 63, JBH 159)

1928/29
105   *v.* Australia at Melbourne (HS 135, JBH 49)
143   *v.* Australia at Adelaide (HS 64, JBH 74)

1930
125   *v.* Australia at Nottingham (HS 58★, JBH 74)
108   *v.* Australia at Manchester (HS 74, JBH 31)

FOR OTHER TEAMS

1st Wicket
1922
120   C.I. Thornton's XI *v.* MCC South African XI at Scarborough (HS
            111, JBH 45)

1925
140   Players *v.* Gentlemen at Lord's (HS 50, JBH 140)

1926
263   Players *v.* Gentlemen at Lord's (HS 107, JBH 163)
157   Rest of England *v.* Lancashire at The Oval (HS 136, JBH 62)

1928
212   Rest of England *v.* Lancashire at The Oval (HS 139, JBH 150)

1928/29
131   MCC *v.* South Australia at Adelaide (HS 70, JBH 64)
155   MCC *v.* South Australia at Adelaide (HS 122, JBH 75)

1929
117   England *v.* The Rest at Lord's (HS 91, JBH 59)

1931
203   Players *v.* Gentlemen at The Oval (HS 120, JBH 110)
227   Players *v.* Gentlemen at Scarborough (HS 96, JBH 144)
243   H.D.G. Leveson Gower's XI *v.* New Zealanders at Scarborough (HS
             126, JBH 153)

PARTNERSHIPS EXCEEDING 250 RUNS

1st Wicket
555   Yorkshire *v.* Essex at Leyton (HS 313, P. Holmes 224★), 1932
347   Yorkshire *v.* Hampshire at Portsmouth (HS 131, P. Holmes 302★),
             1920
323   Yorkshire *v.* Lancashire at Sheffield (HS 195, P. Holmes 125), 1931
315   Yorkshire *v.* Leicestershire at Hull (HS 189, L. Hutton 153), 1937
315   Yorkshire *v.* Hampshire at Sheffield (HS 116, L. Hutton 280★), 1939
309   Yorkshire *v.* Warwickshire at Birmingham (HS 129, P. Holmes 250),
             1931
290   Yorkshire *v.* Middlesex at Leeds (HS 104, P. Holmes 179★), 1928
283   England *v.* Australia at Melbourne (HS 176, J.B. Hobbs 154), 1924–25
279   Yorkshire *v.* Northamptonshire at Northampton (HS 145, P. Holmes
             133), 1919
274   Yorkshire *v.* Somerset at Hull (HS 139, P. Holmes 199), 1923
274   Yorkshire *v.* Gloucestershire at Gloucester (HS 134, P. Holmes 180),
             1927
272   Yorkshire *v.* Leicestershire at Hull (HS 129, P. Holmes 194), 1925
269★   North *v.* South at Sheffield (HS 131★, P. Holmes 127★), 1927
268   England *v.* South Africa at Lord's (HS 122, J.B. Hobbs 211), 1924
268   Yorkshire *v.* Essex at Leyton (HS 129, P. Holmes 136), 1928
265★   Yorkshire *v.* Surrey at The Oval (HS 131★, P. Holmes 127★), 1926
263   Players *v.* Gentlemen at Lord's (HS 107, J.B. Hobbs 163), 1926
253   Yorkshire *v.* Lancashire at Sheffield (HS 132, P. Holmes 123), 1919

2nd Wicket

317	England *v.* The Rest at Bristol (HS 227, C. Hallows 135), 1927
314	Yorkshire *v.* Essex at Southend-on-Sea (HS 255★, E. Oldroyd 138), 1924
288	Yorkshire *v.* Lancashire at Manchester (HS 165, A. Mitchell 136), 1939
283	MCC *v.* Combined XI at Perth (HS 169, Nawab of Pataudi 129), 1932-33
258	Yorkshire *v.* Kent at Folkestone (HS 230, E. Oldroyd 93), 1931

3rd Wicket

323★	Yorkshire *v.* Glamorgan at Huddersfield (HS 147★, M. Leyland 189★), 1928
301	Yorkshire *v.* Middlesex at Lord's (HS 175, M. Leyland 180★), 1939

CENTURY PARTNERSHIPS BY PARTNER
FOR YORKSHIRE

1st Wicket		*2nd Wicket*		*3rd Wicket*	
P. Holmes	69	E. Oldroyd	19	M. Leyland	16
L. Hutton	15	A. Mitchell	17	P. Holmes	3
A. Mitchell	6	M. Leyland	7	W. Barber	2
M. Leyland	4	W. Barber	3	R. Kilner	2
W. Barber	2	D. Denton	1	K.R. Davidson	1
P.A. Gibb	1	K.R. Davidson	1	A. Mitchell	1
E. Robinson	1	P.A. Gibb	1	A.B. Sellers	1
Total	98	A.B. Sellers	1	Total	26
		Total	52		

4th Wicket		*5th Wicket*		*6th Wicket*	
M. Leyland	5	W. Rhodes	2	P.A. Gibb	1
W. Rhodes	4	W. Barber	1	E. Robinson	1
W. Barber	2	F.E. Greenwood	1	A. Wood	1
A. Mitchell	2	G.H. Hirst	1	Total	3
R. Kilner	1	R. Kilner	1		
C. Turner	1	Total	6		
N.W.D. Yardley	1				
Total	16				

8th Wicket		Total	202
E.R. Wilson	I		
Total	I		

FOR ENGLAND

1st Wicket		*2nd Wicket*		*3rd Wicket*	
J.B. Hobbs	15	W.R. Hammond	5	Nawab of	
C.P. Walters	2	K.S. Duleepsinhj	2	Pataudi snr	1
R.E.S. Wyatt	2	E. Tyldesley	2	Total	1
P. Holmes	1	J.W. Hearne	1		
D.R. Jardine	1	Total	10		
Total	21				

6th Wicket			
R.E.S Wyatt	1	Total	33
Total	1		

FOR OTHER TEAMS

1st Wicket		*2nd Wicket*		*3rd Wicket*	
J.B. Hobbs	11	J.W. Hearne	2	E. Hendren	1
P. Holmes	4	Nawab of		Nawab of	
M. Leyland	2	Pataudi snr	2	Pataudi snr	1
R.E.S. Wyatt	2	E. Tyldesley	2	Total	2
E.W. Dawson	1	C. Hallows	1		
C. Hallows	1	W.R. Hammond	1		
L. Hutton	1	M. Leyland	1		
D.R. Jardine	1	Total	9		
W.W. Keeton	1				
A. Mitchell	1				
A. Sandham	1				
R.A. Sinfield	1				
Total	27				

4th Wicket		*5th Wicket*		Total	40
M.S. Nichols	1	E. Hendren	1		
Total	1	Total	1		

SUMMARY OF CENTURY PARTNERSHIPS

Wicket	For Yorkshire	For England	For Other Teams	Total
1st	98	21	27	146
2nd	52	10	9	71
3rd	26	1	2	29
4th	16	–	1	17
5th	6	–	1	7

6th	3	1	–	4
8th	1	–	–	1
Totals	202	33	40	275

Sutcliffe shared century partnerships, for all wickets, with 35 different players. Those with whom he shared 10 or more are as follows: P. Holmes 77, M. Leyland 35, A. Mitchell 27, J.B. Hobbs 26, E. Oldroyd 19, L. Hutton 16, W. Barber 10

TEST MATCH CAREER – INNINGS BY INNINGS

Season	Opponents	Test	Venue	Innings Details	Opening Partnership	
1924	SOUTH AFRICA	1st	Birmingham	b Parker	64	136
		2nd	Lord's	b Parker	122	268
		3rd	Leeds	c Nupen b Blackenberg	83	72
				not out	29	17
		4th	Manchester	Did not bat		
		5th	The Oval	c Ward b Nourse	5	5
1924/25	AUSTRALIA	1st	Sydney	c V.Y. Richardson b Mailey	59	157
				c Gregory b Mailey	115	110
		2nd	Melbourne	b Kellaway	176	283
				c Gregory b Mailey	127	36
		3rd	Adelaide	c Oldfield b Ryder	33	(batted no.6)
				c Ponsford b Mailey	59	63
		4th	Melbourne	lbw b Mailey	143	126
		5th	Sydney	c Mailey b Kellaway	22	0
				b Gregory	0	3
1926	AUSTRALIA	1st	Nottingham	not out	13	32★
		2nd	Lord's	b Richardson	82	182
		3rd	Leeds	c and b Grimmett	26	59
				b Richardson	94	156
		4th	Manchester	c Oldfield b Mailey	20	58
		5th	The Oval	b Mailey	76	53
				b Mailey	161	172
1927/28	SOUTH AFRICA	1st	Johannesburg	c Vincent b Promnitz	102	0
				not out	41	57★
		2nd	Cape Town	c Nupen b Bissett	29	14
				b Bissett	99	140
		3rd	Durban	b vincent	25	67

				c Morkel b Nupen	8	25
		4th	Johannesburg	lbw b Hall	37	6
				c Vincent b Bissett	3	21
		5th	Durban	c Cameron b Vincent	51	2
				lbw b Nupen	23	0
1928	WEST INDIES	1st	Lord's	c Constantine b Francis	48	51
		2nd	Manchester	c Nunes b Griffith	54	119
		3rd	The Oval	b Francis	63	155
1928/29	AUSTRALIA	1st	Brisbane	c Ponsford b Gregory	38	85
				c sub (Oxenham) b Ironmonger	32	25
		2nd	Sydney	c Hendry b Ironmonger	11	37
		3rd	Melbourne	b Blackie	58	28
				lbw b Grimmett	135	105
		4th	Adelaide	st Oldfield b Grimmett	64	143
				c Oldfield b A'Beckett	17	1
1929	SOUTH AFRICA	1st	Birmingham	c Cameron b Ochse	26	59
				b Morkel	114	34
		2nd	Lord's	c Mitchell b Bell	100	8
				c Catterall b Morkel	10	28
		3rd	Leeds	c Mitchell b Quinn	37	42
				c Owen-Smith b Morkel	4	13
		4th	Manchester	b Morkel	9	30
		5th	The Oval	c Owen-Smith b Vincent	104	38
				not out	109	77
1930	AUSTRALIA	1st	Nottingham	c Hornibrook b Fairfax	29	53
				Retired Hurt	58	125
		3rd	Leeds	c Hornibrook b Grimmett	32	53
				not out	28	24
		4th	Manchester	c Bradman b Wall	74	108
		5th	The Oval	c Oldfield b Fairfax	161	68
				c Fairfax b Hornibrook	54	17
1931	NEW ZEALAND	2nd	The Oval	st James b Vivian	117	84
		3rd	Manchester	not out	109	8

1932	INDIA	Only	Lord's	b Nissar	3	8
				c Nayudu b Amar Singh	19	30
1932/33	AUSTRALIA	1st	Sydney	lbw b Wall	194	112
				not out	1	1★
		2nd	Melbourne	c Richardson b Wall	52	30
				b O'Reilly	33	53
		3rd	Adelaide	c Wall b O'Reilly	9	4
				c sub (O'Brien) b Wall	7	7
		4th	Brisbane	lbw b O'Reilly	86	114
		5th	Sydney	c Richardson b O'Reilly	56	31
1932/33	NEW ZEALAND	1st	Christchurch	c James b Badcock	0	0
		2nd	Auckland	c Weir b Freeman	24	56
1933	WEST INDIES	1st	Lord's	c Grant b Martindale	21	49
		2nd	Manchester	run out	20	63
1934	AUSTRALIA	1st	Nottingham	c Chipperfield b Grimmett	62	45
				c Chipperfield b O'Reilly	24	51
		2nd	Lord's	lbw b Chipperfield	20	70
		3rd	Manchester	c Chipperfield b O'Reilly	63	68
				not out	69	123★
		5th	The Oval	c Oldfield b Grimmett	38	104
				c McCabe b Grimmett	28	1
1935	SOUTH AFRICA	1st	Nottingham	lbw b Langton	61	118
		2nd	Lord's	lbw b Bell	3	5
				lbw b Langton	38	24

A MISCELLANY OF ACHIEVEMENT

Scored 1,839 runs in his first season (1919) – a record aggregate for a debut season.

Scored 1,000 runs in all 21 English seasons from 1919-1939.

Reached 2,000 runs in a season on 14 consecutive occasions – 1922-1935.

Reached 3,000 runs in a season three times – the first player to do so.

Scored more runs for Yorkshire than any other player – 38,558.

Scored more runs in a season for Yorkshire than any other player – 2,883.

In 1931 scored 3,006 runs at an average of 96.96 – an average exceeded, among English batsmen, by only G. Boycott (twice) and G.A. Gooch.

First Yorkshireman to score 100 first-class centuries.

Scored most centuries in a season for Yorkshire.

Scored four consecutive hundreds on two separate occasions.

In addition scored three consecutive hundreds on three separate occasions.

Scored two centuries in a match four times – twice for England and twice for Yorkshire.

Hit 10 sixes when scoring 113 *v.* Northamptonshire in 1933.

Scored 1,000 runs in both June and August 1932.

Carried his bat through a completed innings seven times (six for Yorkshire once for North).

In the twenty-three months from May 1931 to the beginning of April 1933 he scored 7,687 runs in 85 matches at an average of 79.24 including 32 centuries, 24 other scores of over 50 and 50 century partnerships.

His partnership of 555 with P. Holmes for Yorkshire's 1st wicket *v.* Essex in 1932 is the highest partnership ever recorded in English first-class cricket.

He and M. Leyland hit 102 in only six consecutive overs for Yorkshire *v.* Essex at Scarborough in 1932.

Made more centuries for Yorkshire (112) than any other player His unbroken partnership of 323 with M. Leyland *v.* Glamorgan at Huddersfield in 1928 remains the record for Yorkshire's 3rd wicket.

The stand of 268 he made with J.B. Hobbs *v.* South Africa at Lord's in 1924 remains the highest opening partnership for England at Lord's.

His first four innings *v.* Australia were 59, 115, 176 and 127.

In their first match together *v.* Australia Sutcliffe and Hobbs put on 157 for the 1st wicket in the first innings and 110 in the second – at Sydney 1924/25.

In the second Test *v.* Australia at Melbourne in 1924/25 Sutcliffe became the first player to score a century in each innings against them.

He was the first England player to score three consecutive centuries in Test cricket and remains the only England player to do so *v.* Australia.

He and J.B. Hobbs were the first opening batsmen to bat through a full day's play in a Test match.

His first three opening partnerships with J B Hobbs *v.* Australia were 157, 100 and 283.

He was the first player to score four centuries in one Test series (115, 176, 127 and 143 *v.* Australia 1924/25).

He was the first player to score a century in each innings of a Test on two occasions (*v.* Australia at Melbourne 1924/25 and *v.* South Africa at the Oval 1929).

His aggregate of 734 runs *v.* Australia in 1924/25 is the second highest by
   an England players *v.* Australia.

His Test average of 60.73 is the highest by an England player who has batted
   in at least 15 Test innings.

He averaged over 50 in all six of his Test series against Australia.

He was the first England player to be dismissed for 99 in a Test innings.

Bibliography

H.S. Altham and E.W. Swanton: *History of Cricket* (Allen and Unwin, 1947).

John Arlott: *Jack Hobbs: Profile of the Master* (John Murray, 1981).

Derrick Boothroyd: *Half A Century of Yorkshire Cricket* (Kennedy Bros [Publishing] Limited, 1981).

Bill Bowes: *Express Deliveries* (Phoenix House, 1958).

Neville Cardus: *Roses Cricket – 1919-1939* (Souvenir Press, 1982).

Dudley Carew: *To the Wicket* (Chapman and Hall, 1946).

Philip Derriman: *Bodyline* (Collins/Sydney Morning Herald, 1984).

Leslie Duckworth: *Holmes and Sutcliffe, the Run Stealers* (Hutchinson, 1970).

P.G.H. Fender: *The Turn of the Wheel, MCC Team, Australia, 1928-29* (Faber, 1929).

Jack Fingleton: *Masters of Cricket* (Heinemann, 1958).

Alan Hill: *A Chain of Spin Wizards* (Kennedy Bros [Publishing] Limited, 1983).

Derek Hodgson: *The Official History of the Yorkshire County Cricket Club* (Crowood Press, 1989).

Gerald Howat: *Len Hutton* (Heinemann/Kingswood, 1988).

Len Hutton and Alex Bannister: *50 Years in Cricket* (Stanley Paul, 1984).

J.M. Kilburn: *History of Yorkshire County Cricket – 1924-1949* (Yorkshire CCC, 1950); *Yorkshire County Cricket* (Convoy, 1950).

Michael Marshall: *Gentlemen and Players* (Grafton Books, 1987).

Ronald Mason: *Jack Hobbs* (Hollis and Carter, 1960); *Sing All A Green Willow* (Epworth Press, 1967).

Don Mosey: *We Don't Play It For Fun* (Methuen, 1988).

Patrick Murphy: *The Centurions* (Dent, 1983).

M.A. Noble: *Gilligan's Men. MCC Tour, Australia, 1924-25* (Chapman and Hall, 1925); *Those Ashes, The Australian tour of 1926* (Cassell, 1927); *The Fight for the Ashes, 1928-29* (Harrap, 1929).

Pudsey St Lawrence Centenary Brochure – *100 Years of Cricket at Tofts Road – 1889-1989*.

Pudsey Britannia Cricket & Bowling Club. *Bazaar Souvenir and History of the Club* (Pudsey, 1913).

A.W. Pullin: *History of Yorkshire County Cricket – 1903-1924* (Chorley & Pickersgill, 1924).

Ray Robinson: *Between Wickets* (Fontana Books, 1958).

Sidney Rogerson: *Wilfred Rhodes, Professional and Gentleman* (Hollis and Carter, 1960).

Herbert Sutcliffe: *For England and Yorkshire* (Edward Arnold & Co., 1935) *English Cricket – What's Wrong & Why!* (Desmond Banks Publications, 1951).

A.A. Thomson: *Cricket: The Golden Ages* (Stanley Paul, 1961) *Hirst and Rhodes* (Epworth Press, 1959).

Ben Travers: *94 Declared* (Elm Tree Books, 1981).

E.M. Wellings: *Vintage Cricketers* (George Allen & Unwin, 1983).

Peter Wynne Thomas: *Complete History of Cricket Tours at Home and Abroad* (Hamlyn, 1989).

Contemporary reports in the *Yorkshire Post* and *Yorkshire Evening Post, Pudsey and Stanningley News,* the *Nidderdale Observer, Bradford Cricket Argus, The Times, The Australasian, The Cricketer* and *Cricket Magazine* and various editions of *Wisden Cricketers' Almanack* and Yorkshire County Cricket Club yearbooks have provided the nucleus of printed sources in this book.

Index

A'Beckett, E.L., 147
Abel, R., 195
Alexander, H.H., 239
Allen, Sir G.O., 117, 143, 236, 242, 263, 285–6
Allom, M.J.C., 284
Alston, R., 16, 177
Altham, H.S., 75, 134
Ambler, F., 33
Ames, L.E.G., 220, 222, 227–8, 232, 237, 242, 247, 251, 253, 256, 271–2
Anderson, G., 47
Appleyard, J., 281
Arlott, J., 86, 236–8
Armitage, W., 27
Armstrong, W.W., 40
Arnold, J., 181
Ashdown, W.H., 255

Bailey, J.D.W., 17, 288
Bailey, T.E., 228
Bakewell, A.H., 181, 246

Ballantine, E.W., 97
Banks
    James, 119
    Joseph, 119
    T., 119
    W.H., 119
Barber
    A.T., 164
    W., 189, 318–9
Bardsley, W., 86, 98–9, 133, 141–2
Barnes, S.F., 33, 40, 51, 100
Barnett, C.J., 186, 191, 249, 260
Bestwick, W., 57
Bettesworth, W.A., 38
Birks, F., 94
Birtles, T.J., 61
Blackie, D.D., 147
Blanckenburg, J.M., 86
Blythe, C., 78, 135
Booth, M.W., 27, 31, 39–40, 57, 62
Bowes, W.E., 11, 15, 38–9, 89, 113, 115, 157–9, 166, 172, 180, 187, 189–92, 197, 204–9, 219–21,

224, 227–8, 231, 235, 238, 242, 244, 258, 269, 283, 298
Boycott, G., 211, 249, 268–9, 276, 295
Bradman, Sir D.G., 16, 87, 131–2, 142–7, 150–4, 215–6, 223, 227, 234, 240–3, 248, 257, 270–3
Briggs, J., 36
Brockwell, W., 196
Brodhurst, A.H., 288, 289
Brodribb, G., 209
Brooks
    E.W.J., 284
    G., 20
Brown
    F.R., 16, 95, 226
    G., 74
    J.T., 35, 36, 193–6, 204
    W.C., 210
Burnet, J.R., 16, 68, 71, 207, 221, 254, 263–5, 287
Burton, D.C.F., 34, 54, 58

Caesar, J., 47
Caine, C.S., 107
Cardus, Sir N., 66, 80, 113, 131–5, 163, 185, 220, 223
Carew, D., 218
Carpenter, R.P., 46
Carr, A.W., 132, 155
Carter, H., 76
Catterall, R.H., 84–5, 312
Chapman, A.P.F., 102, 105, 133, 142, 146, 150–5, 197, 236, 254
Chatterton, W., 196
Chester, F., 137
Clark, E.W., 235–6
Clegg, C.R., 16, 287
Close, D.B., 116, 258, 286
Collins, H.L., 99, 136, 141
Commaille, J.H.H., 81, 136
Compton, D.C.S., 74, 252, 265, 273

Constantine, Lord, 239, 277
Cordingley, A., 25
Cotton, H., 159
Cowdrey, Lord, 258
Coxon, A., 283
Crane, C., 167
Crawford, M.G., 17, 287
Creed, L., 16, 292
Cutmore, J.A., 208

Dacre, C.C.R., 191
Daer, A.G., 203–4
Dales, H.L., 161
Davidson, G.A., 194, 319
Deane, H.G., 86, 91
Denton, D., 39, 60–1, 66, 182, 211, 319
de Soissons, L., 289
Dipper, A.E., 54
Dolphin, A., 61, 164
Doughty, S., 30, 242
Douglas, J.W.H.T., 75, 155
Drake, Alonzo, 39–41, 57, 62
Duckworth, G., 243
Duleepsinhji, K.S., 152–5, 179, 187, 226

Earle, G.F., 183
Eastman, L.C., 201, 202, 206
Eckersley, P.T., 183
Edrich, W.J., 252–60, 283
Emmett, T., 47
Evershed, S.H., 194

Fagg, A., 249–51, 260
Fairservice, W.J., 59
Farnes, K., 207–8, 236
Faulkner, G.A., 231
Feather, R., 17
Featherstone, J., 17, 25, 294
Fender, P.G.H., 145–8, 284
Fingleton, J.H.W., 142, 236, 240

Fisher, H., 206–7
Fleetwood-Smith, L.O'B., 271
Foster
    F.R., 76
    R.E., 97
Freeman
    A.P., 105, 182, 197, 253–6, 285
    E., 59
Frith, D., 19, 290, 291
Fry, C.B., 171, 216

Garland-Wells, H.M., 19, 68, 159
Gibb, P.A., 277, 318, 319
Gill, B., 17, 19–22
Gilligan
    A.E.R., 80, 84–6, 92, 94, 98,
    105, 135
    F., 98
Gimblett, H., 260
Goddard, T.W.J., 186, 190–2
Gover, A.R., 118, 217
Gower, D., 248
Grace, W.G., 143, 156, 195, 215
Greenwood, F., 179, 181, 186
Gregory
    J.M., 75, 98–100, 134, 138,
    140–2, 223
    R.J. 198
Griffith, H.C., 239, 321
Grimmett, C.V., 107, 134, 141,
    147–9, 153, 223–5
Grimshaw, S.E., 172
Gunn, G., 51

Haig, N.E., 219
Haigh, S., 41, 58
Hainsworth, M., 51
Hainsworth, S.B., 17, 50–3, 65–7,
    160, 167, 233, 242, 289
Hall, J., 46
Hall, L., 36, 48, 183, 316
Halliday, J., 46

Hammond, W.R., 37, 68, 142–6,
    149–51, 155, 186–91, 215–8,
    223, 228, 239–40, 246–9, 265,
    270, 275
Hardstaff, J., 265
Harris, Lord, 93
Hartkopf, A.E.V., 100
Hayward, T., 46
Hayward, T.W., 188, 195
Hawke, Lord, 25, 36–8, 53, 158,
    163, 168, 173, 188, 194, 257,
    260, 305
Hearne, J.T., 195
Hearne, J.W., 56, 317
Heath, G.E.M., 267
Hele, G., 240, 247
Hendren, E.H., 56, 71, 84–6, 91–2,
    102, 105, 108, 150, 188, 215,
    219, 223, 283–5
Hendry, H.S.T., 145–7
Hill, C., 145
Hirst, G.H., 21, 29–30, 37–41, 48,
    54, 56–61, 78, 172, 182, 257–8,
    284, 288
Hobbs, Sir J.B., 11, 14, 33, 51, 64,
    67–70, 74–5, 79, 80–110, 113,
    131–7, 140–2, 145–9, 151–6,
    160, 172, 179, 181, 198, 216,
    226–8, 241, 245–9, 270, 273,
    275, 283–4, 289
Hobbs, Lady, 92, 275
Hodgson, D., 160
Hodgson, I., 47
Hollies, W.E., 152
Holmes, E.R.T., 251, 284
Holmes, J., 20
Holmes, P., 11, 51, 54, 56–63,
    65–79, 89, 152, 157–60, 170,
    183–4, 190, 193, 196–8, 199–
    204, 211, 221, 246, 262
Holmes, R., 20
Hopwood, J.L., 183

Horsley, J., 57
Hudson, W., 272
Hunter, D., 38, 48
Hutton, H., 27, 31
Hutton, Sir, L., 10, 13, 16, 27, 31,
    41–2, 49, 110, 120, 132, 168,
    189, 197, 203, 211, 217, 252–4,
    257–8, 262–73, 279, 281, 293,
    295

Ikin, J.T., 272
Illingworth, R., 42, 258, 286
Ingham, R., 24–9, 31, 41, 79, 108,
    121
Insole, D.J., 19, 198, 230, 285

Jackson, J., 46
Jackson, Sir S.F., 96, 165
Jaffa, Max, 16, 292, 295
Jardine, D.R., 11, 149, 187–8,
    232–9, 243, 246–8, 283–4
Jessop, G.L., 37–8
Joel, Solly, 93
Jupp, V.W.C., 188, 210

Keighley, W.G., 282
Kelleway, C., 95, 100
Keeton, W.W., 260, 319
Kilburn, J.M., 16, 68–70, 158–65,
    178, 180–5, 188, 192, 265–6
Kilner, R., 39, 54, 56, 61–2, 66, 78,
    105, 161, 170
Knight, D.J., 75, 284

Laidler, Francis, 124
Laker, J.C., 147, 175
Langridge, J.G., 16, 37, 227
Larwood, H., 66, 141, 153, 155,
    213, 233–5, 239, 242–6, 263
Lawry, Mrs F., 238
Lee, F., 184
Lee, J., 46

Lester E.I., 17, 175, 269–71
Leveson Gower, H.D.G., 156, 160
Levett, W.H.V., 182
Leyland, M., 11, 113, 125, 142,
    186–7, 190, 207–11, 235, 238,
    246–8, 251, 255, 261, 278, 283,
    288
Leyland, Mrs Connie, 125
Lindwall, R.R., 236, 272
Lock, G.A.R., 175
Lupton, A.W., 158, 163, 170
Lyon, B.H., 186, 190, 191

Macartney, C.G., 70, 132–3, 205
Macaulay, G.G., 54, 62, 77, 89, 118,
    161, 164, 182, 186, 191, 197,
    210, 255–7
McCabe, S.J., 153, 239, 249, 271
McDonald, E.A., 76, 100, 113,
    184–5, 213, 221–2, 266
McGahey, C.P., 203
MacLaren, A.C., 96
Mailey, A.A., 97–102, 134, 138,
    148, 218, 225, 241
Makepeace, J.W.H., 75
Mann, F.T., 160
Martindale, E.A., 89, 239, 277, 281
Mason, R., 83, 91, 95–6, 134,
    155–6, 220
Matthews, A.D.G., 210
May, P.B.H., 16, 175, 223, 285
Mayer, J.H., 71
Mead, C.P., 74, 84–7, 188, 215
Middlebrook, R., 16
Milburn, C., 224
Miller, K.R., 236, 272
Mitchell, A., 186, 190–1, 207, 250,
    257, 260, 266, 270
Mitchell, T.B., 16, 232, 237, 242
Mold, A., 36
Moyes, A.G., 241
Mosey, D., 295–6

Murdoch, W.L., 87
Musgrave, J., 46
Myers, Cllr S., 109

Nichols, S.M., 175, 197–8, 204,
    208–9
Noble, M.A., 94, 98, 101–3, 138,
    147
Nourse, A.W., 92
Nupen, E.P., 92
Nutter, A.E., 266

Ochse, A.L., 231
O'Connor, J., 206
Oldfield, W.A.S., 107, 150, 224
Oldroyd, E., 170, 180–1
O'Reilly, W.J., 236, 247, 271
Oxenham, R.K., 147, 150

Padgett, D.V., 175
Palmer, K., 292
Pardon, S., 71, 75
Parker, C.W.L., 186–7, 190–1
Parker, F., 121
Parker, G.M., 82–3
Parker, R., 15, 19, 29, 121, 123
Parkin, C., 51, 60, 281
Parkinson, Sir K., 214
Parks, J.H., 260
Pataudi, Nawab of, 246–8
Pawley, T., 60
Paynter, E., 184–7, 240, 246–8, 276
Pearce, T.N., 203, 16
Pease, Mrs Polly, 121
Pease, R., 53
Pease, W., 121
Peebles, I.A.R., 98, 100, 155,
    214–6, 220
Peel, R., 38, 48, 259
Pollock, R.G., 215
Ponsford, W.H., 87, 99, 141–3, 152,
    223, 248

Poore, Major, R.M., 188
Pope, D.F., 209
Pope, G.H., 175
Pullin, A.W., 16, 78–80, 194

Ranjitsinhji, K.S., 96, 188
Raper, J.R.S., 16
Read, H.D., 197
Reeves, W., 161
Rhodes, A.S., 206
Rhodes, W., 25, 33, 37, 39, 51, 54,
    56–8, 61–3, 74–5, 77–8, 86,
    100, 102, 114, 133, 135, 141–2,
    157–9, 161–5, 168–73, 182, 197,
    206, 226, 257, 284, 288
Richardson, A.J., 98–100, 134–5,
    140–1, 148
Richardson, V.Y., 99, 247
Ringrose, W., 203
Robertson-Glasgow, R.C., 67, 70,
    250
Robins, R.W.V., 98
Robinson, Ellis, 14, 16
Robinson, Emmott, 32, 61–2, 73,
    77, 158, 179–82, 186, 319
Robinson, F.G., 54
Rogers, F.G., 191
Root, F., 51
Rowbotham, J., 47
Russell, A.C., 75
Ryder, J., 105, 148

Salter, C., 28
Sandham, A., 67–8, 284
Schwartz, R.O., 226
Scott, Revd A., 20
Sellers, A.B., 159, 165–6, 190–1,
    201, 256, 269, 287–8
Sheffield, J.R., 198
Shrewsbury, A., 87
Sievers, M., 146
Sims, J.M., 219

Sinfield, R.A., 190–1

Smailes, T.F., 189, 255, 278

Smith, D., 230

Smith, E.J., 203

Smith, H.A., 262

Smith, R., 15, 31, 123

Smith, T.B.P., 199, 204

Snow, Lord, 115–6

Snow, Philip, 16, 115

Sobers, Sir G., 273

Spooner, R.H., 76

Stevens, G.T.S., 161

Strong, Mrs Ruth, 15, 44

Strudwick, H., 283–4

Surridge, W.S., 14, 16, 113, 124, 132, 175, 217, 276, 283

Sutcliffe, Emily (wife), 53, 107–9, 115, 121–5, 209–11, 290

Sutcliffe, Willie (father), 16, 20–23, 27, 53

Sutcliffe, Jane (mother), 16, 23

Sutcliffe, Arthur (brother), 16–23

Sutcliffe, Bob (brother), 17–23

Sutcliffe, John (son), 16, 115, 123, 128, 278

Sutcliffe, W.H.H., 16, 49, 115, 119, 121–7, 128–30, 167, 174–5, 198, 221, 234, 272, 281–4, 292, 297

Sutcliffe, Arthur (uncle), 22, 24, 48

Sutcliffe, Tom (uncle), 22, 48

Sutcliffe, Carrie (aunt), 23, 29

Sutcliffe, Harriet (aunt), 16–7

Sutcliffe, Sarah (aunt), 23

Swanton, E.W., 75, 134, 161

Tanfield, M.A., 199

Tarrant, G., 46

Tate, M.W., 80, 84, 95, 100, 102, 106, 108, 132, 150–2, 155, 284

Taylor, H.W., 83, 87

Taylor, J.M., 99, 102

Taylor, R.H., 207

Tennyson, Hon. L., 93, 154, 174

Thewliss, J., 47

Thomson, A.A., 73, 163

Tillison, Revd G., 297

Todd, L.J., 255

Toone, Sir Fredk, 168

Tordoff, Mrs M, 34

Town, J.C., 109

Travers, Ben, 148

Trott, A., 195

Trueman, F.S., 258

Trumper, V., 103

Tunnicliffe, J., 35–9, 48, 59, 69, 79, 194–7, 204

Tyldesley, E., 91, 188

Tyldesley, R.K., 99

Ulyett, G., 48

Varley, J.W., 15, 118–21, 127

Verity, H., 9, 14, 153, 180, 183, 187, 189–92, 197, 204, 207, 232, 235, 238, 245, 249–51, 255–8, 276, 278, 281

Voce, W., 235

Vogler, A.E.E., 226

Waddington, A., 58, 62, 78, 162, 210

Waite, M.G., 271

Walker, Ernest, 28–30, 34, 48, 108

Walker, E.H., 49

Wall, T.W., 154, 155, 223

Waller, T., 23

Walters, C.F., 16, 216, 246–8

Warner, Sir Pelham, 76, 81, 135, 137, 144, 181, 201, 224

Ward, W., 70

Wardle, J.H., 258

Washbrook, C., 222, 260, 281

Watkins, B.T.L., 191

Watson, A., 36

Watts, E.A., 283
Weekes, Sir E. de C., 273
Wellings, E.M., 114, 165
Wensley, A.F., 227
White, Sir A., 53
White, G.C., 226
Whysall, W.W., 105, 155
Wilcock, Barbara (daughter), 15,
    23, 107, 120–6, 290, 297
Worthington, T.S., 249
Wilkinson, P., 21
Wilkinson, R.D., 74
Williams, A.C., 32
Williams, B., 125
Willsher, E., 46
Wilson, Lord, 275
Wilson, B.B., 60
Wilson, E.R., 61
Wilson, G., 161–3
Wilson, J.V., 175, 280
Witherington, H., 15, 122, 189

Witherington, J., 15, 122, 252,
    278–80
Wood, A., 130, 152, 183, 187, 197,
    279, 282
Woodfull, W.M., 141, 144, 151,
    242, 248
Wooller, W., 16, 125, 285
Woolley, F.E., 37, 51, 59, 76, 84–7,
    99, 102, 105, 108, 152, 181,
    215–6, 228, 254–5, 284
Worsley, Sir W.A., 158, 174, 290
Worthington, T.S., 249
Wright, D.V.P., 256
Wyatt, R.E.S., 16, 66, 68, 87–9,
    117, 155, 187, 208, 216–7, 223,
    226–35, 239, 242–52, 264–5,
    272, 297

Yardley, N.W.D., 164, 174, 189
Young, A., 183

Also by The History Press ...

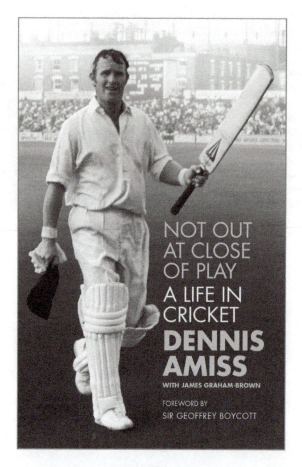

NOT OUT
AT CLOSE
OF PLAY
A LIFE IN
CRICKET
**DENNIS
AMISS**
WITH JAMES GRAHAM-BROWN

FOREWORD BY
SIR GEOFFREY BOYCOTT

9781803990057